SPI
EGE
L&G
RAU

Fat
to Fish

Artie Lange

with Anthony Bozza

SPIEGEL & GRAU

New York

2008

Copyright © 2008 by Artie Lange

All Rights Reserved

Published in the United States by Spiegel & Grau, an imprint of The Doubleday Publishing Group, a division of Random House, Inc., New York.

www.spiegelandgrau.com

SPIEGEL & GRAU is a trademark of Random House, Inc.

Book design by Mauna Eichner and Lee Fukui

Library of Congress Cataloging-in-Publication Data

Lange, Artie, 1967–
  Too fat to fish / by Artie Lange, with Anthony Bozza. —1st ed.
    p. cm.
1. Lange, Artie, 1967– 2. Comedians—United States—Biography. 3. Actors—United States—Biography. I. Bozza, Anthony. II. Title.

PN2287.L2833A3 2008
792.702'8092—dc22
[B]

2008039001

Page 300 constitutes an extension of this copyright page.

ISBN 978-0-385-52656-2

PRINTED IN THE UNITED STATES OF AMERICA

10 9 8 7 6

Contents

The words "genius," "icon," and "legend" are thrown around way too often these days in the world of entertainment and rarely are they appropriate. This book is dedicated to a man who is that rare example of someone who truly embodies all three of those words, Howard Stern.

Howard, this is Artie. Thank you for teaching me and a whole generation of comedians how to be funny.

Foreword
by Howard Stern

Artie is a complicated subject. Most people who listen to my show will ask me to explain why a guy who has everything going for him has so many issues. You know what I'm talking about: the heroin problem that was so bad he would drive all the way to Delaware to score, the coke habit that got so out of control it compelled him to abandon the set of *MADtv* and drive to his dealer in a pig costume, and the Jack Daniel's fixation that caused him to skip dancing with an actual girl at my birthday party and instead waltz around with his whiskey glass, sucking on a straw. All of it—the gambling, the eating, the hookers—forces people to ask: How can a man with so much talent have so many problems?

Artie can get up in front of a crowd and blow people away doing stand-up. He can get on the air with me and crack me up (not an easy thing to do). He'll blast off and do back-to-back impressions of Biggie Smalls, Jeff the Drunk, and the aging porno queen Blue Iris, then turn around and recite entire scenes from *The Godfather* verbatim. He can recall all of Belushi and Dean Wormer's dialogue from *Animal House* word for word. He can tell a story brilliantly and turn any little event into a major routine.

He has the talent, the fame, the great job, and the money. Did I mention the money? According to Artie, he can get upwards of $75,000 a night for a stand-up gig—very impressive. So from the outside looking in, he has it all. So you, like all other fans of Arthur Lange, ask, "Why the weight? Why the drugs? Why the gambling?" You already know the answer, but you want to hear me say it anyway. The answer is simple: He's fucked up! That's it. He's fucked up. He's just like us, only ten million times worse.

Some wonder why Artie doesn't get any help. Everyone has their own theory, but I think it's one of those neurotic things where Artie thinks all funny people have to be depressed to get any kind of laughs. That's just psychobabble, and I'm not Sigmund and Roy, so I won't bore you with my analysis. I don't know anything about it. This book is a celebration—I'll save my theories for his next book. Yes, I believe this book will be a hit, and he'll have a sequel called *I Have Gained So Much More Weight That I'm Not Only Too Fat to Fish, but Fucking, Walking, Talking, and Breathing Seem to Be Out of the Question at This Point.*

But here's the bottom line: Artie is my friend, Artie is the funniest, sweetest motherfucker around, and Artie has the biggest heart on the planet. As I write this, Artie is in Afghanistan entertaining the troops during our two-week summer vacation. He could be luxuriating poolside, but instead he's marching around the desert in a flak jacket that is way too tight on him, high on seventy-five Vicodin. Enough said.

Artie is also a genius. I was lucky as hell that, after Jackie left the show and I was trying to figure out the future of my radio program, Artie dropped into my lap via a guest appearance by Norm

McDonald. At first, Artie was just this brilliant guest, but later he became the perfect fit. If ever there was a perfect match, it's Artie and *The Howard Stern Show*, but if you bought this book you already know that.

So why am I here and why am I writing this foreword? What I'd like to accomplish in these few pages is to give you some idea of how Artie works. I'll try to spell out what it takes to become a superstar comedian and radio performer. Usually, we would keep all of the secrets hidden away, like in *The Wizard of Oz*, but because I like you, I'll pull the curtain back a bit.

Oops, I might have pulled the curtain back prematurely. Skip this and pretend it never happened.

And skip this one too. See, Artie accidentally took too much "medicine" and needed some assistance off the stage. No need to bring that up.

Now, this one's better. This picture kind of says it best. Look at the concentration. The body language. The intensity. Intensity is essential for a successful career. While coworker Benjy might look exhausted from the intense work that is radio, Artie, like a panther, is ready to pounce, thinking up the next big gag or schtick. Do you have a fifth of the concentration Artie has? Of course not.

Okay, here's an important point for all you kids out there who want to be just like Artie: The man knows that great humor needs tremendous discipline. Food is not food to Artie; it's fuel. He needs to stay hydrated at all times. Notice the three drinks. Some may see this and think Artie has issues with food, but they would be wrong. Artie makes the extra effort by juggling multiple drinks because he knows staying satiated is going to blast him into hyperdrive for his comedy. Wisely, the man also loads up on sugary snacks and high-calorie foods that will carry him for at least fifteen minutes or so. Artie makes sure to bring plenty of fuel with him into the studio during every break. I've often thought how dedicated the octopus-like Artie is as he carries his monstrous-sized 6:30 A.M. snack into the studio. Sometimes I think he secretly has a third arm somewhere.

Some of my guys forget to eat during the show and they get weak and useless. This guy always knows how to stay on top of his game.

Like I said, the man knows how to pace himself, and we are only into the first hour of the show. No, it's not distracting to look over at the next chair and see Artie shoveling—I mean, eating—his fuel. It's inspirational.

 Artie Lange

And he never lets the eating get in the way of the show. He can make a point and fuel up at the same time. Some may think this is gross. It's not. It's dedication.

See, this is the look I've come to know. Some people think this is Artie falling asleep from a sugar high, but I know better. This is the look on Artie's face when he's about to come up with another great idea.

Someone once saw this picture and thought Artie was actually being unprofessional by falling asleep during the show. Jerks! Can't they see the guy is dreaming up the next great routine? Sometimes Artie is the most misunderstood guy in show business.

Here's why Artie rules. Right in the middle of the show, he lay down in the green room and worked his ass off coming up with a whole slew of new ideas. I just sat there on the air filling time, waiting for him to finish, because I knew he must really be onto something.

Here's a key point: Being a great asset to any organization means you will volunteer for the tough assignments. If you run any kind of business, you know you need a "go-to guy." While others might shy away from an assignment

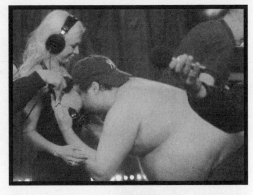

like this, Artie is the guy who bolts out of his chair and into the hot seat without hesitation. Artie's motto: *Anything for the show, baby, anything for the show.*

And notice he doesn't stop volunteering! He could have stopped after the previous incident, but he went the extra mile.

Well, you get the idea—this guy is a winner . . . no assignment too tough. Look at the concentration— the man is a highly trained comedian.

I love the guy.

And obviously, so do all of you.

So spend a few pages with Artie. *Salud* and broccoli rabe, laugh your ass off, and then say a prayer for the man with the biggest heart, my friend Artie Lange.

Too Fat
to Fish

The
Natural

I guess you could say that I won over my first audience at a very young age. I was still shitting myself at the time and I was incapable of wiping my own ass or chewing real food, which, come to think of it, could have been just last week or any other time in my life. But back then I had an excuse: I didn't have teeth at all, so eating anything other than formula or strained mush from a jar wasn't even an option. Even so, my diet didn't stop me from killing them at the Essex County Courthouse in November 1967.

When I was born on October 11, 1967, my dad was on trial, looking at about ten years of hard time for harboring counterfeit money. My dad wasn't a bad guy at all, and he wasn't a crook or a thief or even a gambler. If anything, he had a real weakness for get-rich-quick schemes. He was a sucker for any kind of plan that was too good to be true, and that attitude is what got him into this mess. He got mixed up with the wrong crowd, which is what happens when you do what you're not supposed to do. He had no idea at the time how closely I'd follow that example.

My dad grew up in Newark, New Jersey, which has never been what anyone would call an affluent city. His house was on 14th Avenue, which was a war zone then; now it's like downtown Baghdad—you can't even walk there. Like any young man trying to get ahead, my dad made the most of his opportunities, and since he was always looking for his golden ticket, he decided it was a good idea for him and his friend to rob the local bookie armed with nothing but a piece of pipe. It doesn't take a criminal genius to predict that this scheme wouldn't go exactly as planned. They got there and suddenly wised up and never went through with it, but the bookie was impressed enough by their stupidity and balls that he offered them "employment" in his operation.

I'm not sure what else they did for the guy, but my dad's main responsibility was stashing more than $200,000 in counterfeit money, which he packed into a cabinet above our fridge—not exactly burying the treasure. And that's where the FBI found it when they raided our apartment in Orange on a tip. My mom was very pregnant with me as she watched my dad being hauled off to jail.

My mom worked as a secretary at the time, as she did for most of her life. Without my dad, she was barely going to scrape by, so it really wasn't looking good. Because my dad refused to snitch, the bookie got him a lawyer and took care of his legal fees. That kind of loyalty goes a long way with neighborhood hoods. I can't imagine why. That kind of loyalty does not go over well with cops, however, even for first-time offenders like my dad. Let's just say that from the start he wasn't winning himself any friends in the courtroom.

So as the trial moved along, my family's future was not looking at all good. My dad was facing ten years in prison, my mom was on the verge of having me like any day, and the jury didn't seem too sympathetic to his lawyer's portrayal of him as a guy who was in the wrong place at the wrong time. But the lawyer kept working the first-timer angle, the hardworking-good-guy-who-made-one-mistake angle, and as the trial wound down he figured my dad had a 50-50 shot at walking. And that is when I arrived.

My dad's lawyer was not above using a newborn as a prop, so my birth became his new argument for an acquittal. He told my mom to bring me down to the courthouse for his closing statements and gave her specific instructions. He was going to ask the jury to let this entirely innocent man who'd gotten involved with bad men go free for the sake of his wife and newborn son, and at that moment, she was to stand and hold me up in the direction of the jury. It was my dad's only hope.

That day, my mom tells me, she wore a very conservative dress that might have lead the jury to believe she was Amish of Italian extraction, and she dressed me up in my baby suit, which was some kind of light blue jumpsuit. The lawyer laid it on thick, asking the jury to allow this first-time felon a second chance at life, because, despite his crime, in every other respect he had everything to live for. He talked about me, my father's first son, and how I'd have no father at all if they sent him to jail for this one small misstep. Right then the guy turned to the gallery, and my mom, who was in the front row, stood up on cue, just like they'd planned, and held me out to the courtroom.

Now, I wasn't the best baby, but I wasn't the worst and I was never what I'd call a picture-perfect little angel like the kid on a

package of Charmin. I don't know what got into me, but at that moment, I delivered. My mom stood up and extended me in the direction of the jury, and it was like a light from heaven shone on my face. My eyes lit up, I smiled, I giggled. I had that room in the palm of my little infant hand. They were mine, all right. There was no way they were going to let this little cherub spend his first decade on earth without a father.

My dad walked—no harm, no foul. And after that he straightened himself out for good. He got a job as an antenna installer, which he loved and was really good at. He did that job until he couldn't do it anymore. He was a great parent, my father. He is probably the source of whatever it is about me that anyone who has bothered to pick this book up thinks is funny. He understood my sense of humor and shared the same taste for the strange and idiotic that I do. And he definitely supported my choices, as stupid as they got, which is pretty stupid. He was right there alongside me on the path that led to where I am today.

My dad passed away on February 1, 1990, and when he did, I wasn't anywhere close to where I am now, as a comedian or a person. I was twenty-two, I was a drunk, I was a drug addict, and professionally I wasn't what I'd call "making it." I hadn't done anything at all in showbiz when he died: I got on *MADtv* over five years later. I was doing stand-up, but I was far from where I wanted to be and I wasn't what anyone might call happy. But my dad always had a way of showing me the upside of things. He used to say to me all the time when I'd tell him about doing stand-up, "And you get *paid* to do this?" He got a kick out of the fact that I actually made money to talk shit and make fun of the world, even when I wasn't making much of it. It was something he knew I'd be doing all my life even if no one was listening. I wish he could see me now. Yeah, I get paid to do that, I get paid pretty good. Now it's my *job*, Pop. And it's the only job I've ever really been good at.

Crawl Like
a Man

2

If my father's trial was my first victory as a performer, then meeting Frankie Valli was my first run-in with one of my peers. I was about eighteen months old, so Frankie and I didn't have much to talk about, but how we met is another shining example of just what kind of nut my father was. He was amazing—a legitimately crazy Newark street kid with brazen self-confidence and a wild sense of humor that our family and almost everyone we knew found incredibly endearing. There are all types of funny, and his type got you laughing and made you shake your head at just how fucking nuts he was, but you never lost sight of the fact that he meant his jokes, gags, and teasing in an affectionate way.

For those who don't know, Frankie Valli and the Four Seasons were in the late '50s and '60s what Bruce Springsteen and the E Street Band is to the post–baby boomer generation: The Four Seasons was *the* singing group for people living in New Jersey. Frankie Valli himself grew up in north Newark, in a housing project called the Stephen Crane Village, which was close to where both of my parents were from. My mother grew up just a couple of blocks away on North 7th Street, while my father lived a few miles away in south Newark. My mom and dad were born around the same year as Bob Dylan, but he was never their spokesman: The whole sixties folk scene and after it the hippie, Woodstock stuff didn't really affect them at all. It wasn't just that their upbringing was so different from that of the middle-class rich kids who "tuned in, turned on, and dropped out," it was that they didn't relate to the message at all.

The soundtrack of my parents' young adulthood was simple and it never wavered: early rock and roll. And to them, Frankie Valli and the Four Seasons were the coolest group in the world. To this day, my mother still doesn't like any of the boomer rock associated with her generation, aside from the Beatles, of course, which transcends all. She loves Chuck Berry, all things Motown, Bobby Darin, and all of the great fifties crooners. My father loved the same stuff, though for a brief period of time he grew his hair kind of long and listened to The Doors. I remember him singing "Roadhouse Blues" and "Light My Fire" really loud in the truck on his way to work. But it wasn't any kind of statement other than that he liked the tunes.

The Frankie Valli mind-set was different; it embodied the values of the hardworking families from Newark and Union, who did everything they could to try to get a better life for their kids. It was the background music of their lives and it spoke about their lives, so it meant a lot to them. And because of that, especially among my Italian friends, it means a lot to us.

The sound wasn't current even when I was a kid, but Frankie Valli and the Four Seasons was something that bonded every Italian kid in Union to one another. It was like an unspoken thing, probably in the same way old Italian singers like Louis Prima had meaning for our parents because of their parents. There wasn't a sense of rebelling against your parents' music when it came to Frankie Valli—that would be like going against the family. And if there's one thing all Italians know, it's that you never, *ever* go against the family.

I don't care what anybody says, it's great music. When I was driving around with my friends, we could easily throw in a Frankie Valli tape and listen to it and really enjoy it. My buddy Mike Ciccone and I see eye to eye over this because in both of our houses growing up, Frankie and the Four Seasons was always on and our parents were always singing along. One night when we were about nineteen, we were out driving in Mike's Mustang convertible with the radio tuned to CBS-FM, the great oldies station, when "Rag Doll" came on. We sat there enjoying the harmonies and Frankie's amazingly high voice until the kids who were out with us, sitting in the backseat, interrupted our good time.

"What is this shit?" one of them said. "Get this shit off, put on PLJ!"

My buddy Ciccone was one of those guys who really did not take shit, at any time, from anybody. I will never forget how he calmly lowered the volume and looked over at me, and on cue, we said together: "Frankie Valli is fucking cool, man." There was no way we were going to let anyone talk shit. The others could have gotten out and walked for all we cared.

Those two didn't know what they were missing: The Four

Seasons easily had thirty or forty Top Ten hit records. And now there's the musical *Jersey Boys,* based on Frankie Valli's life story. I have seen it three times now, and I am far from what you'd call a patron of the theater. Really, it is the only Broadway musical I could ever see myself sitting through, because, much like *The Sopranos,* it has what you need to keep me interested: a good story, Jersey references like crazy, and an amazing sound track.

Anyway, in the late sixties, my father started his own business. For years he had hung antennas, run wires, and repaired TVs for American Radio on Route 22 in Union. Once he was married and had a child (me), he took stock and decided he needed to make some changes. He was living with his wife and child in a small apartment on Reynolds Terrace in Orange, New Jersey, and like a guy in a Four Seasons song, my father wanted a better life. He decided to buy his own van and hustle as hard as he could to make it on his own. My dad was definitely a hard worker and an achiever, so he got that van, he worked his ass off, and, once he'd saved enough for a down payment, he bought us a house in the suburbs for thirty grand.

Status symbols were important to my father—like having the most expensive new car that he could reasonably afford and taking the family on a big vacation every summer. For two weeks, usually in August, we would go down to Wildwood Crest, New Jersey. We went to Wildwood each summer until I was about twelve, and I have so many good memories of those summers with my family that mean the world to me. In the summer of '69, I was a few months away from turning two and my sister was just a few months old. My grandmother on my mother's side, Grandma Caprio, stayed home with my sister to give my mom a bit of a break.

Off we went, down the Shore and headed for the Olympic Motel. The Olympic was fine, but it was definitely a motel, not a hotel—nothing too luxurious, just a place to stay right there on the ocean. (In later years we switched to the Crusader Motel.) Wildwood Crest was teeming with people from North Jersey and Philadelphia who'd come to have an old-fashioned good time on the beach. They wanted to play ball, get a nice bite to eat on the Wildwood boardwalk, which was home to some amazing cheese-steak restaurants, or nearby Seaside Heights, which also had great places for cheesesteak. Where you got your cheesesteaks was always a source of debate. In Seaside, there was Steaks Unlimited and Midway, which was a walk-up joint that used synthetic, welfare-style cheese. That might sound disgusting, but let me tell you, when you're drunk, five Midway cheesesteaks are just about the best thing in the world—that welfare cheese goes down real easy. While we're on the subject, though, J.R.'s Cheesesteak and Steaks Unlimited are my favorites, and on the Wildwood Crest boardwalk I prefer the places that use real cheese—some even use mozzarella, which I have found to improve just about anything.

By the summer of '69 my parents' favorite band, the Four Seasons, had hit a bit of a dry patch after a tremendous run of six or seven years of hits. That creative lull happens to everyone at some point, but this was worse, because the music of the time was changing too, so they weren't winning any new fans. Like so many groups of that era, they were forced to play much smaller venues. The week we happened to be in Wildwood, they were playing a five-night engagement at the Starlight Ballroom, which was a decent-sized venue, but nothing worth writing home about.

My mother and father really wanted to go see them, but they had no idea what they'd do with me for those few hours, so they kind of put it out of their minds. Or at least my mother did; my old man was not the type to be discouraged by anything. One afternoon as they were passing the front desk at the motel, they asked the clerk how to get to the Starlight because they'd heard Frankie Valli was playing. There are certain people in this world who somehow earn the trust of strangers without even trying because of the way they carry themselves. My father was one of them.

"I will give you a little hint," the clerk said, leaning forward. "Frankie Valli is actually staying right here in the motel."

"Really?" my mother said, smiling.

"What do you know?" my father said.

There are also certain people in this world who know how to capitalize on a situation regardless of odds or etiquette. My father was one of them too. Being a natural smooth talker, Pop was able to get the room number out of the guy. My father was charming enough that all he probably did was slip the guy a sawbuck. For all you pussies who don't know what a sawbuck is, it's a ten dollar bill.

We went up to the floor and passed by the room but didn't see any action. The next day, we went back, and sure enough, as my father's crazy luck would go, Frankie Valli's door was ajar. My parents debated about what to do: knock and introduce themselves as fans or just wander in like they didn't know he was there, pretending they were looking for someone else. Neither idea made sense to my father. He had a better one.

"Okay, here's what we're gonna do," he told my mom. "That door is open just enough for Little Artie to crawl through. Let's pretend he got away from us while we were walking down the hall, and he just went in there."

"Absolutely not!" my mother half-shouted. "No, Artie, that is just crazy."

"What's he gonna say? It's a kid coming in his room! That way we don't look like two nuts camping outside of his room waiting to jump him or something. It'll break the ice!"

"We are talking about a baby—how are you going to tell him to do that? No, we are not doing that," my mom said.

"Oh yeah? Watch this."

My father took one of my favorite toys and, over the sound of my mother's protests, threw it inside Frankie Valli's room.

"Oh Jesus, what have you *done*, Artie?" my mom said, shaking her head.

My father knew that I went just about anywhere that toy went, and sure enough, I crawled right in there after it. Then they sat there, out in the hall, waiting for something to happen.

"So what now?" my mother asked.

"Shh!" my father said. "He's gonna come out here in a minute holding the baby, and he's gonna look around and ask whose kid he is. And then we're gonna meet him. We'll get an autograph and maybe a picture, and that's it, okay?"

Well, that didn't happen. Five minutes went by, ten minutes, fifteen minutes. My mother, as any mother would, started to get really worried. My father kept reassuring her with statements like: "What? You think Frankie Valli is actually a kidnapper now and he's doing something crazy with him?"

"Who knows?" she said. "You don't!" That's how my mother would deal with him: She'd remind him that his version of a situation wasn't the only possible scenario, and then follow up with about fifty-two completely logical alternatives. Typically, my father would have absolutely no answer for these.

In this case, she had plenty to work with:

"What if he was in the room with a girl?"

"There could be naked people in there!"

"He is a STAR! You have no idea what those people do in their hotel rooms!"

"There could be some shady character in there dividing up money."

"He could be on drugs."

"A million different illegal things could be happening in there, Artie! You don't know!"

At these times my father would listen, usually rolling his eyes, for as long as he could stand it. Then he'd do something about it. In this case, he walked over to the door and pushed it open. He and my mother walked in slowly and didn't see anything close to the Sodom and Gomorrah my mother had imagined. At first they didn't see anything at all. Then they looked toward the bathroom, where the light was on and the door was open. And there I was, sitting on the sink in Frankie Valli's bathroom, playing with my toy, with a big smile on my face. Next to me, in a robe, shaving, was Frankie Valli. He was amusing me with a blob of shaving cream.

"Okay, little man," he was saying. "We're gonna find your parents right after I'm done shaving, but I hope they're not far, because I'm in a hurry, kid."

As someone who has become a bit of a celebrity, if this were to happen to me, I would have called the FBI. But there was Frankie Valli, in his room, in a robe, shaving, when a toddler crawled in unannounced. And then the kid's parents show up? I'm much too suspicious—that would be too much for me. But this was a different time, and my father had that crazy Newark mentality that Frankie Valli definitely recognized and I'm sure could relate to. I've made my mom tell this story so many times that I have to believe her when she swears that, as insane as it sounds, it was not an awkward moment.

"Oh, we're really sorry," my father said. "We were looking all over for him—thank you so much for taking care of him. We are really sorry he crawled in here."

Frankie, from the beginning, was completely cordial and they started talking like it was no big deal that they were in his hotel room under the strangest possible pretenses. At some point in the conversation, my mother and father admitted that they were big fans.

"You know what?" Frankie said. "You want to come to one of the shows?"

"We'd love to!" my mother said. "We just can't find a babysitter for our son."

"Well, don't worry about that," Frankie said. "Bring him. We'll leave him backstage with some of the girls we have on tour. He will be completely safe, I promise you. Just bring him along, and you'll come with us. Why don't you get everything you need and we'll go down to the show in a few minutes."

Just like that, my parents went from wondering if they'd even be able to get tickets to meeting Frankie in his room to attending the show as Frankie's guests! And it wasn't just for that night—Frankie invited them down to two or three shows. He saw that they were a young couple, in love but struggling with money, and he was very, very generous with them. One of the nights after the show he asked them to come out to dinner with him, the Four Seasons, and everyone else on the tour, and since they were all just people from Newark, my parents fit in just fine. Even though Frankie Valli and the band were hitting some hard times, they weren't anything less than gracious and humble.

At some point, my parents and I were hanging out with Frankie and his crew, on the terrace at the motel. My father had bought a camera for my mom in the motel lobby, and she took a bunch of pictures. She got me, my father, and Frankie Valli, as well as a few of me alone with Frankie, and then my dad took a few of my mom and Frankie. Actually, my parents took pictures in every conceivable configuration of themselves, me, and Frankie Valli. Most of them were lost in the shuffle over the years, but for most of my childhood the best ones were proudly displayed in our house in Union in one of those square plastic picture cubes.

Talk about status symbols: Displaying a big plastic cube full of pictures of Frankie Valli in your home in North Jersey was like driving through the ghetto in a brand new Bentley. People would come over and pick up the thing and say, "Wow! How do you know Frankie Valli?"

"We're friends with him," my father would proudly say. "We were on vacation together there, down the Shore."

The truth was, after that week, my parents completely lost touch with Frankie Valli and never saw him again. I asked my mother if they got Frankie's contact information and tried to see him again, but she said no. She talked my dad into just being happy with the time they had had with Frankie there that week. She didn't want to stay in touch and bug him, which in modern terms we call stalking. My mother also wouldn't ever have wanted Frankie to think they were taking advantage of his generosity.

They might not have spent time with him again, but they continued to watch Frankie's career closely and remained big fans and supporters. When *Jersey Boys* opened on Broadway and Frankie was back in the news, I mentioned to Howard how I'd met him as a toddler and I had my mom dig out the one remaining picture we still have with him. It was up on the Stern Web site for a while, and now here it is, forever in print.

I've stared at this picture so many times over the years, because it shows my father in his heyday. He's twenty-four or twenty-five years old, and as you can see, he looked like a movie star back then, my old man. He's in great shape from climbing roofs, and there I am, sitting on his knee, blond hair, dressed in all my little baby-rabilia. And there's Frankie Valli looking at me, smiling, trying to make me laugh. I get so unbelievably emotional when I look at this that sometimes I just start to cry. That moment captures so much: It's my family, it's my father, and it's Frankie Valli, a New Jersey hero who was to my father what Bruce Springsteen is to me. I'm there with my hero, meeting his hero. It's hard for me to see myself

as just a cute little kid, unaffected by life, without a care in the world. I had no idea then what I would later do to myself and my body as an adult.

When *Jersey Boys* opened in 2005, it became an instant success, taking in something like 400 grand in ticket sales in just one day. It's still packing houses on Broadway, and it's gone on to be a huge national touring production as well. As soon as I heard about it, I immediately got tickets to take my mother to see it for her birthday. Four of us went: my mother; my beloved godmother, Aunt Dee, who is my mom's younger sister Diane; my sister, Stacey; and me. I've seen it two more times since, and I assure you, it must be good for me to be recommending it here in my book. Did you think when you picked up this book that Artie Lange would be giving you tips on great Broadway musicals? Really, if you get a chance, see fucking *Jersey Boys* when you're in town because it is the most fun you will ever have, whether you like the music or not.

All of that attention a few years ago put Frankie Valli back in the public eye again: He was on a few talk shows, he got a small role on *The Sopranos,* and he released an album covering love songs from the sixties. This was around 2006–2007, when *The Stern Show* was making the move over to satellite radio. One day Gary Dell'Abate, the show's producer, came in and said to Howard during a break, "Would you like to have Frankie Valli in as a guest?" We'd just had Paul Anka on, who had delivered in such an amazing way—he really was one of the best guests we'd ever had. Howard did one of his classic, brilliant interviews, and Anka told great stories about Sinatra and the old days. People at the show had been on the fence about having him, but Anka blew other guests away. So when Frankie Valli came up, I stepped in.

"Oh man, that'd be great," I said. "Look, you know, I got this great story about meeting him as a baby, and I could bring in the picture of me and him and see if it jars anything in his memory at all when we do the interview. Would it be all right if I had my mom up here to say hi to him in the greenroom after? She literally has not seen or talked to him in person since this week that she and my father and I spent with the Four Seasons at this motel in the summer of '69."

Howard, as anyone who's met him or heard him in action knows, is *always* thinking—that guy's mind is just incredibly quick. "That would be great to do on the air if your mother agrees to it," he said. "Let's do it."

I called my mom that afternoon, all excited to make this reunion happen. Now, my mother really hates being on camera and hates attention—in that way and so many other ways, she's the complete opposite of me. It took some time and a lot of badgering, but eventually I convinced her to come up to the show that day and see what would happen. Then, of course, some shit luck went on and for whatever reason Gary wasn't able to book Frankie. Then

Frankie's character on *The Sopranos* got whacked, so he wasn't in the public eye anymore. But the musical is still going strong and I'm still holding out, hoping that one day Frankie Valli will come up and do *The Stern Show* and I'll be able to reunite him with my mom. It's sappy and odds are that he doesn't remember a thing, but it would mean a lot to her and to me and to the memory of my dad to be able to stand there with him and show him that picture. It would be a special memory coming full circle. In my life, things like that are what I live for and what I look forward to. In the meantime, I've always got the musical.

Mr. October

3

As a child, as far as I was concerned, my dad had an amazing job and we had all the money we needed. My life was so fun and carefree that I never realized that we weren't rich—until I met someone rich. Still, I've never met a rich kid who grew up as happy as I did. When I started going to New York City to do comedy, and later on, when I moved to L.A. to do *MADtv*, I met plenty of people who grew up wealthy. These people came from families that had several homes, a staff of servants, and took vacations in beautiful, exotic locations all around the world. My family had one house, and my sister, Stacey, and I had a maid—we called her "Ma." When we vacationed, there wasn't much of a debate between

Fiji and Bora Bora—we relaxed strictly at the Jersey Shore. When I encountered rich people for the first time, I discovered that not only do they holiday in places that are hard to find on a map, they also use the names of seasons as verbs. When they asked me, "Where did you summer and winter growing up?" I would usually say, "As a child? The same place I springed and autumned."

Rich people know how to relax. That's all they do growing up, relax. I wish my mother knew how to relax because now I have the money to let her take it easy. I wish she liked tennis or golf. Maybe skiing or world travel. Unfortunately, she doesn't. My mother likes cleaning tables with Pledge. If I'm ever blessed with a child, I'm going to enourage that child to take it slow. I'd like to see someone in my family fucking relax! Even if it's thirty years from now.

As I mentioned earlier, our family's favorite destination down the Shore was Wildwood Crest, New Jersey. We'd head out there for the last two weeks of every summer and check into the Crusader Motel, and sure, it was only a motel, but it was right on the beach. While my mother and sister sat on the sand, my father and I would play baseball for what seemed like all day.

As a kid, I was obsessed with baseball, and not much has changed since then. Like a lot of fathers and sons, my dad and I bonded over baseball more than anything else. Since my father spent his days climbing roofs and installing antennas, he was in great shape, which made it easier for him to keep up with an eleven-year-old boy out on the baseball field all day long. We would start out playing catch, then he'd hit me grounders. After that, he'd usually follow up by hitting screaming line drives for me to chase down and that sort of stuff. Eventually, he'd work up to what he'd call the scorchers, which were shots he'd just slam into the field as hard as he could. Then he would pitch me batting practice for about an hour. He was the coolest ever, my old man. I'd hit balls all over the field, and he would go shag them down. Finally, if you can believe it, he'd come back in from the outfield and hit me fly balls, which he'd call "sky-ers," for another hour or so. My father was a really good athlete, so his pop-ups really were sky-high. Eventually, I learned how to judge them properly and catch them well. It was great training for when I started to play on teams, which I did all through school.

My dad and I were constantly in search of a perfect surface where we could get good hops. A lot of the time, we would end up on private golf courses where he'd hit me grounders on one of the greens. That was hilarious. Let me tell you, the hops we'd get on these well-groomed putting greens were amazing, but it was definitely challenging, mostly because I was in charge of watching out for cops coming to arrest us. My father was a real inner-city guy, so he had no concept that what we were doing was just so obviously wrong. He saw it as creating a slight inconvenience to the golfers. Before he'd start hitting me balls, he'd tell me to look out for, as he'd put it, "the golf fags."

I liked to make my father laugh whenever I could, and during our practice I usually succeeded by doing play-by-play sportscasting as I ran around catching fly balls. Playing baseball with him was great, but being able to make him laugh was the best. It put me on top of the world: Those moments were when I first realized the power you can have over people if you are able to make them laugh. If something pissed my father off—like, usually, me—I realized that I could get out of trouble if I could make him laugh when I 'fessed up to my crime. He'd always encourage me too: Driving back from the ballpark in his truck with the ladder between us resting on the dash, he'd say, "Sport, if you don't make it in the majors, you'll probably have a career as a comedian." My dad's encouragement is definitely why those were the only two things I've ever wanted to do with my life. I never went through a period where I wanted to be a doctor, a cop, or even a rock star. All I wanted to do was play shortstop for the Yankees from the time I was about five.

Then I turned fifteen and realized how silly that was and just gave up on it. And let's face it, that's the luckiest fucking break Derek Jeter ever got.

The second my Yankees dream ended, though, the other one kicked right in, and once it did, I was really fucked. Historically, a successful life in comedy is a dream that's as pondered and unpursued as a career as an astronaut. For me, it became an obsession that consumed my life, as you will soon see. For now, though, I want to stick to baseball.

So I'm about to share with you the very craziest experience I ever had with my dad. Clearly, my father was as much a best friend as he was a dad. And as you can probably tell by the golf course story, he had his own set of rules for everything.

On October 18, 1977, my father took me to the final game of the World Series, the Yankees vs. the Dodgers at Yankee Stadium. That Yankee team of the late seventies has got to be one of the coolest clubs in the history of sports. They had Willie Randolph, Reggie Jackson, Mickey Rivers, Lou Piniella, and of course my favorite, Thurman Munson. He was by far my favorite; the day Thurman died, August 2, 1979, I do not mind telling you, I wept. I was eleven years old and it was *devastating*. If someone ever invents a time machine, my requested trip back in time is simple: I want to go back to 1977 and see any Yankees home game so that I can witness Munson hit a two-run double to right center field. I know what you're saying: "How do you know he'll double in the game you're transported to?" To me, this is a nonissue, because as a fan, I recall that Munson hit two-run doubles in every game that year just as easily as he showed up to play.

I don't care what anybody says, 1977 was a magical year. The New York area was sweating through the hottest summer ever and a midsummer blackout caused a lot of babies to be born in April of 1978. That year, the serial killer, David Berkowitz, the Son of Sam, terrorized the city. But every single thing that sucked that summer seemed to do nothing but make the Yankees better. The year before, they'd gotten to the World Series for the first time in twelve years. And when they did, they were swept four games straight by the fucking asshole Cincinnati Reds. Munson hit .529 in that series, and that fact alone, in addition to the fact that Johnny Bench batted .531, made me want to drive to Cincinnati and punch everyone in the city in the fucking face. I took that shit seriously after that loss. I refused to even watch *WKRP in Cincinnati*, which is a perfectly acceptable show.

The next season, in '77, after falling behind some, the Yanks came on strong in September and won the division. And then they won the pennant against George Brett and the jerk-off Royals to get themselves in the Series again. And that time, they were playing against the Los Angeles Dodgers, another team that I could not fucking stand. The '77 Dodgers were nothing but clean-cut, California dude players—chumps, like Steve Garvey. I hate him. He had a haircut like a Marine for no good reason. He was always clean-shaven and well-groomed. Steve Garvey and the fucking L.A. Dodgers were the anti-Munson, so I could not wait to see the Yanks kick their asses in the Series. That is how I felt, and how intensely I felt it back then at nine years old. Sure it was juvenile and the kind of reasoning that only a kid can have, but please believe me when I assure you that nothing at all has changed.

In 1977, my father was thirty-four years old. He worked long hard hours to pay the mortgage and support his wife and two kids, but regardless of whatever stress was going on for him, he was always capable of acting enough like a kid when he was with me that I never knew about it. He was always ready to play no matter how tired he was and he was always planning something special, but his scheme that October took the cake. After the Yankees beat everyone and got into the World Series, my father told me he had a surprise for me. This was right around my birthday, October 11, so I figured it could have been anything—a new glove, a new bat— but it was much, much better than that. That day, my father walked up to me and pulled the impossible out of his back pocket—tickets to the Series, the Holy Grail for any boy in the tri-state area. He had two tickets to every Yankees home game in the World Series that year.

My dad was so far from a high roller his entire life—there was no way he'd won these tickets in a card game or scalped them from some exclusive ticket broker. In the middle of the year, he had sent away in the mail for them just in case the Yankees made it to the Series again. He'd paid $10 apiece for them, and fittingly, they were in the very last row of the very last section of the very upper deck, right above third base. Those seats were sky-high, literally hovering above the South Bronx. But even if we saw nothing, it still meant that we were going to be inside the fucking Stadium for the World goddamn Series of 1977, the Yankees vs. the Dodgers.

My dad would come home from work early every night we had tickets for the games, and he and I would get ready together. I was unbelievably excited. We lived in Union, New Jersey, which is a working-class suburb a few miles west of Newark. Without traffic, we could make it to Yankee Stadium in about half an hour. With traffic, it might take two days. My father hated public transportation, so he insisted on driving to the Stadium. For an 8 P.M. start we had to leave at 6 P.M. because we weren't going to miss anything. My father hated the thought of ever taking a bus or a train to get anywhere, probably as a result of the fact that he was what some people call "nigger rich." No offense to African Americans or any-thing—that's just how I've heard the phrase used. Whatever you want to call it, the message was clear: My father was the kind of guy who never saved a dime. He behaved like a rapper who'd just gotten signed. He'd spend all of his cash on Cadillacs that he'd trade in every two years. Where my father was from, having the newest Caddy was a huge status symbol, so, naturally, he liked to drive his car everywhere. On October 18, 1977, his Caddy du jour was a '76 Coupe de Ville. He worshipped that car.

On top of all the other crazy shit that was going on in New York City in the late seventies, the city itself was broke. Entire neighborhoods looked like abandoned war zones. And the part of town that was the shining example of this problem, the one hit the worst of all, was the South Bronx. The blocks around the Stadium were nothing but crumbling brick apartment houses with no residents. There were vacant lots full of cinder blocks and rubble everywhere. The area was full of drugs and drug addicts, and it seemed like heroin was slowly killing everything. But right in the middle of this pile of shit was the most famous address in the world of sports: 161 River Avenue, Yankee Stadium. All of this native scenery made it a very difficult job to park the Coupe de Ville—no spot ever seemed to be safe enough or big enough. But there was no question about doing it any other way, because my dad thought parking garages were a huge rip-off. And he was right—it was as true then as it is now.

Over the years, I have gotten some psychotherapy, mostly because I was ordered to do so by either the court or my job. After sharing just a few stories about me and my family during those visits, I figured out pretty quickly that my father was definitely obsessive-compulsive. It wasn't a commonly known affliction back then, but in retrospect, it's clear to me that he had it bad. A prime example: For a guy who loved cash and having it on him and around him all the time, he was completely grossed out by it. He considered all money to be filled with germs that could spread sickness. After he showered and got ready for a night out, my dad could not and would not touch money. Either my mother dealt with the money for the night or he wore gloves—always a brand-new pair of the work gloves he'd wear to install antennas. It was crazy. If he and my mom went out with other people, they'd be all dressed up for a social experience, and there he'd be with his hands covered in sparkling-clean new work gloves.

I remember him wearing a pair like that each night we went to the Series. He wore them to pay the tolls, of course. He even planned ahead on how to further avoid touching money in spite of the gloves: Before we left, he had me line up quarters on the dashboard. When we got to the George Washington Bridge, all he had to do was reach over with his gloves on and grab them to pay the toll instead of fidgeting with his wallet. He would put a few extra quarters up there too for the guys who squeegeed your windshield when you got off the Jerome Avenue exit in the Bronx, the exit that everyone going to the game had to take. When the kids asked for it, he just lowered the window and pointed to the quarters and let them reach in and grab the money themselves. Looking back, if one of those kids had a knife or any kind of weapon, they could have done serious damage. But stuff like that didn't concern my father. He was more inner city and ghetto than anyone in the Bronx. He grew up in Newark. When it came to matters of the city street, he was always in control. He made you feel comfortable. If he was around, no one could hurt us. I still felt that way even after his injury; even with him lying there paralyzed from the neck down, he gave me a feeling of security. If someone broke into the house while he was hurt, I thought he would somehow still be able to protect us. He was my hero, always capable in my eyes.

In any case, each of the games went like this: After we encountered the squeegee gangs and had driven around for what seemed like hours until my father found the one fucking parking spot in the South Bronx where it was impossible to get a door ding, we'd walk to the Stadium. And we always made it in time to catch some batting practice. I remember that before Game 1 we saw Bucky Dent take his warm-up—he would become the World Series MVP in 1978 when the Yanks beat the Dodgers. We sat down about five rows behind third base, and I remember my father marveling at how close to the field we were and how expensive those seats must be. Ironically, we were sitting exactly where my season tickets are now located. I got there permanently, Pop. I know that he would love knowing that his son has those seats now. Also that first night, Bucky turned on one and hit a scorching line drive into the stands that hit a guy three rows in front of us right in the head. This man was probably about fifty years old, and he was bald, and I can still recall just how scary the sound was when the ball hit him smack in his temple: It was like a soft piece of wood cracking in two. The guy went unconscious immediately, and my father helped the cops get him out of there. Stuff was getting crazy. I could not stop looking around at everything, the field, the players, all the action in the outfield. My father could tell that I was loving it. His son was as big of a baseball fan as he was, and that made him ecstatic. To him it also meant I probably wasn't gay. Talk about a perfect son!

The World Series that year was phenomenal. In the first game, we watched Paul Blair win it for the Yankees with an extra-inning single between short and third that drove Randolph home. The place went nuts. We were in baseball heaven, even though our seats were geographically as far away from home plate as you could get, which technically was closer to heaven than home plate—it didn't matter. In the seventies, the upper deck at Yankee Stadium had its own charm. That first game was the first time that I ever smelled weed. And it worked on me a little too well, because the contact high I got cost my father at least $30 in hot dogs and pretzels.

When I've told this story before, most publicly on *Letterman*, I recalled how my father made me hold his beer while he rolled a joint. I'm embarrassed to admit it now, but I lied to Dave. The truth is, my father never touched drugs and barely drank. But the guy in front of me sure as hell did both, and he asked me to hold his burning joint by the roach clip while he put mustard on a hot dog. My dad looked on and smiled and didn't care at all. He loved crazy people. Besides, what's more American than baseball, hot dogs, and weed—especially all at the same time?

The Yanks and the Dodgers split the first two games and then the Yankees took two out of three in L.A., which brought it back to New York for Game 6, with the Bronx Bombers up three games to two. They had the chance to take it all in that sixth game. As a fan, part of me was upset that we didn't finish them off in L.A. on their own turf, but in a bigger way, I was thrilled to have the chance to see another game, possibly the final game, at home. If they took it, it would be their first World Series win in fifteen years!

So there we were, on October 18, 1977, ready to go, with the quarters on the dash and my father in a brand-new set of work gloves as we drove the Coupe de Ville once again into the Bronx. We dealt with the squeegee kids, found the best anti-door-ding parking spot, got in early to have a couple of hot dogs and watch batting practice, and then we settled into our nosebleed seats to watch what would become the history-making Game 6 of the 1977 World Series.

The great and controversial Reggie Jackson had already hit two home runs in the Series and he seemed primed to do something big that night, because if there was one thing about Number 44, he did not disappoint. His first time up at bat, Reggie walked. It seemed like the Dodgers wanted no part of him. They should have made way better sure of that, because the rest of the game belonged to the man Thurman Munson called "Mr. October." Reggie's next two times at bat, he hit home runs, both of them screaming line drives into the stands behind Yankee Stadium's famously short right-field fence. By the time he got up for his fourth at bat, the whole place could smell victory. The Yankees had the lead. And as Reggie Jackson stepped to the plate, we Yankee fans, who can never get enough excitement, were not only rooting for a win, we wanted a third Reggie Jackson home run.

My father and I were on our feet chanting, "One more time! One more time!" and "Reg-gie! Reg-gie! Reg-gie!" Everyone else there was doing the same thing; it was pandemonium. My father put me on his shoulders so I could see better, and Mr. Roach Clip looked back at us and said, "Man, can you imagine what's going to happen if he hits another one? We will fucking tear this place *down*!" Mr. Stoner's sentiment was cool and all, but thank God he was proven wrong on the destruction end of things. On the first pitch from Dodgers relief pitcher Bob Welch, Reggie unloaded that classic swing and hit a picture-perfect sky-high home run to dead center field. From the moment it left the bat, there was never a doubt where that ball was going. It touched down in the section of Yankee Stadium behind the center-field fence, the batter's eye, where the fence is at its very farthest point from home plate—it's something that is hardly ever done. I think Reggie was only the second player ever to have done so in the history of the park, the first being the Orioles designated hitter and current Yankees announcer Ken Singleton.

We might not have torn the place down, but it nearly collapsed all on its own. As soon as that ball left the park, the entire crowd started jumping up and down and screaming; you could feel the upper deck shaking as if there were an earthquake. It was actually pretty scary, but none of that mattered. I was ten years old, sitting on my father's shoulders at Yankee Stadium after watching Reggie Jackson round the base for the third straight time that night. I was in baseball little-boy heaven—three homers on three consecutive pitches. If I could somehow capture a fraction of that happiness

again now, I would not be up at 3 A.M. on a work night writing this story with a tall glass of whiskey keeping me company.

With the ninth inning upon us, the Yanks were up 8-4 and just three outs away from their twenty-first Series title. To commemorate that moment, my father saw the opportunity to do something that was so unbelievably and uniquely him that to hear the retelling is almost, but not quite, as good as shaking his hand. My father was crazy, but in a wonderful and loving way; yet still, what he had in mind, if a social worker or a cop had overheard his plan, would have no doubt ended up with him being thrown in jail. But it was this kind of thing that defined who my father was, and lucky for him, this was New York in the crazy seventies, which was a time before the country had agreed to collectively stick an uptight ruler up its ass.

Just being in the Stadium for the last out was not enough for Artie Lange, Sr.: What he really wanted was to see the end of the game from the front row. My father was a master at conning people and sneaking into places he was not allowed, so this did not seem at all out of the question. Combined with the fact that, back then, security was nowhere near as stiff at baseball games as it is now, it wasn't very tough for anyone to bullshit or tip a guard to get up front. It was no effort at all for my dad, so before I knew it we had snuck and weaved our way up to the first row, just left of the Yankees' dugout, with just one out left. It was nothing short of amazing to be right there, with all of the crowd's energy and excitement all around us. You'd think that would be cool enough. Not for my old man. He wanted more.

As Lee Lacy, the player who would end up making the last out for the Dodgers, stepped up to the plate, my father turned to me with this intense look on his face.

"Now, listen, when the game ends I will not be able to get on the field," he said. "But *you* can."

"I can?" I said. *"Really?"*

I looked at the field and saw a bunch of New York City cops lined up with their billy clubs out, just waiting to smack the shit out of anybody who tried to run onto the field.

"Listen," my father continued. "When the last out is made, I am going to throw you onto the field."

"Okay," I said, looking up at him, thinking that, since my dad was suggesting it, this plan was absolutely fine. "Okay! Yeah."

"Now, when you get on the field, I want you to run to shortstop and just wait for me there," he said, looking me in the eye. "The cops will not hit a kid. They never hit kids, so you've got nothing to worry about. Eventually I will be able to get out there on the field, and when I do, I will meet you at shortstop, okay?"

I nodded my head. "I got it," I said.

"Remember," he said, pointing at the field. "Shortstop."

There were two outs when, on the last pitch of the game, Lacy squared to bunt and popped it up right to Yankees pitcher Mike Torres. Torres caught the ball easily to end the game, and he and Thurman Munson embraced at the mound and started the celebration. When I saw that they'd won, I practically went numb. I started screaming and jumping up and down uncontrollably; it was such an overwhelming feeling of elation that I was incapable of containing myself in any way. To this day, I have never been as happy as I was at that moment. I think that deep down, subconsciously, I have been chasing that feeling ever since. That type of rush, the kind that overcomes every bit of your being, is the same rush you get when you first chase money and gamble. And heroin? Don't even get me started. I've done both of those over and over again, and even at their best they didn't measure up to a fraction of what I felt that night. I think most people's happiest times occur when they're children. Whether you're rich or poor, we're all kids for a while; it's an experience we all share. From six to fifteen, nothing means shit no matter how you grow up; we are basically carefree. That is why the most despicable crime in the world is for an adult to abuse a child mentally or physically. Aside from the obvious wrong in that, anyone who does something inappropriate to a child also robs them of something they can never get back: the only time in life when anyone can ever be 100 percent happy. Not to sound like a negative prick, but once you become an adult, particularly if you do not have money, life becomes just one stressful, unending parade of depressing bullshit.

I didn't put all of that together as a ten-year-old. I was too busy losing my mind with joy. My heart was racing, and the fucking night just kept getting crazier. For a second, I thought my father forgot about his plan to storm the field. I thought I was off the hook. No such luck. As I lost myself in celebrating, I felt my father's hand on my lower back.

He yelled in my ear, "I'll meet you at short!"

He threw me up over the line of cops and onto the field as naturally as if he were shooting a free throw. I somersaulted onto the on-deck circle and looked back at my father. There he was, grinning ear to ear as he pointed at me and yelled, "Run to short!" I turned around and booked as hard as I could to shortstop, and saw firsthand that my dad was right about the cops. They didn't bother me at all, but all around me they were taking down anyone who looked like they might be a member of Led Zeppelin. No, it was worse than that: They were hitting any adult male on the field as hard as they could with their nightsticks. It was a fucking war zone. Right next to me, some guy stole Willie Randolph's hat right off his head. I saw Reggie barreling into people looking like Earl Campbell running into linebackers. I was confused, scared, and ten years old. I felt like Willem Dafoe at the end of *Platoon* when the chopper takes off, leaving him to get shot to death. I wanted to drop to my knees in slow motion and raise my hands to heaven just like Dafoe. But I didn't do that; somehow I kept running. I made it to shortstop and waited there just like my father said. It was really freaky, especially to a kid: I kept staring at this fat guy who'd been knocked out and was lying on the ground by third base with blood coming out of his head.

After about fifteen minutes, I was ready to start crying. The only thing that stopped me was the knowledge that my father was Superman and he would be showing up to handle the situation any minute now. Then I felt a tap on my shoulder; I turned around and there he was. Just like Reggie, my father did not let me down.

"We won!" he yelled. He was beaming just as big as I ever saw him. Then he put me back on his shoulders and the tears that were seeping from my eyes immediately turned to tears of joy. After that, we walked around the field until they turned the lights off and kicked us out. But before we left, my father told me to run into the Yankees' dugout and sneak a quick drink from the water fountain.

ny others, we dug up a patch of the infield grass to

got home sometime around 3 A.M., my father,
laid down the law.

about going to school tomorrow," he said. "I don't care
what your mother says." He was definitely in best-friend mode at
that point.

Instead of going to school, I spent the day with him and we
planted the Yankee Stadium grass in our front yard. Our family is
long gone from that house, but that patch of history is probably still
part of the lawn at 433 Huntington Road in Union, New Jersey.

———

That night was the pinnacle of my childhood, and I am so thankful
to have shared that moment with my father. Exactly eight years
later, on October 18, 1985, my childhood and the carefree part of
my life officially ended. On the eighth anniversary of that day, my
father fell off of a roof while installing an antenna and became a
quadriplegic for the rest of his life. It happened one week after my
eighteenth birthday. A week after my tenth birthday, we'd cele-
brated Reggie's three World Series homers together. One week after my eighteenth birthday, I watched him spin around on a special
bed with a metal halo screwed into his head to prevent further
damage to his spine. Happy days for my family and me were over
for a long, long time.

My father remained alive and suffering for four and a half years
after the accident before passing away from an infection caused by
a bad bedsore and complications from diabetes. He'd been diag-
nosed with diabetes when he was twenty-five and had administered
himself a shot of insulin every day since. Though it ultimately
played a role in his death, it never slowed him down in his life.

My father died on February 1, 1990, at age forty-six, and those four and a half years between his accident and his death were nothing less than a living hell. Not a moment went by when I didn't feel crippling guilt for not being there with him, holding the ladder that day. I used to work with my dad a lot as soon as I was old enough, and holding the ladder was usually my job. It ate me up that if I'd gone to work with him that day, it never would have happened.

On the morning of October 18, 1985, I wasn't with my dad because I did something unique, for me at least: I went to college. Even though I'd had to go to summer school to graduate from Union High, I was able to gain admission to Seton Hall University in South Orange, New Jersey. It had nothing to do with my nonexistent academic prowess; my Uncle Frankie supposedly knew someone who knew someone in the Admissions Office. That's how I got in, and in that it was typical: With my family there was always a scam.

I went to college for exactly four weeks, and the only grade I can speak of is an A that I received for an oral presentation I made in one class. I forget what the assignment was exactly, but I was the subject of my presentation. I did what I've done in front of people ever since: I told stories about my family and about my life. It was the first time I got a bunch of laughs in front of a crowd of total strangers, and it felt amazing to get that reaction from people. It's a power trip that you never get over.

I also tried out for the baseball team, which didn't work out so well. Seton Hall has a great sports program and trying to join without a scholarship is pretty rough, but I did my best, and even though nothing came of it, I realized how much I loved playing ball. During my one-month college career, I also realized just how much I hated school. It bored me to death. The only highlight was that one day I got laughs in front of my class, and in the long run it was the only education that I really needed. That experience convinced me that I could be a comedian and just as soon as it happened, I began to think up ways that I could quit college. I definitely couldn't just leave; I needed some kind of excuse, since my uncle basically got me in. And then fate handed me the perfect one, which I wish it never had—namely, helping my family deal with the tragedy of my father's accident.

That horrible Friday, I daydreamed through my classes as usual, had lunch with some friends, and then drove home at about 1:30 P.M. When I walked through the door, I was greeted by the sight of my mother sitting in the kitchen, crying.

"Mom?" I said. "What is it? What's happened?"

"Daddy had an accident," she said through her sobs. "He fell off a roof."

I could tell by how hard she was crying that everything was not okay. "Ma," I said, afraid to ask my question. "Is he . . . dead?"

"No, Artie, he's alive . . . but it's not good," she said. "It's not good at all."

My father was laid up at St. Barnabas, the same hospital in Livingston, New Jersey, where my sister and I had been born. I drove over there with my mother in the car I owned at the time: a fire-engine-red 1976 Buick Special that I would total precisely eight days later. It was the last decent car that she or I would have for the next ten years.

October 18, 1985, was the day of my dad's accident and my very last day at Seton Hall. From that moment until his death, I dealt with my guilt by engaging in every single piece of shitty, self-destructive, self-pitying *Wah! Wah! Wah!* type of behavior there is. Drinking, drugging, gambling, and bar fights that led to arrests became my everyday routine, and that was just what I did at night. My mother and sister, however, responded by being strong—no, *very* strong—women.

While our family struggled to maintain a shred of the kind of life we used to enjoy, my sister put herself through FIT in New York City by bartending. Her hard work and achievement helped my mother's mood greatly, because my mother did everything in her power to shield her children from this tragedy. But that was simply impossible. For those four and a half years, not a day went by that my mother did not look completely exhausted—and each and every day I hated that. But there was no escape.

Medicaid provided my father with the minimum care they could, which meant that at night my mother had to set alarm clocks to go off every two hours so she could get up to turn my father in his bed. It was the only way to keep him from getting sores. My father was a well-built, heavy man and she did it all by herself, *every two fucking hours*. That was her night. And her day was just as busy. It began at 6 A.M., when she woke up, made him breakfast, fed him, got him ready for the nurse, then showered, got dressed, and went off to work as a secretary. She'd come back home on her lunch hour to make sure that all was well and that the nurse was doing her job properly, then returned to work for the afternoon. When she got off at 5 P.M., she'd come home, the nurse would leave, and my mother would make dinner for herself and my father. Then the evening cycle began again. Medicaid did not provide for care on the weekends, so for those two days my mother was on duty for forty-eight hours straight.

We weren't at all rich before, but now we were struggling on top of the strain of caring for my father and keeping our family afloat. My mother had to deal with shitty cars that always broke down and asshole government workers, because if the welfare and Medicaid checks didn't keep coming we would have lost the house. All the while she kept up a brave facade so my sister and I would never know just how bad it really was. Every single day I felt like such a failure, so helpless. I was supposed to be the man of the family, and I was so far from doing what even the generous might call a passable job of it.

After a relentless period of continuously fucking up, however, I got back on track and made making it in comedy my one and only obsession. It wasn't the promise of fame or of achieving a career or a purpose in life for myself; all I wanted to do was make enough money to buy my mother some relaxation and peace. That was the light at the end of the tunnel, that was the goal, that was how I kept the pressure on myself.

It's amazing how time plays tricks on you: When you're a kid, a day seems to take a year, and a school year is an eternity. When you're an adult, when times are good, entire years go by in what feels like the space of one season. But the worst trick time plays on you is just how slowly the worst times in your life take you to live through. Those feel like one endless, horrible moment that just won't stop.

The night before my father died, I had dinner with him and we watched TV together in his room. After a while, I told him that I was going to my friend Mike Lawlor's house to watch some college hoops. I made sure he was okay and said goodnight to him and started to leave. But as I got to the door, he did something he never did—he called me back.

"C'mon," he said, a genuine tone of sorrow in his voice. "Take a few more minutes and talk to your old man."

I gladly sat back down, and we talked for a while longer. He had, from the moment he'd been injured, done the best he could to keep up his sense of humor, which wasn't easy under the circumstances. But tonight he was very sad, much more so than usual, and he didn't try to hide it.

We talked a little, but for the most part we sat there in silence together. I could tell that he didn't want to be alone.

"Well," he said, trying to smile, "you'd better get going if you want to catch the game." As I got up to go, my father made one more request.

"Put your hand on my hand, Sport," he said.

I held his hand and watched him struggle to bring my hand up to his mouth to kiss it.

"I love you, Son," he said. He started to cry.

"I love you too, Pop," I said, unable to hold back my own tears.

We cried for a few minutes before we both got it together. Then I fixed his blankets and made him as comfortable as I could in preparation for a night's sleep—giving my mom a rare break. I said good night, went to the door, turned out the lights, and that was the last time I saw him alive.

I went drinking over at my buddy's house, watched a couple of college basketball games I'd bet on, and, after losing both bets, returned home drunk at about 4 A.M. On my way to my room, I looked quickly toward my father's room and everything seemed calm and as normal as it could be. I went upstairs and fell asleep until three hours later, at 7 A.M., when I awoke to the sound of my mother and my Uncle Rich knocking hard on my bedroom door. I was not happy about that at all.

"What?" I yelled. "What is it?"

"Artie, there's an ambulance outside for your father," my uncle said.

I opened the door and standing next to Uncle Rich was my mother, crying.

"He's gone, Artie," she said, sobbing. "He's . . . gone."

I ran downstairs to my father's room and found two paramedics and two police officers next to his bed. The police tried to stop me from coming into the room, but when I explained who I was, they let me approach. And there was my hero, the toughest motherfucker I would ever know, lying there, lifeless. He had died sometime in the middle of the night while I was at my friend's house doing shot after shot to help me deal with losing bets on two fucking college basketball games. Four and a half years of paralysis had turned my father's powerful, muscular arms to jelly. His face looked fat and his stomach was distended like that of a starving African child in a UNICEF ad.

I closed my eyes and started to cry as hard as I ever have. It wasn't just the shock of the loss, it was the way that he'd gone—much too soon and so unlike the way he'd lived. I wasn't going to accept that. I wasn't going to let that become my father in my mind. I wasn't going to open my eyes until I remembered him the way he was when I first got to know him. I fought against my grief until I saw him again: in the early seventies, with his hair long, his face young, walking with a strut in his step like a typical guy from the streets of Newark who thought he was invincible. My dad was Superman to me, and in my mind he always will be. And that's all that counts.

Even though my father was an atheist, in his final years he came to believe in God and at least tried to make peace with Him. So I did what I thought was right and what I thought he'd want me to do: I made the sign of the cross. Then I grabbed his hand.

"I'll see you again someday, Pop," I said. "We'll play catch." I covered him with the bedsheet and that was the last time I ever saw his face.

My dad had asked us not to have a wake because of the condition the accident had left him in. We complied, and instead we had a mass in his honor at the Holy Spirit Church in Union, where, as it happened, I had raised hell as a CCD student ten years before. My father was the type of guy who'd amassed a lot of friends over the years, so the service was very crowded. I delivered the eulogy, and though it was hard to choose just one story to explain everything I wanted to say about my father, I chose to share the one that says it all to me: the night my dad and I went to Yankee Stadium and watched Reggie Jackson hit three homers to win the World Series.

What happened to my father is nothing you can prepare for and nothing you can predict, but as life-changing and devastating as it was to all of us, it never robbed us of our memories. I've got thousands of them to keep me smiling through the tears. And if it ever gets really bad, I've got a pretty simple, always reliable solution. If I want to stop crying and start laughing, all I need to do is recall October 18, 1977. My dad and Mr. October never disappoint.

Union's Most Wanted

4

F lashing back to August of 1985, I can really appreciate now just how carefree and easy I had it. Little did
I know that everything I took for granted would only
last another two months. Why would I think I was anything
but invincible when I was loving life that much? I was seventeen years old and had just graduated from high school. Well,
that's not exactly right: I had to go to summer school to get my
diploma, but on August 7, summer school let out and I was
completely free. I had a job working a few hours a week at a
restaurant called Beacon Hill, where I washed pots and pans.
Every once in a while, to add to my financial portfolio, I worked
construction at a job my Uncle Frank got for me unloading

Sheetrock and insulation in the scorching sun. The future looked bright, man, especially from the driver's seat of my ride. At the time, I was rolling in my first car, which I'd bought the year before on my birthday. It was a blue 1974 AMC Matador with a 305-horsepower V8 engine, a radio that pumped, and ice-cold air-conditioning. That car was so kick-ass that to this day it remains the best six hundred bucks I ever spent in my life, hookers included. The first five cars I bought in life I paid for in cash then waited for change from the guy.

I had a girlfriend at the time too—a nice Italian girl from Union named Sue Pacardi. We'd started going out that April and were kind of an item, enough to go to the prom together and everything. It was high school, so at first it was a casual relationship that I didn't take all that seriously. On prom night, as so many other Jersey kids do every single year to this day, my friends and I went down to Seaside Heights and checked into the Franklin Motel on Franklin Avenue. At some point that weekend, and I have no idea exactly when, I fell completely in love with Sue. At least love is what I thought I fell in. Maybe what I did was fall out of my happy-go-lucky teenage daydream and into reality for a minute, just long enough to realize that Sue was leaving town to attend college in South Jersey on the second-to-last day of August. From that moment on, I thought about her constantly and about how my time with her was running out. It also became clear to me pretty quick that Sue wasn't feeling the same kind of *Romeo and Juliet* devotion to our relationship that I had recently developed, but I wasn't going to let that stop me. Instead, it became my inspiration. After we got back from prom weekend, I tried to spend as much time with Sue as possible in an effort to make her fall as hopelessly in love with me as I now was with her.

Keeping up our romance once Sue left for college would have been the tough, typically useless endeavor it is for so many kids that age, but of course I was more than ready to give that a shot. But I was alone on that one too, because as the summer days sped by, Sue began to give me subtle signs that she wanted to break up before she left for school. She was a tough chick to read, and it was hard to understand what she really meant, especially when she'd say things like "Artie, I want to break up before I leave for school."

Whenever she brought it up, I told her that I understood and I kept up appearances, but secretly I was devastated. I was determined to change her mind, so whenever we hung out together, I tried to impress her with stupid stunts, because to me that was the one skill I possessed that was going to make me more desirable in her eyes. Whenever I was in her presence that summer, I was constantly looking for opportunities to pull off some kind of wiseass maneuver that would win her heart. One of the grander gestures I could only attempt at my friend Mike's place of employment, so visiting him soon became a thing to do.

My friend Mike worked in the housewares department at the Bradlees department store in town, where one time he'd shown me how to get on the intercom to make a storewide announcement. All you had to do was pick up a courtesy phone wherever you found one and dial 6. That was it; some chime would go off and then you were on the store's PA system. Security wasn't too tight back then on the Bradlees airwaves.

Mike regretted sharing that little piece of employee know-how with me, because I used it as often as possible, usually to get him in trouble, until he was eventually kicked out. For instance, once I stopped into the store with a few friends, picked up a courtesy phone, dialed 6, and cheerfully said, "Hello, shoppers, welcome to Bradlees! We'd like to announce a special promotion. For the next thirty minutes only, every item in our housewares department will be absolutely free! That's right, everything in housewares will be free for the next thirty minutes. Just stop by and ask for Mike. He'll be happy to help you." We all found that shit hilarious, but it's pretty safe to say that those pranks had a lot to do with Mike later needing to seek gainful employment elsewhere in Union's retail landscape.

Anyway, one day in the summer of '85, I walked into the store with Sue, that very same Mike from housewares—who, by the way, is also known as Shecky—and another friend of mine, Chico. To impress Sue, without a word I walked over to a courtesy phone, dialed 6, and said: "Um, hello, Bradlees shoppers! I'd like to announce that it's homosexual night here at the store. All fags get 10 percent off any purchase. That's right! Just walk up to the checkout, show us that you're a fruit, and we'll give you 10 percent off! It's our way of saying thank you to all the fruits shopping here at Bradlees tonight." That definitely got me big laughs from Sue and my friends, but it also got me caught red-handed by two plainclothes security guards. Sue watched as they hauled me off to their back office, ripping my Thurman Munson shirt in the process. I went from hilarious hero to total loser in the blink of an eye. Pulling off a prank is great—if you pull it off. There's probably nothing worse in the world of class clowning than getting busted in the act and humiliated by the very authority figures you made such a huge effort to ridicule. I didn't go to the big house—that came later on in my glamorous life. The guards let me off with a warning, but they did make such a huge show of publicly scaring the shit out of me that I had to declare that grand plan of mine officially a failure.

I grew more and more desperate to win Sue over as the summer went by, so by the last week of August I was in a state of silent panic. That is how I'd characterize my misguided, bizarre mind-set, and it is the only explanation I can find for the completely retarded stunt that I resorted to one sunny afternoon just before she left. The day started out pretty normal, as I recall: I made plans with some friends to play whiffleball in my backyard around 1 P.M. I then spoke to Sue, who halfheartedly asked me if I wanted to come along with her while she ran errands in her mother's car, a '77 Ford Granada. Parents love a car like that, because it's slow and boring and safe. They feel entirely comfortable loaning a car like that to their teenagers, because the only kind of death it will cause is dying of embarrassment. Sue had quite a few items to buy and loose ends to tie up before making her big move to college, so this run was going to take all morning.

I agreed to go with her before she described the dull and tedious list of stops we'd have to make—not that it would have made a difference to me. I was being presented with an entire morning to work my magic every which way on her. There were going to be opportunities to woo her left and right; surely this would be the day that Sue fell forever for Artie. It didn't quite work out that way, but not for a lack of trying: From the moment she picked me up, I looked for any excuse to show off my absolutely charming sense of spontaneity. Sadly, I found no openings apart from my usual and constant busting of chops all around. And I was even coming up short in that department. I really hadn't considered just how boring a morning of precollege errands can be.

As should be apparent by now, Sue was way more mature than I was. She already had her own bank account and a checkbook, which to me was very impressive. The final errand of the morning was stopping off at the bank to deposit a check. I'd gotten nowhere in my mission, and I was very aware of the fact that this was the end of the ride, so to speak, so I decided to go into the bank with her and at the very least bust some more chops.

When we got inside, Sue went to the back to do her banking while I walked around like a boob, unsuccessfully avoiding boredom. The only thing that aroused my interest was a teller in one of the front windows—a really cute broad in her mid-twenties with dark hair and nice tits. I looked around, saw that Sue was occupied, and then went over to the table that held all of the different slips and picked up a pen.

I was already a huge fan of Woody Allen by then, and I especially liked the film *Take the Money and Run*. In one of the funniest scenes in the movie, Woody's character, Virgil Starkwell, writes a stickup note on the back of a bank deposit slip, but his handwriting is so poor that the teller can't read it. She thinks that the word "gun" is the word "gub" and reads it out loud and asks him what a "gub" is and blows his whole plan. If you haven't seen that movie, you should. I highly recommend it.

In a misguided homage to that scene, I thought the best thing I could possibly do at that moment would be to write a fake holdup note on the back of a deposit slip and hand it to this cute teller. Like a moron, I figured it would go down like this: I'd hand it to the girl, she would laugh, knowing right away that it was a joke—she'd probably even seen the movie. And even if she didn't, what I'd done would be so funny to her that she'd become terribly attracted to me. Sue would then see me pull this prank off, and the combination of my successful gag and the cute teller digging me would win her over instantly and, college be damned, she would be mine. In my mind, this plan was extra crazy, but it was what the situation called for, so it made complete sense.

I remember the note I wrote almost word for word, mostly because a judge read it back to me about fifty times in juvenile court, as you will soon see. It went like this: "I have a gun. Put $50,000 into a bag, turn around, and count to a thousand. Please act casually. Thank you for your cooperation." And I signed it, "Artie Lange, Jr."

I wish I was bullshitting you with this one, but I'm not. I really am *that* retarded. I didn't consider that this teller might freak out because probably, at least once, she'd worried about having a gun stuck in her face at work. No, to me the fact that I'd signed the note was indication enough to anybody that I was joking. Brilliant! Assured that I had finally come up with the grand slam of gags, I walked up to the window and handed the girl my note. I then slammed into a brick wall called reality: My signature as the foolproof indication that this was a joke meant shit to her. The first thing that this girl read was "I have a gun," and it was over—she turned white as a ghost, started shaking, and looked like she was about to start sobbing. I immediately panicked and grabbed the note out of her hand.

"It's a joke!" I said, trying to keep my voice down. "Really, it was a joke. It's just a joke. I am so, *so* sorry."

The teller took a deep breath and looked relieved and started to calm down a bit. It seemed like she believed me. About this time, I saw Sue coming my way.

"I am really sorry," I said, trying to smile benevolently. "I was just trying to make you laugh. I wasn't serious at all—I promise." Then I got away from her window as fast as I could. I crumpled up the note, threw it in the nearest trash can, and walked over to Sue. That was another sign that I'm both retarded and not cut out for a life of crime: I stupidly left behind the piece of evidence that would come back to bite me in the ass.

Sue knew nothing at all about what had happened, and I chose not to tell her, thinking, as we got back into her mother's car, that I'd dodged a bullet. Sue drove me home to my whiffleball game and told me she was heading to Mandee's on Route 22 to shop for clothes for college.

"Great," I said. "I'll call you later."

I headed into the backyard and played whiffleball with my buddies Deeg, Shecky, Larry, and Kevin. Those guys are not relevant to this story in any way whatsoever, but I promised them that I'd put their names in my book. So now that I've done that, we can move on.

As my friends and I ascended into whiffleball heaven, the real drama was unfolding elsewhere. Back at the bank, the teller might have managed a half-smile and acted like it was okay at the end of our ordeal, but she failed to mention that during her initial panic, she remembered enough of her training video to trigger the silent alarm that went straight to the local police station. Thirty seconds after Sue and I walked out of the bank and drove away, a mini SWAT team pulled up to the back entrance prepared to handle an armed bank robbery in progress. When they didn't find one, the teller explained what had happened, but if there's one group of people that sure as hell wasn't going to see the humor in a shit-headed prank like that, it's a SWAT team. I have no idea how convincing the teller was in upholding my innocence, but it wouldn't have mattered if she were as earnest as Sally Field accepting her Oscar, there was no keeping those cops from arresting me.

It really was my lucky day, because not only was I, Artie Lange, Jr., officially the jerk-off who'd left signed evidence of his misguided practical joke right there in the bank, I had also messed with a teller who'd managed to write down the license plate number of Sue's mom's car as we drove away. It says nothing of that broad's grace under pressure: Sue's mom's Granada had as much pickup as a covered wagon, so if she'd wanted to, the girl could have cried for a few minutes, then sharpened a pencil, walked around the desk and outside to the sidewalk, put on her glasses, and written down the plate number before we were out of visual range. It was some getaway car, let me tell you. The thing is, even if she hadn't written that down, it wasn't going to take Sherlock Holmes to find us, considering that the bank had Sue's home address.

I'd guess that it took the SWAT team thirty minutes or less to figure all of this out, drive to Sue's house, and surround the place like it was Waco. Her parents, thank God, were at work, but her sister Teresa was not. Now, I loved Teresa, I really did, but there's one thing that I have to say about her: To this day, she is the loudest broad I have ever met. Normal people have what you'd call a speaking voice, a whisper, and a yell. Now think of the average person you know yelling your name across a crowded party, at a sports event, or just before you're about to step in front of an oncoming bus. Teresa's whisper was as loud as that. She could carry on a conversation comfortably over the sound of a jet engine.

That afternoon the cops stormed into Sue's house and found Teresa, who was pretty high-strung and probably screamed and had a panic attack as they explained to her that they were looking for Sue, her mother's Ford Granada, and an unidentified male her sister had been seen with. All three were wanted in connection with an attempted bank robbery. In a frenzy, Teresa called my house, and I answered the phone on an extension that we had in our garage. I wasn't at all happy about it, either, because I was in the middle of a nothing-nothing whiffleball game that was heading into the eleventh inning. It was a classic whiffleball pitchers' duel.

"Yeah, hello?" I said.

The moment she heard my voice, Teresa unloaded a primal yell that pierced my skull. It was so loud that all of my friends heard it and got quiet.

"ART-IE!" she shouted. "The cops are here looking for Sue. WHAT THE *FUCK* DID YOU GET HER INTO? Whatever it is, I know it is YOUR *FAULT!* What is it, Artie? Is it *DRUGS?* If Sue gets arrested and cannot go to college, I will not be able to move into her bedroom and I will NEVER FUCKING FORGIVE YOU! I know it's *FUCKING DRUGS!*"

I had no idea what was going on, and there was no way I was getting a word in edgewise. It wouldn't have mattered—I did not possess what it was going to take to calm Teresa down—but I tried anyway. And then it hit me: The teller must have called the cops. But the cops didn't have Sue yet, so I thought that if I found her first there was a chance I could turn this around somehow. I told Teresa not to worry, though I doubt she heard me over the sound of her own screaming. I hung up, borrowed my buddy Deeg's blue 1980 Camaro, and raced to Mandee's on Route 22. I found Sue in the dressing room trying on a shitty mid-eighties, $14 blouse the likes of which you'd find on an extra in a Bangles video. She was surprised to see me but not surprised by the story. When I told her the whole thing, she just started laughing; she knew she hadn't done anything and that I was the one in trouble so there was no need to make a huge deal of it. She was a really cool chick.

We did, however, have to deal with the cops, so on the advice of my buddy's uncle, who was a lawyer, we called the police station and revealed ourselves as the teenage Bonnie and Clyde they were hunting for. They told us to come down to the station to surrender ourselves, which we did. Sue was so upbeat about the whole situation that I started to think maybe this plan hadn't backfired after all. Maybe I'd actually done it; maybe I'd finally managed the grand gesture that was bold and funny enough to win her heart. Sue laughed all the way to the station and all the way inside—until they handcuffed us together. Then her carefree attitude about it changed to terror.

"Artie, why are we handcuffed?" she said. "I didn't do anything. What's going to happen to us? Why am I in handcuffs?"

"I don't know!" I said. "Why are you asking me? I have no idea what the fuck is going to happen." It really didn't help any to say that to Sue.

The cops left us cuffed to each other for an hour, just sitting in the station. Then they separated us for our individual interviews. I don't know how Sue held up, but when I got into the detective's office, I just lost it. Sue's father was a greenhorn, right off the boat from Italy. He owned a barbershop, but you never know in Jersey—he could have been a connected guy, brought over for God knows what. On top of that, her old man did not like me one bit. There was no way I wanted to answer to his wrath should his daughter get charged with a crime. Whenever I saw her father, I'd say, "Hey, Mr. Pacardi!" He'd look at me like he'd just smelled dog shit and grunt. Clearly, he did not want me around.

During my interrogation, I begged the detectives to throw the book at me, just as long as they let Sue go. I told them the whole stupid story. I told them that it was a joke, I told them about the Woody Allen movie, and I told them that I had been doing nothing but trying to flirt with the teller girl. They said they'd need to think about what to do with us—both of us—because this was a very serious matter. What seemed like a joke to me was nothing to joke about, they said. Then they continued to scare the shit out of us for a few more hours before eventually freeing Sue with no charges and knocking mine down to a disorderly-conduct charge. I was assigned a court date in November, just three months away.

We'd driven to the police station in my friend's car, so I drove Sue home and saw my worst nightmare standing there waiting for me: her father. Teresa had told him the whole story, but he wanted to hear it from us. Oddly, he seemed okay with the whole thing after we explained it firsthand, probably because Sue wasn't in trouble in any way. Those few minutes explaining the story were terribly awkward and uncomfortable, and when they were over I thought I was off the hook. I turned to leave, but Sue's dad stopped me. He wanted to talk to me alone.

Mr. Pacardi led me into one of those family rooms that Italian families have but never use, and like most of them, this one had vinyl covers on all of the furniture. That room exuded the same kind of stillness as the entrance of a funeral parlor, and all I could think of were the scenes from mob movies where the unsuspecting goodfella walks into a room and gets whacked. I had no idea what Mr. Pacardi was going to say, I just knew that I'd rather have my appendix removed with a butter knife than sit through it. It wasn't going to be good, because the guy had a look of pure anger and disgust on his face: He looked at me like Mike Tyson looked at Trevor Berbick during their weigh-in that year. And we all know how that little get-together turned out.

Mr. Pacardi didn't sit down and he didn't offer me a seat. He just stood there in front of a vinyl-covered couch and in heavily accented English said, "I want to tell you some-thing."

"Mr. Pacardi, sir, I'm very—" I said.

"Shhh!" he said, staring through me with that evil eye. "You listen-a me." He pointed a finger at me. "I say one thing. . . . When you robba bank, you *no* take-a my daughter."

"Sir," I said, "I wasn't robbing a bank. It was only—"

He cut me off again, waving his finger and saying, "No, no, no! You say nothing. I know you. You are *a-craze*. Do you hear me? You are a-craze. Just no take-a my daughter when you robba bank."

I saw no way out other than agreeing with him. "Yes, sir, I will never take your daughter with me when I rob a bank," I said. "And I will take all the blame from the cops for this. No one will ever know that she was even with me."

For the briefest of moments he looked satisfied, and then he grunted in my general direction. "Get out," he said.

When I got home, my parents had just come back from the Jersey Shore, so I told them the story—carefully. It didn't matter: My mother went absolutely ballistic. My old man was pissed too, but he wasn't pissed that I'd done it; he was just pissed at me for getting caught.

I found myself a lawyer on the recommendation of a family friend, and that was the end of that. I had to wait for the November court date, but the best part of the story was yet to come. Two days later, in the local paper, *The Union Leader*, there was a story about the whole thing, right there on the front page. The headline read:

Hold-up attempt 'was only a joke'

Union police are investigating a
hold-up attempt during which a man

before fleeing empty-handed.
The hold-up attempt took place

Ave.
According to police, the man at-

The story was there just as it happened. Because I was seventeen and still a minor, legally they couldn't print my name. Sue, on the other hand, was already eighteen, so they could print hers. And print it they did: "Driving the alleged getaway car was the man's girlfriend, Sue Pacardi."

As I read that, my only thought was that Sue's father was going to gut me like a fish. Thank God Sue found the whole thing so hilarious. She told her dad that it was all in good fun and that he shouldn't fuck with me. Call me crazy, but I took that as a sign that I'd finally impressed her.

In the end, it didn't change the state of affairs between us much, and it definitely came too late: A week later, Sue went to college in South Jersey. As if on cue, I tried to keep it going for a while, but as she had informed me all those times that I chose to ignore, Sue had plans for her life. I had plans for mine too, but they were very, very different.

I was a dreamer. I wanted to go to New York City every night to try to become a comedian. I never wanted to go to college. I wanted to start living life and to learn as I went. In my eyes, I'd try to make it in New York City, but even if I failed, the experience itself would be interesting and any success I might find along the way would allow me to travel and see the world a bit. I saw our town the way Bruce said it in "Thunder Road": It was a town full of losers and I was pulling out of there to win.

Sue's plan was much more conservative. She wanted to go to

college, major in marketing, meet a guy there, marry him young, and have kids. And basically, that is exactly what happened. About three weeks into her first year in college, Sue met the guy she'd marry six years later. They had kids and bought a home close to where she grew up, and that is her life. I still see Sue every once in a while. She has adorable kids and she seems happy, and that makes me really happy.

One thing's for sure: She dodged a huge bullet by dumping my ass. I wanted my life to be interesting and different, but little did I know just how soon that would happen. As I said, my father's accident, which occurred just two months after Sue left, changed everything for us. It was our family's Armageddon and the start of a long, dark, winding road of self-discovery for me. I neither experienced nor pursued anything even remotely close to the orderly, stable future that Sue had planned for herself. High school crushes and dreams of making it in showbiz hit the back burner for a good long while. By the time my father died, my journey had led me to become nothing but a broke twenty-two-year-old drunk with a gambling problem, and very little future at all.

As for the end of the bank story, however, here it is, and it's pretty good. By the time my November court date came around, my father had just fallen, and he was lying in the hospital, paralyzed, which made my having to answer for my idiot behavior in public about a month later all the more depressing. I stood in front of the judge at Union County Courthouse in Elizabeth, New Jersey, with my lawyer at my side and my grandfather, the great Sal Caprio, lending moral support.

The judge, to put it mildly, skewered me alive. Since I'd been stupid enough to throw the note away in the bank trash can, the cops were able to retrieve it. In front of an entire courtroom full of juvenile delinquents who'd done much more legitimately tough and illegal things, the judge made an example of me by yelling at the top of his lungs.

"Mr. Lange!" he bellowed. "Let me read something to you: 'I have a *gun*. Put $50,000 into a *bag* . . .'" I think he truly enjoyed the note, because he must have read it fifty times in the twenty minutes it took to sentence me. Then he called me a moron: Without any kind of warning or any kind of reason, just like that, he said, "Mr. Lange, you are a moron." Nothing more, nothing less—I was a moron; that was his verdict. What a wonderful morning that was.

I was sentenced to twenty-five hours of community service and assigned to clean up all the garbage on the front lawn of the courthouse there in Elizabeth. But my first day of community service couldn't have been better: It was St. Patrick's Day, 1986. I was ordered to report to the head janitor, who would be my boss for the duration of my "term." When I found him, he and his fellow workers were still so drunk from the parade that they marked me down for ten hours of service after I'd worked only two. That was a nice mistake. Thanks to that, it took me only four more days to work off my debt to society.

But even in service to my community I could not escape the ballbusting idiocy that has made me the man I am today. You see, back then and to this day, I had the kind of friends—and now the kind of job—where merciless ballbusting is expected. That's just what we do. It didn't matter that I'd just had my ass handed to me by a judge or that my family was reeling from tragedy. While I was cleaning up that front lawn, my jerk-off friends saw a golden opportunity and drove by whenever I was there to throw White Castle bags, used napkins, and whatever other shit they found in their cars out the window at me. They would then slow down and pull over to get a great view of me cleaning it up. My friends are a fun bunch of guys, they really are. Next time something bad happens to you, I'll be sure to send them over to cheer you up. The funny thing is, the judge could have yelled at me all day and made no impression on me at all other than hammering home what my dad had tried to teach me: If you're gonna fuck around, you'd better not get caught. It took my own kind to deliver the message, and they had to do it with bags of greasy old fast food. Cleaning up their crap while they watched did it, all right, as only mocking from your peers can. I heard the message loud and clear as they laughed at me from the curb: Could I be a bigger shithead?

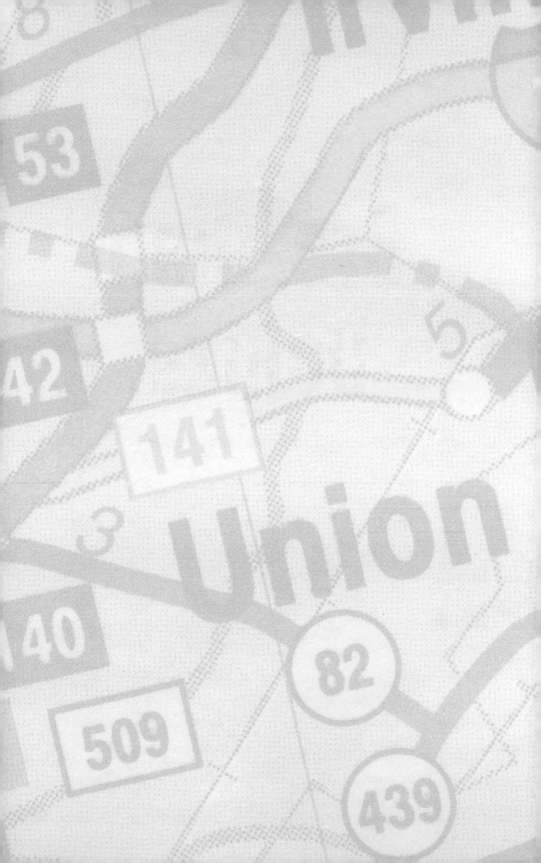

Brazilian Deluxe

5

When a bunch of guys get together regularly at a bar or wherever, they eventually get around to talking about their first time. It's inevitable. *The Stern Show* is a good example, because, aside from Robin, it is definitely a bunch of guys who get together regularly, and as any listener can tell you, the subject certainly comes up from time to time. On the show, Gary and Benjy have actually brought in the girls that they lost their virginity to, and Howard has asked them, in cringe-worthy detail, every single fact surrounding the big event. When the question came my way, I just sort of brushed it aside. It wasn't tough to do—I had done the same with my buddies since forever. Whenever that conversation came around, I'd handle it with a statement like "Yeah, I lost it to some broad I did it with just once. It was just some girl I met down the Shore."

The "how'd you lose your virginity?" conversation was always something of a touchy subject with me for a few reasons—the first being that, as far as I was concerned, it happened for me very late. It might not have been late in some communities, like the ones where kids are locked in cages until marriage, but compared to the average kid growing up in my town, there was no contest; I lost it pretty late. I had some friends who first did it when they were thirteen. Can you imagine how hard it was to be friends with these guys? In teenage boy terms, they had discovered pussy—the meaning of *life*—when they were in junior fucking high! I was still keeping a record of my whiffleball batting average, when suddenly my buddy Joey got laid and instantly he didn't care at all about that stuff. I couldn't understand why and I made fun of him for it.

"Dude, I'm at .387, you're at .380—you gotta catch up," I said to him.

And he just gave me a look that said, *Uh, yeah, Art, I've actually stuck my hard cock into pussy, so you know what? I'm gonna concede the whiffle batting title to you. Enjoy those small victories, bro.* He'd held in his hands the Holy Fucking Grail of male adolescence. Whiffleball paled in comparison.

My lack of experience in that department was extra torturous for me considering that I actually had a girlfriend in high school—Sue Pacardi, the girl from the bank robbery. Sure, I got to second base, I did some heavy petting or whatever you want to call it, but I was as close to having actual sex with Sue as a four-year one-on-one game of Spin the Bottle would have gotten me. Getting a girl's clothes all the way off was a pipe dream. I had this overly attentive Italian mother who'd shown me how to put my jacket and shirt on properly and how to fold it when I went on a trip, so technically I'd have been better at helping a girl put her clothes on than I was at getting them off.

So here we go, it's time for me to come clean about this virginity thing, because I'm sick of carrying it around inside of me. For the first time ever, anywhere, to anyone who cares, I'm telling the truth and admitting that I didn't lose my virginity until about a week after my nineteenth birthday. Like I said, where I came from that was late—maybe not for people living in the 1930s and 1940s, but for teenagers living in the eighties, it was pretty fucking late, man. Forget about today, when it seems like every time you look in the paper there's something new about kids having sex with teachers or kids getting caught having sex, doing things that most adults don't even do—all in like seventh grade. Nowadays, they call a female teacher who forces a seventh-grader to have sex with her a criminal. Back in the late seventies, we would have called her the coolest fucking teacher ever. If I had the same kind of success rate I had as a teen today, I can't even imagine how much of a loser I'd be.

Add to that the fact that I lost my virginity to a full-blown Brazilian hooker and you may get an idea why I have yet to break this heartwarming tale out at holiday cocktail parties. Say what you will about it, I don't care, because this girl was unbelievably fucking hot. She was in this country illegally—big surprise—and was eighteen at the time, at least according to her. For the sake of many things, we're going to call her Mary, and predictably, I fell completely in love with her. She barely spoke English, and that could not have mattered less to me. I was devoted to her from the moment she made a man out of me.

Right after my eighteenth birthday, a few months after I graduated from high school, my father, as you know, fell from a roof, and my mom, sister, and I had to deal with all that came with him being permanently paralyzed. None of us knew which way was up for a while, and during that time, I forgot all about juvenile goals and pranks. But when I did resurface and resume life in the usual way to the extent I could, losing my virginity became an obsession. It was just something I had to do and, more than ever before, something I had to do right *now*. I'm sure it was that lesson life teaches you when you or a loved one experiences a tragedy: Do not take your time here for granted. If my dad could go from the most strapping motherfucker that ever was to someone who needed care 24/7 in the blink of an eye, it could happen at any time to anyone. It made me reassess my life goals, and having sex became the number-one priority. It became clear to me that there was no way in hell that I was going to let myself die a virgin, nor was I willing to enter my twenties a virgin either. I had to lose my virginity while there was still an "een" at the end of my age, end of story.

At the time, I had no prospects at all, but not for lack of trying, all of which did wonders for my self-esteem, by the way. Just shy of my nineteenth birthday, I really began to panic. I remember sitting one afternoon methodically going over my options, taking into account the ever-shrinking time left. At that point, if the opportunity presented itself I would have fucked Rue McClanahan. And that was the day I decided, "Fuck it, I'm doing this on time. I'm having sex with a woman, even if it has to be a hooker." For some reason, I figured that hookers were something I could figure out without any guidance, so if worse came to worst, I'd just find a whore on the street and end this virginity bullshit before my twentieth birthday.

Salvation came, ironically enough, through holy matrimony. My buddy Shecky's brother was getting married in November 1986, and he had his bachelor party on a night that is a legendary moment for New York baseball fans. It was held on October 11, at one of the shittier union halls in Elizabeth, New Jersey. I have no idea about the hierarchy among organizations like the Knights of Columbus and the Elks, but I can tell you that the union that owned the place where they threw the bachelor party was much further down the food chain. I can't imagine that they were even nationally recognized, because, to be kind, this place was the recreation center that time forgot. Elizabeth, New Jersey, is generally a nice, working-class neighborhood, but a large part of it—the part that no one likes to talk about—is a really shitty ghetto. And that's exactly where this hall was. Clearly, the best man, who, like the groom, was only about twenty-five, had gotten his shit together late, because this room wouldn't be anybody's first choice.

Like many of my life's more memorable experiences, the backdrop to this one was a history-making baseball game: the night the Mets beat the Red Sox and won Game 6 of the World Series. For those of you who know nothing about baseball, and I'm sorry for you, I'm talking about the infamous game where Mookie Wilson's grounder rolled through Bill Buckner's legs and the Mets won. That error changed the momentum of the Series, and the Red Sox could not come back: The Mets took Game 6 and went on to win Game 7 the very next night.

At the bachelor party, the game was a major focus of the evening, because people there had bet on it and quite a few of the partygoers were Mets fans as well. I was not one of them. I'm proud to say that from the moment I could first recognize a pinstripe it was only the Yankees' navy and white for me. The Mets and their stupid orange and cheap blue always were and still are such an abomination to me. I'm so anti-Mets that I was actually rooting for the Red Sox that night, and no one there could fathom that I, a die-hard Yankee fan, could do such a thing. Whatever—those people are fucking idiots. The Red Sox might be the Yankees' archenemy, but it seemed so obvious to me that the fucking Mets team that year was worth hating much, much more. I mean, Lenny Dykstra, Keith Hernandez, and Darryl Strawberry? That whole fucking team was just a bunch of gung-ho cheerleader types. I couldn't stand those motherfuckers.

Years later, when I found out that they were all doing blow and getting into bar fights when they weren't playing ball, I felt like an idiot. If there's one thing I've always valued in baseball players, it's the ability to be a fucked-up badass and still put up the numbers. Now, I still think the Mets as a club fucking suck, but that late-eighties team, I have to admit, was cool as hell. I was just too much of a dumb fuck to know that at the time. But that shouldn't be a surprise to anyone, especially me. The only guy I hated back then and still hate is Gary Carter, because it's clear that the guy has always been an uptight motherfucker. Never trust a catcher who never needs a shave. They're just not right.

In any case, that night, in a shitty room in Elizabeth, New Jersey, about forty guys stood around watching the Series instead of celebrating Shecky's brother's final night of single life. The party didn't look to be shaping up into anything much—it just felt like we'd gone to a really crappy bar, where the drinks were free, to watch the game—until the best man told all of us that four whores were coming down. Apparently, they were going to do some kind of lesbian show that they'd encore by blowing guys or doing whatever else we could negotiate with them in what the best man called "the back room." That got my attention, all right. It looked like I'd get out of my teen years with some degree of self-respect after all.

A hooker was a sure thing, but I was nervous about it anyway, so the next time I needed a piss break I went to check out this "back room" the guy had mentioned. I came out of the bathroom and looked down the hall—nothing, not even a broom closet. I was a little drunk, so I figured I'd missed the door or the hallway to this place. But as I looked around, I slowly figured out the obvious: the "back room" was the john. Now, that would have been fine if we were somewhere with a passable can full of high-end amenities, like a door that locked. But we were working with a "back room" that even the cheapest hooker would never call her boudoir by choice:

There were a few stalls, a dingy trash can, and an atmosphere that reeked of the skeevy and grotesque. It was a clear indication of where the night was heading: This run-down, perfectly innocent catering hall was about to become a pit of vice.

In addition to the whores, someone had arranged for a few really low-level gangsters to show up to run gambling tables. They hauled in blackjack and roulette set-ups, and a few people started playing craps in the corners. There was liquor, there was blow, there was weed, and there were a couple of big kegs: It was the most low-rent, fake version of Vegas there ever was. The crowning glory was the pint-sized black-and-white TV at one end of the room that everyone crowded around. The game had become such a big deal that most of the guys couldn't care less about the other distractions.

I was one of them—until the whores showed up. There were four of them, and two of them were kind of cute and younger. Or maybe I should say *young-ish*: Like a medium-hot girl who likes to go out on the town with fat friends who make her look better, the other two hookers were such train wrecks that the better two looked fresh as spring daisies. One of the old ones wasn't just old, she was elderly—and she had a lot of miles on her. And the other one, I swear to God, looked *exactly* like Larry King. She was wrinkled and just monstrous, and her tits were hanging down below her knees. Of course, she was the one who came up to the best man and said in a classic smoke-and-whiskey-drenched voice, "We're going to put on a lesbian show first, and then we will hang out with all of you *individually*."

Guys, as a rule, are idiots. Simple, stupid idiots. We reacted as if we were at a friend's house and his mother had asked us for some help with the chores. "Okay," the best man said. "What do you need for that? Do you need anything from me?" In response, the woman let loose a line that became an instant classic among my friends. She looked at him very intensely; you could tell she was seriously thinking about it.

"Okay," she said in a really gross, sultry kind of croak. "Do you have any rope or bungee cord?" I wasn't sure I'd heard her correctly.

"Uh . . . yeah," he said. "I think I do."

She and the guy went out to his car and found some rope in his trunk. Then they pulled an old banquet table to one end of the room and she got naked. A few guys proceeded to tie her down, following her very specific instructions.

"You," she said to one of the guys, "wrap that bungee cord around my wrist—twice. Good. Now hook it to the table leg. Now you—tie my ankles to the table with the rope. Do it tighter."

It all got disgusting real fast. First of all, the table was old, rotting wood and so nasty that all I could think about were splinters getting stuck up her wrinkled ass. Then, once she was spread-eagled and strapped down, she announced in her Wicked Witch voice: "Any of you can do what you want to me. You can fist me, you can lick me, you can stick anything you want up my pussy and my ass. Anything—as long as it's not sharp." There were definitely options in that department, because she'd arrived with a few different dildos, Ben-Wa balls to slip in her asshole, and butt plugs. And apparently, if none of that was satisfying, you could just shove your arm in there.

Bachelor parties are a unique and often uncomfortable male-bonding tradition, because they are where you find out once and for all who in your crew is a true pervert. My experience has been that it's usually the nerdiest, most laid-back, passive guys you know. This party was no different: There were a couple of really conservative-looking twerps there who became as happy as kids on Christmas as they got, literally, elbow-deep in this broad's cunt. Those two led the charge into hell, because after them, people started taking pictures with their arms all the way up her, treating her like she was a photo op at a tourist destination. It was pretty awful.

While that was going on, the other three girls tried desperately to lure the rest of us away from the ball game. They got topless and started shoving their tits in people's faces and rubbing up on everybody. It was a great role reversal: Their power as chicks had been stripped away, since all of us preferred to watch baseball on a shitty, small black-and-white TV than pay them any attention at all. It was more than just a game, though—it was turning out to be one of the best World Series games of all time, so it didn't help them any that none of the girls were what I'd call a young Carmen Electra.

I remember every detail of that game, and it went like this: The Mets were down by two runs and down to their last out. Gary jerk-off Carter got a hit, then Kevin Mitchell got a single, so there were runners at first and second. Then Ray Knight singled, driving Carter home and Mitchell to third. Then Bob Stanley threw a wild pitch, sending Mitchell home and tying the game. After that Mookie Wilson's hit rolled through Buckner's legs, sending a run home and winning it for the Mets. Stanley's wild pitch was the error that won it for the Mets, I don't give a fuck what anybody says. It wasn't Buckner letting the ball roll through his legs, it was Bob Stanley's wild pitch—that was the big error. That tied the game and gave the Mets momentum, and it would have gone into extra innings. And besides, Wilson might have beaten out the throw anyway. I remember it clearly: Buckner was hobbling to get that ball, so his throw wouldn't have been anything special.

In any case, the Mets won and everybody went fucking crazy. Every guy in that room started yelling, either in anger or from joy, depending on how they'd bet that night. We kept on like that for a good ten or twenty minutes afterward, in spite of the fact that there were tits being shoved in our faces on all sides. Aside from a few pervs with their hands up the old broad, no one could have cared less about anything but the game. Then that wore off and everyone started to branch off and involve themselves in whatever vice— gambling, drugs, hookers, all of them—they preferred.

I played blackjack and a little craps, the whole time trying to plot how I was going to make my "transaction" occur. I did not put my fist or anything else in the woman on the table, though I definitely marveled at that freak show like it was an exhibit in a museum. While I was gawking, one of the two cuter chicks, the one who looked Hispanic, came up to me topless and in that hot accent said to me: "You wanna blow job?"

I didn't even need to think about it. "Yeah," I said. "Let's do this." She told me to go into the bathroom and wait in a stall, which I wasn't happy about, but I'd gotten a blow job like that before, so it wasn't unfamiliar. The familiar ended when she put a rubber on me before she began to blow me. When I saw the rubber, I didn't think there was any way this was going to work. But it did: I was pretty pent up, plus, even though she wasn't some great beauty, I found the girl kind of sexy. Most of all, she was just really good at her job. In about fifteen seconds I came, because let me tell you, she was that fantastic. But the best part was the price—$5. A really good blow job for $5? *That* is a bargain. When she came in to do it she was nude except for her thong, and when I gave her the money I wondered where she was going to put it. Before she started in, she took off one of her five-inch heels and dropped it in there with about twenty other crumpled five-dollar bills. I'm not gonna say that there were a bunch of horny fucks at this party, but when the girl left she was about 6 foot 7.

The sad truth is that $5 is probably half of what I had on me. If I'd had more, I would have definitely gotten another blow job. I wasn't going to let that kind of talent, at that price, get away. I decided that I'd at least find out how much she'd charge me to take my virginity.

I walked up to her when nobody was nearby and asked her, very politely, "So, uh, how much would it be to like bang you?"

"That would be fifty dollars," she said. "You wanna do it?" I didn't have overly sentimental expectations for my first time, but attempting it in the lovely rear lounge at this place was too much. So I asked her for her phone number in the same way you might ask for it from a guy who had a landscaping or driveway-paving business. "Listen," I said. "I might be able to use your services. I'd like to call you next week."

I got her number, and it turned out that she lived in Elizabeth, over by the Camelot Diner on Morris Avenue, close to the border of Union and less than a mile from my family's house.

"That works out great," I told her, still acting like I'd be calling to get an estimate for the deck I planned to add to my house.

It took me a couple of days to get up the nerve, but when I eventually called her, she said that she wasn't going to be around that night. I knew deep down that my courage wouldn't last, so I didn't want to make a plan with her for a few days down the line. I had free use of my father's handicap van that night, and since it had a ton of room in the back, I figured that tonight was the night: I'd throw a bunch of sleeping bags and some pillows back there to avoid paying for the hotel room that I could not afford.

"I can't tonight," she said. "But my sister Mary is here, who is younger than me. She is eighteen and she is very, very beautiful."

"Oh yeah?"

"Yes, you come talk to her," she said. "I bet that you will like her."

It was taking a risk, because I had no idea what her sister looked like, but I figured that a whore's concept of beautiful was probably different from mine. But being cautious wasn't really on my mind now that victory was within reach—being a virgin was killing me. "Fuck it," I said. "Tell her I'm coming over." To me there was no way I could be disappointed, considering what I imagined she'd look like. I fully expected to have sex with someone who looked like Luis Guzmán.

I drove the van over to their apartment complex. I buzzed up, and she came down, and I was immediately in disbelief. This girl was *beautiful*. She looked kind of like Eva Longoria, that type of hot. She said she was eighteen, and I wasn't about to bounce her if she wasn't carrying ID. I could tell she was no child, so there was nothing sinister going on. And how much older was I at nineteen anyway? I think I might have actually drooled watching her walk to the van, and she could tell: My eyes were lit up like Times Square.

"You like me, right?" she said.

"Yeah!" I nearly shouted, I was so excited. "How much would you charge me to have, you know, full sex?"

"This is fifty dollars," she said. "You want sex and blow job, is seventy-five."

"Fine," I said. "I brought cash with me. I have it right here!"

I didn't care for one minute that $75 was easily half of my net worth in life—probably more. And the virginity thing was still a concern, but her beauty transcended my mission. I just had to fuck this girl—she was that hot. The only conceivable problem was whether or not she'd do it in the handicap van.

"We don't have to go anywhere, you know," I said, trying to make the back of my dad's van sound like a four-star hotel. "We can do it right here in back. It's very comfortable."

The language barrier was a problem, because, unlike her sister, Mary barely spoke English. She looked at me, looked in the back, and then just looked hesitant. I gestured to the low-budget harem bed made of sleeping bags that I'd put together.

"We will stay right in here," I said louder and slower, like idiots do when they talk to foreign people. And then I tried to reassure her: "Don't be nervous, everything will be okay." At this point, I was praying to God that Telemundo had never aired *Silence of the Lambs*.

"I will not drive to any remote place where I could kill you or anything. We could park at maybe . . . the diner? The Camelot Diner, down the road?" I pointed.

"Camel-o?" she said. "Okay. Camel-o."

"I fuck you in van?" I said. "Is okay? I bang you in truck? No one around, at Camelot, I fuck you in truck, okay?"

"Okay," she said. "Fuck in truck. Camel-o."

Let me tell you, arranging for paid sex is both more humiliating and ultimately more rewarding when you have to think, speak, and hand-gesture your intentions as slowly as if you're a retard. You really feel like you've earned something when you finally get it. As a matter of fact, there would be fewer misunderstandings in marriage if negotiations like that took place right at the altar. The priest could take care of it. Just before the vows, he could say something like:

"Miss, do you understand that you are offering to blow and fuck him for a period of at least one year?"

"Yes."

"Sir, do you understand that she's offering to blow and fuck you for a period of one year and it will cost you a house in the suburbs, a minivan, and a Honda Civic?"

"Yes."

"Do you also understand that in exchange for her blowing and fucking you, you must agree to work nonstop and listen to her bitch every five seconds?"

"Yes."

"Do you also understand that after a period of one year, further blowing and fucking will cost you one necklace per year?"

"Yes."

"And do you also understand that over the next several years you are required to give her two or three children that will cost you a hundred grand a child?"

"Yes."

"And you also understand that after a period of several years the fucking and sucking will cease, but this arrangement will still cost you eighty percent of your worth?"

"I do."

"You may kiss the bride."

It's depressing, yes, but God knows it's the fucking truth.

Anyway, when we arrived at the Camelot Diner, which is still there, by the way, but is now called the Tropicana, I found an appropriately quiet spot in back by the dumpster. This wasn't some big parking lot; people were definitely going to be driving by pretty close to us, but no one was going to think anyone was in the van, so it would probably be okay. There were homes right there too, because Elizabeth is basically the inner city, so if someone looked out of their window at the right angle they might see something. I didn't care. I locked the doors, and then I figured I'd better be straight with her.

"Me," I said, pointing at myself. "First time."

"Eh?" she said.

"First time," I said. "Now, first time." I then used the universal sign for banging, which is putting your finger through a hole you make with the index finger and thumb on your other hand.

She smiled at me, just coy and adorable. *"Lo se,"* she said. "I know this."

"Really?" I said. "You *know*? How?"

"Lo se."

I was nervous as hell. I had been obsessed with getting to this point and getting laid—not even by a girl this hot—and now all I could do was stall. I tried my best to make small talk, as if she actually understood or cared about one word I was saying. Like her sister, Mary was really good at what she did for a living, because after a few minutes she ignored me altogether and just handled the situation.

"Dinero?" she said. "What you want?"

"I would like the deluxe, please," I said, like an idiot. "The intercourse with the blow job on the side."

"De-whats?" she said. I don't know if I said it because I'd seen it in some shitty teen-sex movie, or just because we were at a diner where my favorite meal was a cheeseburger deluxe. In any event, she took the money and counted it, and that seemed to get the message across.

"You want fuck and blow job?"

"Yes, I do," I said. In hindsight, I should have asked her for some french fries too and really tried to confuse the foreign cunt. "So, uh, you like New Jersey?"

After another painful minute or two of trying to make conversation, this girl just leaned over and started kissing me on the lips, which unbeknownst to me was a real treat. As I got older and more experienced with whores, I learned that kissing was not something they did regularly. It's way too intimate. Of course, anyone who saw *Pretty Woman* could tell you that too. That's about the only realistic detail in that film, as far as L.A. street hookers go. If you don't believe me, ask Hugh Grant.

At nineteen, I was thin and I wasn't bad-looking. I'd probably have had a shot at Mary, since I wasn't yet grotesque, as I am now. I swear to Christ, when I was younger I really was kind of a good-looking guy. Then one day in the mid-nineties I woke up and I'd become Vic Tayback. The honest truth is, I thought she was attracted to me; I thought this was like the best date I'd ever had and maybe the start of a relationship. You tend to lose your ability to reason clearly when an incredibly hot woman puts the moves on you, whether you're paying her or not. But I realized that her attraction to me might not be all that strong when I noticed that she'd stopped kissing me until, much like her sister, I put the $75 in her shoe. I swear to God, I should have paid these broads extra to fuck me with no shoes on, just to see where they'd put the money.

Once business was settled, we moved into the rear "lounge." We sprawled out on the luxurious sleeping bags, and she took out a rubber. She put it on me with her mouth, which a lot of whores have done to me since. That's such a skill; I suggest that whores everywhere make it a permanent part of their routine. Whores who know how to do it right, please teach your friend-whores.

We started rolling around, her long jet-black hair was loose, she got naked, and then I got on top of her, and because I was a complete and utter novice, it took me a little while to find the proper hole. I didn't need a guide-in though; I did get it on my own, and once I was in there, I've got to tell you, I lasted probably a good minute and a half—which is way longer than a lot of other people have told me they lasted when they lost their virginity. I can be straight about this: My manly staying power wasn't due to my iron-clad concentration or some kind of tantric sex self-hypnosis I learned about from Sting. It was strictly the awkwardness of the situation, because I was preoccupied with the fact that we were fucking in my father's handicap van. I can clearly remember my schizophrenic train of thought as I was banging her. It seesawed between *I can't believe I'm fucking a chick this hot,* and *Jesus, look at those tits,* to *I'd better not leave any stains back here* and *Is tomorrow when I have to drive Pop to the rehabilitation center?* I was somehow in the situation and watching it from a distance at the same time. I was happy to be having sex, but where I was doing it was at once funny and unbelievably depressing.

I never shared this story with my father before he died, and sometimes when I recall it, I think I should have, because he probably would have found it hilarious.

Let me tell you, once I was finished banging Mary, that same delusion that hit when she started kissing me returned—twice as bad. I suddenly felt such a connection to this girl that if I thought she understood more than every third word I said, I'd have told her

all of my hopes and dreams and asked her to be my wife. Instead, we sat in silence for a while and sort of cuddled. It was the most intimate moment I'd ever shared with a woman. Then she started giving me kind of a hand job, which got me hard again, then she blew me without a rubber on. I now know that no matter what you're paying, this is very, very rare for a hooker.

In my mind, at that moment, she was no longer a hooker—she was a girl who clearly liked me. She was really into it, I thought. She was probably acting, but it sounded to me like I might have even satisfied her on some level. I was so happy with the way my first time went. It was a milestone, like the first time I was asked to appear on *Letterman* or when I played Carnegie Hall. I felt such an instant bond to this girl that I considered offering to help her study for her SATs. I'm sure someone of her background would have been impressed with my combined score of 860.

"Look," I said to her. "Is it okay if we do this again?"

"*Sí,*" she said. "*Sí,* is okay. I like you." Then she gave me a kiss on the cheek. That did nothing to help me stay focused on the reality of the situation.

After I dropped her off, I went straight back to the Camelot Diner and ordered a bacon, egg, and cheese on a hard roll with a large chocolate milk. I have eaten that delicious, nutritious meal many times since, but it never came close to tasting as good as it did then. This was back when people were civilized and you were allowed to smoke inside, so afterward I lit up a cigarette. God, was that fantastic. As my friend Dan the Song Parody Man says, "A cigarette after dinner is one of the forty best cigarettes of the day."

About a week later, I called Mary again. I had somehow gotten together the necessary $75 and the same exact scenario happened once again—including my meal afterward at the Camelot. And that wasn't the last time either, because she and I had a thing going: It was more drawn out each time we got together. We spent more time talking and I got to know her a little. She told me that she and her sister were in the country illegally, which gave her an edge that I found incredibly sexy. There was no doubt about it, I was really smitten; I just thought she was a doll. She was adorable and I liked her personality, so I tried to talk to her about how we could get her a green card to stay in the country.

I didn't care if I had to keep paying her for our "dates," I wanted this girl to be my girlfriend. My friends might take some work, but I figured I could easily bullshit my mom about it. There's no rule that you have to tell your mother that your girlfriend is a whore. Besides, this chick was young; she didn't look haggard. She didn't look like she'd done the rope and bungee cord bit at bachelor parties yet, that's for sure. I started thinking of how our relationship could develop, which was completely crazy. I concluded that the best thing to do was just dive in. I seriously considered just asking her to marry me.

Mary and I did it a total of four times. The last time we got together, I actually sprung for a room. It wasn't much of a departure from the van—in fact, in some ways, it was worse. It was a shitty, small motel called the Garden State Motor Lodge that is still there on Route 22 eastbound in Union, a couple of miles before you hit Freilinghausen Avenue in Newark. That was where some of the more happening kids in high school took broads to get laid. I was really into this girl, so I splurged: I went for one of their top-tier, $18-a-night rooms. This place was one of those establishments where rooms were also available by the hour. I'm pretty sure that's the deal I went for. It paid off too—my girl gave me the usual, plus a free blow job. The time before, she also didn't charge me for the blow job, which was wonderful. It was this kind of treatment that convinced me that we should definitely get married. I mean, how many guys' girlfriends don't charge them for a blow job on their fourth date? Think about how much it costs just getting to the fourth date.

The day after our rendezvous at the Garden State Motor Lodge, I was on cloud nine and decided to proceed with my plan to introduce her to my family, which was my first step at making this a real, eventually non-payment-based relationship. I was unsure about it, though, because of the profound sadness in our house. My mom was a tower of strength—she was the only thing keeping us all together—and I thought that bringing an attractive girl over so I could tell my mom I had a girlfriend might improve her mood.

I've never asked my sister, but I'm pretty sure she didn't lose her virginity to a male whore. She probably went a more conventional route. Oh, wait—my sister as well as every other girl I'm related to has never had sex. I've never done anything normally in my entire life, really. I am a fucked-up person, let's face it. Quite frankly, I'm lucky to have any sort of job at all, much less a job working on the coolest radio show ever and making the kind of money I make today. Back then I already knew that I was fucked up, and I knew that losing my virginity the way I did was fucked up, but I thought that I could turn it around. Even though I wasn't going to school like my sister, I'd at least show my mom that I'd met a nice girl and might have a shot at getting married and having some kind of a normal life.

Of course, this story has a sad ending like most fucking things in my life do, particularly when women are involved. About a week later, I called Mary's apartment, and her sister told me that Mary had gone back to Brazil. My heart dropped. I swallowed hard and almost couldn't speak.

"Really?" I said. "What happened?"

"Well, she has a boyfriend back there," her sister said. "He was going to come over here and then he does not. He knows nothing about what we are doing here, okay?"

"That's really too bad," I said.

The sister spoke English pretty well compared to Mary, so she was able to explain their situation.

"She's not coming back," she said. "We are really nice people. We are very religious. We are doing this only to make money so we could get over here, and her boyfriend wants her to go back. But she said you are very nice, and if you want to come by, I will be happy to help you out." Now that's my kind of religious chick.

"Yeah, maybe we could do that," I said, knowing full well that I had no intention of it. "I'll call you." I didn't want to flat-out turn her down, but as far as I was concerned, she wasn't even in Mary's league. I remember hoping that things would get better for Mary in her village, but to be honest, it sounded like the best career a woman could land back there was becoming a heroin mule. And now, years later, after all of my struggles with drugs, I'd like to think that possibly I've done some heroin that sweet Mary shit out at a Best Western in the South Bronx, perhaps at gunpoint. It might sound strange to you, but I guess I'm just a hopeless romantic.

I was instantly depressed, because those "dates" with Mary were just about all I had to live for. I ended up calling her sister back the next day. I told her to have Mary call me if she ever returned to the States, and gave her my phone number. At that point, I had my own phone line in our house, which rang only in my room. I kept that number for another ten years and never got a call.

It took me a while to get over Mary, and as you can tell, I'll never forget her. More than a few times in the months and years to follow, I'd drive by her apartment complex. I kept thinking each time I passed by that I'd see her back in town, just walking down the street, heading home. In the back of my mind, I never totally believed her sister's story. I thought maybe I'd creeped her out somehow, or that she could see I was getting attached and had her sister make up a story. My self-esteem is always good in a pinch.

Nothing can change the fact that I had four wonderful meetings with this girl and she helped me become a man. And she did it while there was still an "een" at the end of my age! Thank the Lord for that! Besides, I guarantee that none of my friends lost their virginity to a chick hotter than Mary. She had a nice ass and she had beautiful thighs. She had real tits that were a solid C cup, young and perky. She was built just exactly the way I like a chick to be built.

In the years to come, one of my favorite bars became a place called McGee's, which later became Suspenders, that isn't far from the Camelot Diner. I spent far too many nights there in my twenties, drinking and getting arrested for drunk and disorderly, for fighting, and also for a DUI. On the nights when no one ended up in jail, my buddies Chico, Shecky, Deeg, and I would usually end up at the Camelot eating cheeseburger deluxes, chocolate milks, cheesecakes, and chocolate layer cake well into the night. I never said anything to them, but I was usually sitting there wishing Mary would walk in. In my drunker moments I'd daydream it: She'd stroll through the door, looking every inch as hot as she was, we'd go out into the parking lot, and then I'd say to her, much like Abe Vigoda said to Robert Duvall in *The Godfather*: "Mary, could you throw me one for old times' sake?" And much like Duvall said to him, she'd say: "Can't do it, Artie."

Well, that never happened. Instead, I spent many of those nights fending off questions from my friends about how I lost my virginity. I was always so vague that I'm not sure even I remember the bullshit story I used. I think it went something like this: "So, yeah, it was the summer of '85, and I was down the Shore one weekend. This chick was a friend of a friend. I can't even remember what high school she went to, but it was just that one weekend and then she never called me." Yeah, that sounds about right.

I was so embarrassed about the real story, even ten years later, that I still couldn't admit it. It's not like my friends hadn't done dumb shit. I certainly could have told my buddy Deeg—he's the only other guy who went to my high school and wanted to get into show business. We got real tight in our late teens and twenties by walking that road together. We went on auditions and took acting classes in Greenwich Village for the few weeks we could afford to. We had a bond, because to do that at all, we had to be able to embarrass ourselves in front of each other all the time. Deeg is a great guy and he would have understood, but for some reason, I could never get up the balls to share it, even though for years I was dying to tell someone this story.

As for my squiring skills, after Mary, I went into a big drought. I thought that all I needed to do was lose my virginity and then I'd just be having sex all the time, forever. I figured that once I'd done it, I'd have some kind of natural sex knowledge that broads would sense. I wouldn't act any different, but I'd have an invisible manly swagger as a non-virgin that would make me irresistible. I think it's what's affectionately known as having "stank on your down-low."

That didn't happen, but about a year later I went on a ski trip against my will. Skiing just ain't my thing. Let me put it to you this way: For years my manager tried to get me to do the Aspen Comedy Festival and I told him that the two groups of people I hate most in this world are comedians and people who ski, so it sounded like a living a hell. I do not ski, nor will I ever, but this one time I got talked into it by my buddy Al, his girlfriend Toby, and Deeg, just as a way to get the fuck out of town. We drove up to a place called Owl's Nest in Ontario, Canada, where I spent my time drinking in the lodge. And that's where I met the second girl I ever had sex with. I got her drunk one night on Absolut vodka, and I made Deeg spend the night in Al and Toby's room. I won't name names, but my buddies definitely remember her, because that story has never really gone out of rotation, mostly because on the drive home we were trying to figure out who the girl looked like. An hour into it, I had it: She looked exactly like Elton John. To this day, if anything about Canada or skiing is mentioned, one of my friends will start singing: "It's a little bit funny, this feeling inside...."

There was one remarkable thing about that experience: The girl was a virgin. She's the only virgin I have ever slept with. I do see something humorous in the fact that my virginity was taken by a complete pro and the next time I had sex, I played that role—just not nearly as well. As far as my sexual history goes, I didn't start putting up any real numbers until I began going into New York City to try my luck doing stand-up. Once I was involved in the New York scene and doing coke and hitting after-hours clubs, it became much easier. Anyone who was or is involved in that scene knows it's a no-brainer: You meet broads and you have cocaine relationships, which revolve around doing lots of cocaine and then fucking. Those are never a sure thing, however, because usually girls who want to hang with you for coke love coke way more than they love fucking.

In my struggling years in New York, I probably put up another seven or eight broads, which for me are strong numbers because I've never been a ladies' man. However bold I may be when I'm on stage or making a fool of myself for laughs, it goes right out the window in the presence of a beautiful woman. And time and success have done nothing at all to change that: I'm still unbelievably shy around women. It's the classic scenario: As a performer, I'm more comfortable on stage in front of 5,000 people than one-on-one with a hot chick.

When I got my role on *MADtv* in the summer of 1995, I was twenty-seven years old. My "number" at that point was eleven. Only two of them were repeat customers—three of them, if you include Mary the hooker. I had only three repeats (I would like to have said "threepeats," but I didn't want to have to pay Pat Riley a licensing fee), but by that point I had been to a lot of bachelor parties, so I'd been blown by about fifty different women. I'm sure many of my fans will be disappointed to hear that of the eleven I had sex with, only two were whores, which makes that nine regular chicks I was able to talk into bed.

I did find out, when I moved to L.A., however, that if you're a regular on a network show, you can be the world's biggest retard and still get laid. And that's a good thing for me, for obvious reasons.

Still, my numbers should be much better. At the age of forty, thirteen years into show business, I have somehow moved up the ladder into the major leagues of entertainment, but my numbers haven't really jumped accordingly. I went from doing stand-up to a network show to having a network deal to being in studio movies and then to a regular spot on the biggest radio show ever. When we talked about numbers again recently on the air, I was vague about it because, for the first time in my life, I actually couldn't remember. I secretly felt so cool that I had actually lost count of how many chicks I've banged. I tried my best to add it all up tonight, and I'd say I'm up to around eighty. If I'd never gotten into show business, of course, I'd probably still be lingering down around eleven. But, now that I'm thinking about it, eighty is a *really* low number considering the career I've had. I've spent the last seven years doing *The Howard Stern Show,* and that is the ultimate—the best regular gig a comedian can have. Doing *Howard* plus all the stand-up I do, I've seen every kind of groupie, because a headlining comedian in a good club can get sex, drugs, anything. I figure that a guy who was at all good with women and had my same career for the past thirteen years would be up over a thousand. While eighty might be a lot for a normal guy, remember that we're talking about eighty put up by a guy who, in his forties, still sucks with women and is in a line of work where it's easy to get broads. It's much more realistically pathetic when you see it that way, don't you think?

Too Fat to Fish:
My Days as a Longshoreman

6

I grew up with about fifty-two guys named Mike, so pretty early on each of them was given a nickname to tell them all apart—Shecky, Joker, Deeg, Dut (rhymes with putt), and Goof, to name a few. Of all those illustrious nicknamed Mikes, Goof plays a major role in this story.

At the time of my father's death, I was twenty-two years old, unemployed, and I owed bookies and shylocks money. I was a drunk who started doing drugs a little too much and gambled with money I didn't have. All I hope is that there's an afterlife so my father can see that the son who was such a fuck-up when he died went on to make something of himself.

But at the time of this story, that was a long way off: By 1990, a bunch of my friends had gone through college and were ready to graduate. I had done nothing for those four years except try stand-up twice, with miserable results, and take one acting class in Greenwich Village with my buddy. I couldn't stay enrolled in it for very long because I didn't have enough money, so all I'd really done was get a four-year degree in vegetating. While Pop was alive, time stood still for us, but once he was gone, it was like I woke up and realized that the world had been passing me by. His death lit a fire under my ass, so about a month after he died, I saw an ad in the paper and went to a club in Greenwich Village that was having a stand-up comedy contest sponsored by a radio station on Long Island.

I was one of ten contestants, and it was officially the third time I ever did stand-up. Three years had gone by since I'd last tried it, and I'd done so badly that it took me that long to forget it. But I just said, "Fuck it, for my father I'll try it again." I came in sixth place, which wasn't great, but at least there were four people in the world shittier at it than I was. It was incentive enough to try it again.

I also decided to get myself a job of some kind, and Goof was there for me: He asked his father to give me a job in the machine shop he owned in Roselle, New Jersey. The only opening I could fill was sweeping up, doing basic machine work, drilling stuff, working on a lift, and loading and unloading this powder that is used to sandblast stuff on major industrial construction jobs. Goof's dad had a side business where he would buy all this sandblasting powder in bulk, then package it up in huge buckets and secure it to pallets that were sold and loaded onto trucks. Part of my job was sweeping up around that operation.

I started two days after my father's memorial mass and got six bucks an hour under the table. That sparked exactly one year of absolute nothingness, just a shit-awful loser bullshit year in my life. I worked at that job for $6 an hour and I could get there whatever time I wanted as long as I finished all the work I had for the day. Here's how my typical workday went: I would get there at noon, do my work, and be finished by about 7 or 8 o'clock at night. A lot of nights Goof would come over from the machine area and help me finish up so we could get out of there quicker and start our night of drinking. For dinner we'd order a bacon pizza from Domino's and bring it back to the area where all the sand was stored. I will never forget all the bacon pizzas we consumed that year, because each and every one ended up being coated in that disgusting sand, which seemed to settle evenly over the top of the bacon and cheese the second we'd open the box. God knows what was in that shit, because it actually changed the color of the pizza from a healthy white and red to this toxic shade of magenta. I've never seen that color anywhere else in the natural world. Between that, the eight packs of Marlboro Reds I was smoking a day, and the Old Grand-Dad or Jim Beam I'd bring to work to get loaded, I probably took ten years off my life in that one year alone.

On a good week, I'd make probably about 250 bucks, cash, almost all of which I spent at local bars around the Union area. One of them was this place where the bartender would give us free drinks all night. He started serving us when we were like fifteen and he just didn't care. He was running a racket and a half in there: Every single buddy of his who came in drank for free and he pocketed all the tips directly. The bar was always crowded, but the owner couldn't figure out why he was barely breaking even. A real whiz with numbers, that guy.

We'd also go to this sports bar and drink ourselves into oblivion. We'd do blow whenever it was around and I'd gamble with money that I didn't have. I did have the distinction, however, of being the first one of my friends to put in a "100-timer" gambling. The smallest bet a bookie takes is called a "time." That is not to be confused with a "dime," which is a bet for 1,000 bucks—fifty dimes and fifty times are very different things. Dimes are for high rollers, and times are for people who are not high rollers, like me and my friends. In our world, though, if you bet twenty times, you *were* a high roller, because that is a 100-dollar bet. One hundred dollars to us was a hell of a lot to put on the line. There was also a "vig" you had to pay the bookie if you lost, which was a one-dollar charge per five-dollar "time." So if you lost 100 bucks, you really lost 110. A vig is like a tax for losing that basically gives the bookie and the shylock an advantage, meaning they will probably always be in the money, even if more people win than lose that week. Vigs only counted on bets of fifty dollars or more at a rate of five bucks per fifty lost. Everyone knew that if you bet less than fifty bucks you were a fucking pussy anyway, and they felt too sorry for your loser ass to charge you a vig.

During this period, my buddies and I got a number for a bookie on Staten Island whose name was Bobo, and we bet on and off with him for like eight years, until one day he just disappeared. The number didn't work and no one knew what happened. But before Bobo fell off the face of the earth, I became the first of my friends to bet a 100-timer, and I bet it with Bobo.

It was a 10-buck vig for every 100 bucks you bet, so a 100-timer would be betting $500. If I lost I'd owe $550, and if I won I'd win $500. None of my friends had come anywhere close to that. Considering that I had about $80 to my name, they couldn't believe what I was doing. Bobo took the bet, which I had to place through a couple of our friends, who acted as middlemen for all the bets we placed. Bobo would send a guy down from Staten Island to take the bets and collect or pay out each week, and they'd meet him in the McDonald's parking lot on the Parkway in Union. Our friends never actually met Bobo—no one we knew had ever seen him—they only dealt with Bobo's guy.

The game I bet on was the Giants versus the 49ers in about Week 10 of the season on *Monday Night Football*. Obviously, I thought I had a sure win on my hands, but this was both the year that my judgment was about as clear as my vision after a bottle of Jack Daniel's and the season when the Giants overachieved and beat the 49ers in the NFC Championship before beating the Bills in the Super Bowl.

Bobo's line on this regular season Monday night game was the 49ers giving three and half points to the Giants. Now, some lines had them giving four, and the *New York Post* and the *Daily News* had given them four and a half, but Bobo's line was three and a half. I have always liked the Giants and they were playing out in San Francisco, so I said fuck it, the Giants will definitely cover three and a half points. To anyone who doesn't know what I'm talking about, it meant that if the Giants won outright and you bet the Giants, you won, and if they lost but by only three points, you won dough too since the points given was three and a half. If they lost by more than three and a half points, then you lost your money and you paid the vig.

All the Giants had to do was not lose by more than three and a half points for me to collect. We watched the game at a bar, and in a shining example of my shitty luck that year, it turned out to be a grueling defensive battle that the Giants lost, 7 to 3.

And you know what? I blame Joe Montana. That motherfucker is responsible for me losing more fucking money in my life, that fucking ass-wipe. I cannot stand watching him interviewed even today. Fuck him. So, anyway, I lost $550 and I had only $80, and what unfolded next has become a classic story among my friends.

I was in that state of mind that people who have been on the skids know well: It's when you just don't give a fuck at all and you handle situations that you should be taking more seriously as if they're a joke, because you really don't care what happens to you.

When you feel that way, you're actually hoping for something or someone to make a decision for you, because you don't give a shit about doing anything for yourself. My nonchalance worried my friend who had to meet Bobo's guy.

"Artie, what the fuck am I gonna tell this guy?" he said.

"Tell him I don't have the money. It's not like you'll be lying," I said.

"Are you serious?"

"Yeah. Can't I work it off or something?" I was acting like Bobo had a restaurant and I could just do dishes for a few weeks to cover my dinner tab.

It wasn't too far from the truth in the end: The middleman who represented Bobo each week actually had a roofing business, and when he met my friend he came up with a solution.

"Yeah, tell your dumb fuck friend Artie that I'm working two six-day weeks up at this place in Clifton," he said. "I'll give that jerkoff 250 bucks each week and he can work it off."

I accepted and spent two weeks roofing with this fucking guy up in Clifton, in really shitty, late-fall weather. It was glamorous work, climbing my ass up and down a ladder on a roof with a steep pitch, carrying these enormous fucking bags of shingles. Six days each week, I worked a fourteen-hour day. I was expecting $250 a week, so I'd be even after two weeks, but when I shook his hand that last day, he told me otherwise.

"Well, thanks, man, I really appreciate it," I said. "We're even, right?"

"Even?" he said. "What the fuck are you talking about, jerkoff? You still owe Bobo the fifty-dollar vig."

That was the kind of prick I was dealing with. I don't know who I borrowed it from, but I came up with the $50 vig and then I was even. And then, in one of my rare rational decisions from that period, I actually stopped gambling for a while. I think I made it through to the playoffs before trying my hand again.

In the meantime, I lived vicariously through a few of my friends who tried to get one over on Bobo by betting on hockey games. These geniuses figured out that the NHL held one day game a week, on Wednesday afternoons, while every other game in the season was played at night. Bobo didn't pay much attention to hockey, so one time, for a goof, they bet with his middleman on a game that had already happened. With Bobo you had to call all of your bets in by 7 P.M., so they watched the game that afternoon and bet on the winner, because there was an outside shot that Bobo would think the game was on for Wednesday night. Sure enough, Bobo looked at the scores the next day, not knowing about the day game thing, saw that they'd won, and paid them out. That was it; they were in on a sure thing: As long as they didn't arouse suspicion, they could probably keep it going for a while. But that wasn't enough for these guys—they wanted to win big. They put one over on him once, so they thought they were the shit and started betting on that Wednesday-afternoon hockey game every week, well into the spring, each time for more money.

Soon, like classic shitheads they bet one-timer bets on every other game, but on those Wednesday games, they'd bet enormous fucking amounts. If they'd had any brains at all, they would have bet a steady number on those Wednesday games and the guy never would have noticed. But they couldn't do that—they'd bet $200 a game, when a forty-timer was a huge thing. It doesn't say much about Bobo's accounting department that it took them about five or six weeks to notice that these two *gavones* were winning like sixty-time parlays, which means that not only were they betting the team that won, they were also betting the over and under in the game, which is the point spread. A parlay means the two bets are connected, so unless you win both, you lose all the money. These are what we call long shots. And these guys hit five of them in a row, which is what we call astonishing—and nearly impossible. So Bobo's crack team of bookies started to wonder what the hell was going on with these kids and if they knew somebody playing in the hockey game every Wednesday night.

Bobo decided to do a little homework, so he picked up the paper and realized that these two smart-ass kids from Jersey had been duping him for the last two or three months, betting on games that had already happened. Even though they were betting well above their means, we were all pretty small-time, so they'd probably only taken him for about $800. Anyway, Bobo wasn't happy and his middleman called our friend to deliver the message.

"Listen, motherfucker," he said. "Your buddies fucked up and they won again this week. They are not getting that money, and Bobo wants the money they've ripped him off for. Bobo is fucking LIVID. Your dumb fuck buddies are gonna meet Bobo himself, not me, at that fucking McDonald's this week, you hear me? They don't show, you're all fucking DEAD."

"I got nothing to do with this," our friend said. "I didn't rip him off."

"Bobo don't fucking care, you hear me? You're all answering for this, asshole. Go to the back of the McDonald's, the booth on the left-hand side."

"Okay," my friend said, pretty worried. "How am I gonna know who he is?"

"He's fifty, bald, with tattoos. Fucking be there." The guy hung up.

My friend the middleman and my friends the hockey bettors were scared shitless. There was no way they were going to meet Bobo. My friend who got the call had to go, so I went with him, even though we weren't the assholes ripping him off. It didn't matter to Bobo, we were all getting punished that week: He didn't pay anything the rest of us had won, plus we were getting a talking-to.

My friend and I went down to the McDonald's at the usual time, went into the back, and saw a guy who matched the description. Our hearts were pounding as we walked over to him. He told us to sit down. He was sitting there with a Quarter Pounder with Cheese and an order of large fries in front of him.

"You want a fry, kid?" he asked me.

"Yeah, sure," I said, and took one. I thought that was very nice of him.

We sat there in awkward silence as Bobo looked down in concentration, refusing to make eye contact with us for about two minutes. Then he looked up.

"You two motherfuckers tell your fucking friends something from me," he said real low, leaning forward and staring us in the eye. "If they EVER try something like this again, I will find out where they live and I will fucking kill their parents! If they got kids, I will fucking kill their kids in front of them. I will make them fucking watch and then I will tear their fucking hearts out!" He started yelling real loud and got a bit red in the face.

"I will rape their fucking *grandmothers,* you hear me? I am not here to be made a fucking fool of! I will hit them with a bat as hard as I can in their fucking face!"

My friend and I were kind of looking down out of respect for Bobo as he went on, threatening to rape and kill people, but then both of us looked up at him and then at each other and just started hysterically laughing. It was Ash Wednesday and Bobo, being a good Catholic, was sitting there, with an enormous ash-cross on his forehead, threatening to murder our unborn children and behead our deceased relatives. He'd obviously gone to church, got his ashes, and didn't stop to think just how ridiculous he would look screaming at us with a cross on his forehead. We didn't know what to do, because there was no way we were going to stop laughing: We had that uncontrollable laughter that nerves and ludicrous situations bring on. All we could do was put our heads down and hope that Bobo would think we were trembling with fear instead of shaking in hysterics. But we were no longer looking at him, and he was getting really pissed. He started shouting louder and louder and his face got redder and redder, which made that enormous black ash-cross look even funnier.

"You motherfuckers better show me some *respect*!" he screamed. "You are not getting a fucking CENT of the money I owe you this week! You tell those motherfuckers to get me my money or I'll kill them and kill their family! Now get the fuck out of here! Get out of my sight!"

We got up and made it to the door, but as soon as we were in the parking lot we burst out laughing harder than we had before. We could barely move; we had to lie on the hood of my 1970 Chevy Nova for about an hour laughing.

"I don't even think he knew it was there!" my friend said.

"His wife probably told him when he left this morning, 'Make sure you go get ashes, Bobo, it's Ash Wednesday today,'" I said. "'And bring home some soda bread!' I'm sure he was, like, 'Okay, honey, I'll get the ashes, then I have to go threaten to rape and kill a couple of kids' families over in Jersey, then I'll pick up the bread. See you tonight.'" And Bobo's Ash Wednesday cross was just enormous—it was as big as the cross that Jesus fucking climbed up the mountain with.

That was the pinnacle of 1990, that year of shit for me. Then, in February 1991, a friend told me that he'd put in a word for me with his father since he knew that the job in the machine shop with Goof was a dead end. All my friends knew that I'd tried stand-up again but nothing much was happening with that so I needed a good job. He told me that his dad had openings for longshoreman jobs down at Port Newark, and everyone who knows anything about that knows that those jobs aren't exactly advertised in the paper. You have to know somebody, because they are positions coveted by any guy who has no college degree. If you get one, you're set—the union is so amazing that you're taken care of for life.

My buddy's father was very respected in the union; he got Port Newark and Elizabeth running really well in his years in office. It was no longer the way it was in the old days of *On the Waterfront* with Brando and Johnny Friendly. Nobody ripped off anybody anymore and the union insisted on honest, cooperative relationships with management. Somewhere along the line, they figured out that in the long run it was better for their guys to keep the peace instead of stealing a piece of everything that came through there.

Since my friend's dad was putting in a word for me, I was able to go down and start working part-time, just by showing up and saying that he'd sent me—he had that kind of standing in the union. I'd be able to work my way up, and when a permanent position opened up, I'd be in there for life. At the time, the part-time rate was nineteen bucks an hour, and there was always a lot of overtime: You could get time and a half for a while and then double time kicked in. There were guys down there who could not spell their fucking names who were making a hundred grand a year with overtime.

I got a position at the orange juice pier where ships came in from Brazil and unloaded liquid orange juice concentrate. When a ship came into the port, it took three hours to tie it up and hook up huge hoses, through which three million gallons of orange juice concentrate would flow into refrigerated tanks. It took about four days for all of the orange juice to be pumped out, and according to union law four longshoremen were required to be there the whole time to supervise the operation.

For those four days, you slept there and you were on the clock, being paid, 24/7. To pass time, the tradition was that you played cards. I would play 500 rummy, and I tried to learn how to play pinochle with Chick, the old-time Italian longshoreman who enjoyed whipping my fucking ass. Chick was as good as a professional cardplayer—and a prick about it too. You'd play 500 rummy with this guy and he would let you get up to 400, almost 500, before he'd methodically take your heart out with his hands. He'd let you get, like, ten points from victory, then beat you and leave you owing him money. Chick could also play speed chess, which was fine with me, because he really enjoyed kicking this management guy's ass all the time and the rest of us really enjoyed watching it. This guy was an engineer who'd graduated from Yale, and Chick would take him for 200 bucks a week. The guy kept coming back, thinking he was going to get one over on this old Italian guy, but he never did. It killed the guy that Chick, who had probably barely made it to seventh grade, was beating him every single day on his lunch hour.

Every day on the way to work, Chick listened to CBS-FM in his Lincoln Continental as he made the five-minute drive from the Down Neck section of Newark, where he lived, to the port. He'd listen to the famous *Harry Harrison in the Morning* show and absorb whatever oldies they were playing. Since Chick worked right next to me putting lids on these huge drums of orange juice concentrate, I'd hear him, for the entire morning, sing whatever song it was that he'd just heard in the car on CBS-FM. If the song didn't interest him, or if he wanted to break it up a little, he'd do a jingle that he'd made up about Harry Harrison. He'd do all of this at the top of his lungs.

For four hours, since he always added curses to whatever he sang, he would belt out things like this:

"Kathy's clown, Kathy's motherfucking clown!"

"Hey Jude . . . hey fucking Jude-y fucking Jude-y fucking Jude-y,

Jude-y, Jude-y, Jude-y. Cocksuckin' na-na-na. Na na na-na! Fuckin Jude!"

But my favorites were the jingles:

"Harry Harrison! Harry fucking faggot Harrison! In the cocksucking mooorning!"

You had to find a way to enjoy it, because no one was telling Chick to stop—he ran the place. Every morning, lunch trucks would come at about 10:30, loaded up with potatoes-and-egg sandwiches or peppers-and-egg sandwiches, and Chick would buy everybody a first-break snack. You'd try to give him five bucks for your sandwich and he'd get truly offended, like close-to-violence offended.

"Get the fuck outta here with your five dollars!" he'd shout at you. "You think your piece-of-shit five dollars is going to make me rich? Fucking eat the sandwich!"

Since I was the low guy on the totem pole, he'd usually ask me to go get the lunch. There was an Irish kid who worked with us who would order potatoes and eggs with ketchup on it, which is like sacrilegious to Italians. It's the same as putting cheese on linguine with clams—you just don't do it. I didn't feel good about it, but I ordered it for the guy anyway. The owner of the truck was this Italian guy, and when I put in the order for ketchup, he stopped what he was doing and looked at me like I'd just told him to go fuck his mother.

"I do not do ketchup," he said.

"Listen—I know, it's not for me," I said. "The guy's Irish who wants it. He doesn't know what the fuck he's doing. He asked for ketchup."

"Fuck him—I do not do ketchup."

"Man, come on, just give me a couple of ketchup packets. I gotta bring everyone lunch."

"I will give you no ketchup. Not on my sandwich. You are not going to ruin that fucking sandwich!"

"Are you really going to make me go somewhere else for ketchup packets?"

"No," he said, staring me down. "I do not want to hear about you or anyone else putting fucking ketchup on my sandwiches. I will not enable you to do that. Fuck that, you get no ketchup from me."

Every day, I would have to go to the fucking diner down the street, buy a cup of coffee, and ask for ketchup packets. It took me an extra twenty minutes, all because this fucking Irish guy who had no idea how to properly eat an Italian potatoes-and-egg sandwich had to have ketchup on it.

There was another character down there unlike anyone I've ever met who we'll call Tony D., who was always butting heads with the management people. He was an older guy who liked busting all the younger guys' chops about broads and whatever else came to mind. We were split up into two teams: I was part of the crew that loaded these huge fifty-gallon drums with orange juice. The other crew loaded and unloaded trucks. Tony was on the truck side of the operation. Whenever our break ended, Tony would still be on our side of things talking shit, so one of the management guys, all of whom were these nerdy Ivy League types in white coats, would have to walk over to him and timidly say, "Tony, you've got to get back to work on your side now."

Tony D. loved this—he waited for it, each and every break. He'd get right up in their face, half kidding and half serious, just to fuck with them.

"I'm breaking balls here! Are you telling me I can't break balls?" he'd say. "That will be the fucking day when I can't break balls. FUCK YOU!" At this point, he'd turn away, too angry to go on. He'd actually turn toward us and give us a wink, leaving the management guy to kind of whimper away, looking like he was going to cry.

I became close friends with a few of the guys I worked with

down there, one of whom was a senior longshoreman. This guy was basically the foreman of the group and essentially my boss. One Friday at the end of work, he asked me if I wanted to go fishing with him the next day. Now, I had never gone fishing and didn't really give a shit about learning how to fish, but he was a good guy, not to mention that he was my boss and I wanted to get in good with him. I told him sure, and he said he'd pick me up at 5:30 the next morning. We'd launch his boat from Elizabeth and we'd go fishing for bluefish and tuna.

Like I said, fishing was just not the kind of thing I did, and having never done it before, I agreed to it without giving it much thought. With the same lack of thought, I then went to happy hour with the guys from work like I did every Friday and started to get ossified drunk. In those years, I really took Friday happy hour to heart: I would get so drunk that more than once I bet twice on the same game. I did it this night too: At 5:30, after a few drinks, I called my bookie to bet on a game. Then, at 7:30, just before he stopped taking bets, I called him back and bet on the same game, but this time I bet on the opposite team. Now, the only thing that could possibly happen, given that the guy took both my bets, was that I would lose. I was basically giving him the vig. It would have made more sense for me just to call the guy and tell him that I'd like to give him fifty bucks. I did it three separate times that year, all of them during Friday-night happy hours, which should give you an idea of how much drinking went on.

"Wait, what did I do?" I asked him the next morning after that third time.

"You called me at 5:30 and bet one team, then you called back at 7:30 and bet the other team," the guy said matter-of-factly.

"Can I ask why you let me do that?" I said, annoyed. "You know I forget shit when I'm drunk—you should have reminded me that I'd already placed a bet."

"I am trying to teach you a lesson about drinking and gambling," he said. "They don't mix."

"Wait a second—am I getting life lessons from a bookie? I feel like I'm at the end of an episode of *Diff'rent Strokes*."

"You've gotta learn, man," he said. "Only way to learn not to be a dumb fuck is the hard way."

"Listen, buddy, do me a favor? From now on, don't teach me life lessons, just tell me I'm a drunk and that I've already bet and then hang up on me."

Drinking was definitely the thing after work on Fridays, mostly at a couple of bars right there in Newark—this place Zip Zip, or Tony DeCanicca's, which had great *zuppa di pesce*. We lived pretty large all around: We got an hour and fifteen minutes for lunch every day, which was another great union perk, and sometimes we'd go, all a mess in our work clothes, to these formal restaurants. There was the Spanish Tavern, Iberia, and a few great Portuguese and Italian places. We would eat like kings, with waiters in tuxedos serving us, then we'd go back to work at the port.

My favorite lunch down there, though, was at this amazing deli called Amelia's run by this little old Sicilian lady. Amelia made a different special every day, and every once in a while she'd make a big vat of broccoli rabe and the special would be a sandwich of broccoli rabe with fresh mozzarella on amazing bread from Napadano's, this great old bakery down the street. Then we'd walk across the street to Nasto's, this chocolate factory in the middle of Down Neck Newark, and get a huge ice-cream sundae. After a lunch like that, let me tell you, the last thing you'd want to do is fucking work, let alone put your tool belt on over your fucking gut. All you are really qualified to do after a lunch like that is sleep for twenty hours.

There was another little home-cooking place we liked too, called Cookie's. It was run by a 350-pound Italian woman whose sons were part-time bookies who never worked. Cookie had turned the basement of her home into a little restaurant, probably to support them, and every morning she'd fry 200 meatballs and a bunch of green peppers in oil. When I first started working at the port, I didn't have a driver's license because I'd lost it after being busted on a DUI charge, so my foreman, the same senior longshoreman who invited me fishing, would drive me to work. Every morning we'd stop off at Cookie's so he could put in a bet or pay off or collect from one of her sons, and soon enough I started doing the same thing.

We'd stop over there at like 7:30 in the morning since we had to be at work by 8, and if we got to her place at the right time, she'd be coming out of the kitchen with 200 freshly fried meatballs and peppers, and she would say, "Help yourself." It smelled so good that I'd start grabbing meatballs with one hand and putting them on a plate while forking into the peppers with my other hand. I'd end up, for breakfast, eating about ten of these things with five helpings of peppers, about three pieces of bread, and a soda or root beer to wash it all down. These were not some kind of gay turkey meatballs like you see these days, by the way. They were unbelievably beautiful, real meatballs made of beef and veal. It was the breakfast of champions and the best way to warm up for my hour-and-fifteen-minute lunch.

Anyway, the night before this fishing trip, I was out with all of the guys and my foreman and by 10 P.M. I was stone-drunk off my ass. I had done a little blow that night too, since there was some going around, so I was nowhere close to getting a good night's sleep before the big adventure. That's not what I told the foreman, though. When he came up to me, slapped me on the shoulder, said good-bye, and told me he'd be over to pick me up bright and early at 5:30 A.M., I couldn't have been more enthusiastic.

"Dude!" I said. "I'll be ready! It's gonna be great!" All night long I had talked up how much I was ready for it and looking forward to it, assuring him that I was really into fishing.

I ended up going out to a go-go bar in Linden, New Jersey, called Cheeques—which is pronounced "cheeks," by the way—with my friends Chico and Shecky and another one of the many Mikes. I did not get home until 3 or 3:30 A.M., and when I did I was drunk, high, and covered in cheap lipstick from the many dancers I had paid to kiss me on the cheek. I passed the fuck out in all my clothes, and by the time 5:30 came around, I'd barely gotten a nap in and was nowhere close to being sober. I was lying there like a Neanderthal, sweating like a pig, with puffy eyes, my hair all over my face, and my mouth wide open. The phone must have rung for a few minutes before it woke me up, but when it did it scared the shit out of me. At first, I had no idea where I was. Then I picked up the phone.

"You ready to go fishing?" my boss said. "It's 5:30—I'm on my way over."

If it had been anyone else in the entire world but my boss, I would have told the guy to fuck off and slept all day. But somewhere in the haze clogging my brain, I remembered the drunken promise I'd made the night before.

I cleared my throat, got one eye all the way open, and hoped I sounded more tired than drunk. "Oh yeah, come on over," I said. "I overslept, but I'm ready."

"All right, move your ass. I'll be there in twenty minutes."

I got up, tried to see through my skull-splitting headache, and made it to the shower. I kind of stood there under the water for a few minutes, then I threw on some sweatpants, brushed my teeth, and took a look in the mirror. It wasn't good at all. I looked like George Clinton when he got busted for crack. The shower hadn't come close to washing away the reek of liquor, and I had the worst bedhead I've ever seen on someone who wasn't homeless. For a minute, I wondered if shaving might improve things.

"Fuck it," I said, and walked downstairs.

Now, because my mother is both a crazy person and an insanely clean Italian woman, she was already up at 5:30 A.M. on a Saturday, vacuuming. As a working woman, my mother never got the chance to vacuum during the week and always had a full schedule of things to get done over the weekend, so she would get up at the crack of dawn on Saturday mornings and start cleaning. It was another reason that I liked to get passed-out drunk on Friday nights—so I could sleep through the noise. I snuck downstairs, knowing full well that there was no way I was going to make it out of the house on her watch. She had her back to me as I came down the stairs, but she seemed to sense me coming. It wasn't any kind of mother's intuition—given my condition, it was probably just her sense of smell. She is one of those weird people who hate the smell of tequila, sweat, and stale orange juice. She took one look at me, death warmed over, stopped the vacuum, and stared me down for like a full minute.

"*Where* are you going?" she asked. She looked at me with the utmost suspicion, like I was an intruder in her home. She probably thought I was sneaking out to buy drugs.

"I'm going fishing, Ma," I said.

"What?" she said, crossing her arms. "What are you doing?"

"I'm going fishing, Ma. I got invited by my foreman at the job."

"No, you are not, Artie," she said, now glaring at me. "You are not going fishing."

"What do you mean I'm not going fishing?" I said. "I got invited fishing. I'm going fishing."

I'd like to remind you that I was twenty-three years old and until this point not only had I never gone fishing, I'd never shown an interest in anything that could be considered a hobby besides playing baseball, busting chops, drinking, and doing drugs.

"Artie, you are NOT going FISHING." Panic was creeping into her voice. At the time, I was somewhat heavy, definitely heavier than I was in high school, but svelte compared to how I am now.

Still, to my mother, I was much too heavy and out of shape to do anything physical. Fishing isn't exactly running a 5K, but the water, in her mind, spelled certain death for her son. I could see her wheels spinning, thinking of what she could say to me to keep me from going.

"You listen to me, Artie," she said, working herself into a yell that could strip paint from the walls. "You are not going fishing! You are not leaving this house! You are too FAT to fish! Do you HEAR ME? You are TOO FAT TO FISH!"

Something clicked in my ma. Maybe it was just seeing me looking like that much of a mess, wondering what the hell I was doing to myself at night, or maybe it was the fear of losing me after losing my father. Whatever it was, to her, in that moment, allowing me to go fishing was like allowing me to walk off a cliff.

"Ma, it's my boss, I've got to go!" I tried to reason with her. "He's going to be here in like five minutes. I've got to get in good with this guy."

"I don't give a shit, Artie! You can't swim! You don't like water! YOU ARE TOO FAT TO FISH! I have never seen you do a thing. You have no interests, you have no hobbies. You aren't interested in anything but fooling around! You are not leaving this house! You will drown and die! YOU ARE TOO FAT TO FISH!"

"Ma, I can swim!"

"No, you can't!"

"Ma! You've seen me swim!" I yelled. "I swam every year in the ocean down the Shore!"

"I don't care, Artie! You are fat! You will die!"

She kept on like that for half an hour straight, and I couldn't get a word in edgewise.

"You are going to fall out of the boat and you will DROWN! Is there even a motor on this boat?"

"I don't know, Ma."

"You don't *know*? And you plan on going *fishing* on this boat? You don't even know HOW to fish! Tell me, what are you going to catch, Artie?"

"I don't know, Ma. Tuna and bluefish?"

"No, you won't, you will catch *nothing*! Because you're not *going*, because you're TOO FAT TO FISH!"

Whatever other points my mother made about why my plan was so outrageous, she kept returning to the fact that I was too fat to fish. It was like the chorus to an insane song she was singing. She got so worked up and loud that my sister Stacey woke up and lay in her bed hysterically laughing. She got so loud that my next-door neighbors woke up and started laughing because all of our windows were open. She just kept screaming the phrase "too fat to fish."

This was a battle that I was not going to win, so I called my foreman and luckily caught him right before he left his house.

"Hey, man," I said.

"I'm leaving now. What's up?"

"Well, I can't go," I said. "This is real embarrassing, but my mother will not let me go fishing with you today."

"Oh, come on, fuck you." He started laughing. "That's a good one. I'll be right over."

"No, I'm serious, man, she won't let me go."

"What are you, five years old? You need a note from your ma, Artie?"

"C'mon, man, you're Italian—you know how Italian mothers can get."

He got quiet for a minute. "She's really not letting you go?"

When I put it that way, the guy understood what I was saying, but for good measure I put my mother on the phone.

"Artie is not going fishing today. He's not going anywhere on a boat with you because he is too fat to fish and will fall out of the boat. But go have a nice time." Luckily, my mother wasn't the type to embarrass me.

I went upstairs, my hangover now infinitely worse after all that yelling, and ran into Stacey, who was about to piss herself laughing.

"Do you realize that she screamed at you for like forty minutes?" she said, doubled over. "What the hell was that? People heard her down the block!"

"Yeah, I know."

I passed out again, in my clothes, and slept until about 3 P.M. And when I woke up, my mother made me a mozzarella omelet and I ate it and was never happier in my life. Then I went back to sleep.

That night over dinner, my sister started laughing again.

"Ma? Do you realize what you sounded like this morning?" Stacey asked. "I ran into the neighbors, and they heard the whole thing and were asking me about it. You just kept screaming that Artie is too fat to fish. Where did you come up with that?"

"I don't know," my mother said, half smiling. "I just had to stop him any way I could."

"But, Ma, do you realize what you *sounded* like?"

It finally dawned on my mother, and when it did, she started laughing. Then I did too and pretty soon all three of us were sitting there at the table, red-faced, not able to breathe over the fact that she not only made that up on the spot, but forced me to call my boss and tell him, as a twenty-three-year-old man, that I could not go fishing. And then she told the guy herself that I was too fat to fish! The ballbreaking started the minute I walked into work Monday and it never stopped.

Things at the port remained more or less the same until the Brazilian guy whose orange juice we were unloading got an idea in his head about cutting operating costs to increase his profit. The name we will give this guy is Camacho, and he was paying his Brazilian workers like one fucking dollar a day to pick oranges for fifteen hours; then, in Newark, he was paying us $19 an hour, or $38 an hour with double time, to fucking play pinochle and 500 rummy. He thought that if he could get scabs in there to break the union, he'd be making much more money, which of course he would be. In Camacho's eyes, he was ripping people off at one end and getting ripped off at the other end. In our eyes, we were doing a fucking dangerous job and we deserved that money, which was a wage we were proud of the union for getting us.

Sure enough, in time this guy in South America tried to break the union. One day, we showed up for work and were locked out. Then, about an hour after we were supposed to be at work, he brought in about thirty Portuguese men in armored buses with big grates over the windows and doors. They pulled right up and let these scabs out. We were told that these guys were going to work for half our wage and that the operation was no longer a union shop.

I feel privileged to have been there during that time, because, let me tell you, longshoremen know how to fucking strike. We immediately picked up rocks and started throwing everything we could get our hands on at this fucking bus. The Portuguese guys were scared shitless, but the drivers got them in the gate and they locked us out. Someone in our crew put in a call to the powers that be, while the rest of us continued to disrupt the work being done in every way we could. This was the start of weeks of bitter striking. Every day we were out there picketing with signs, and guys were slashing tires and doing all kinds of shit—it was serious. One day this guy got pulled out of a truck and the longshoremen just beat the crap out of him. I didn't really want to hurt anybody and I didn't know what the fuck to do: I really wanted to make it as a comedian and didn't want to get arrested. So I kept my distance and threw things and watched the nutty shit the other guys did. These guys were fighting for their jobs. Who could blame them? It wasn't just a job, it was all they had. There were guys down there with not a lot of skills and families to support. There was nowhere else in the world they could land another gig like that; they were fighting for their livelihood.

The union was great—they were very protective of our positions and promised us that it would blow over. If it didn't work out, they said, we'd get work for equal pay elsewhere.

At this point, I had about $6,000 saved in the bank. Enough was enough, and I thought it was my time to go. I was about to turn twenty-four, I lived with my mother so I didn't have to worry about rent, and I had six grand. I decided that I'd get in my car every single night and go into the city to open mic and amateur comedy nights. I had thought about it nonstop for the past two years—how could I not, staring at the New York skyline from Port Newark every day? I'd think to myself, *It's right fucking* there, *what are you doing* here? I knew I'd be leaving a job that other people would kill for, that would take care of me for life, but I kept thinking that I wouldn't be able to live with myself if I pussied out and didn't try my best. That was it: I was going to start from scratch, with no family or friends to give me advice about show business, and I was going to try to make it as a comedian. At the same time, I knew I was crazy for thinking of leaving.

I'd been working for the union from February of '91 to September of '92, working on the docks with a real cast of characters. All I'd had to do was show up and mention my friend's father's name and I was given a job. In 1991, I made about $60,000. If you had 700 hours in for the year, you qualified for what's called a container check, a truly amazing thing that the longshoremen's union does for its members. My buddy's father was instrumental in getting this thing going. He'd worked with the union and port management to clean the place up, and once he did, he went back to them with a plan to keep things that way. His point was that the port was busier than ever, that everybody was prospering, so he suggested that at Christmastime, each longshoreman be paid a penny or two cents for every container moved through the port in the year. Management agreed, so around Christmas in a busy year, a container check could be worth four or five grand.

In '91 it was like $4,500, of which I gave $2,000 to my mother as a Christmas present. I had not been able to help out much since my father's accident, because I had been so self-destructive. I had taken that union job specifically to be able to pay her back and help her out, and I was happy finally to be able to do that in some small way. It came at a good time, too, because my mother had a lot of expenses that year: We were still dealing with welfare and Medicaid, and it was all really depressing.

My mother, to her complete credit, never once discouraged me from following my dream. I don't think a lot of mothers, if I were their son, would have done the same. As a matter of fact, she was upset that I was working at the port to help support her. As I've mentioned, she desperately tried to protect me and my sister, financially and emotionally, from my father's accident—which of course was completely impossible. My mother looked at my work down at the port, as well as some of the drug, drinking, and gambling problems I had, as by-products of my father's accident. I think she saw these things as her failure. But she was wrong; that shit is just in my personality and I would have gone through that rebellious time no matter what. My mom didn't see it that way and she felt guilty, so when I told her that I wanted to take my savings and live off of it for as long as I could while I pursued my dream, she was elated and supported it wholeheartedly. It would have been nearly impossible to get through all the rejections and hard times that lay ahead of me if my mother didn't believe in me.

Before I could start chasing my dream, I had to take care of one last thing: I had to tell my buddy's father, the great man I'm indebted to for life, who'd gotten me the job, that I wanted to to quit. I felt incredibly guilty—he had done me such a huge favor. I had to quit the proper, respectful way. I had to thank him and explain my reasons for leaving. I was scared shitless, because I knew he'd be mad. I ran through different ways that conversation would go down, with me attempting to explain why I needed to try my best to be a comedian, but there really wasn't any way I could make it sound like a reasonable decision.

I waited outside his office for like two hours, which did nothing much for my nerves. I'd brought him a nice bottle of wine that I gave him and then sat down, probably looking as nervous as I felt.

"Thanks for the wine, Mike," he said. "So how have you been?"

"Oh, fine, I'm doing all right."

"Glad to hear it. So, Mike, what can I do for you?"

For the entire meeting, the guy called me Mike, which had me on the verge of laughing the entire time. He'd gotten another friend of ours, one of the million Mikes, a job too, and clearly he'd gotten us confused. But I wasn't about to correct him. He was a nice enough guy, but he was one of those really impressive, really intimidating union guys. He was an incredible public speaker whenever I saw him at union events. From the moment he shook your hand, you could tell that he was not a guy to be fucked with.

"Listen, sir," I said. "This has been the greatest couple of years of my life, because I made all of this money and was able to help my mother out and save some money for myself for the first time in my life."

"I'm glad to have helped you out, Mike. I'm glad I could give you that opportunity."

"Well, sir, I don't know if your son ever told you about this, but I'm an aspiring comedian," I said. "I really want to get into show business, and the only way I can do it properly is to quit right here and now, get a part-time job, and go in and out of New York City whenever I can to auditions."

He looked at me like I had three heads. "What?" he said. "I'm not sure I heard you right—what are you going to do?"

"I need to quit the job to be able to go to New York and make it in show business."

"Listen to me, Mike," he said, very seriously. "This is a *great* job. People kill for this job. You are not appreciating what you've been given."

"I do appreciate it, sir. I really do," I said. "I wouldn't be able to even attempt to pursue this if it weren't for this job. I've saved up enough to give me some leeway until I get a part-time job while I try to make it."

"And what are you going to do for the rest of your life?" he said.

"Well, I'm going to try to make it in show business. I'm going to do whatever it takes."

"I don't even know what to say to that, Mike," he said. "What are the odds of that happening? You're just going to waltz into New York City and make it?"

Everything he said was right, and he wasn't insulted as much as he was concerned. After all, he had about a hundred names ready to take my spot.

"Mike, I want you to rethink this," he said. "Have you told your mother about this?"

"Yes, sir."

"And what did she say?"

"My mother is actually supportive of it."

"You're a real good friend of my son, Mike, or else he wouldn't have asked me to help you out after your dad died," he said, looking at me very seriously. "Listen, I love you and there's nothing I wouldn't do for you. That's why I'm going to be honest with you, since other people might not be. Listen to me: There is about a fifty-million-to-one shot that you are going to make it in show business. It's not easy; if it was, everyone would do it."

"I know that," I said. "I'm ready for that. I'm going to give it my all. You know, in high school I was kind of a class clown. I could get laughs and stuff."

Around this guy I was not, however. I was nothing but shy.

"That's *it*? A class clown? You really need to rethink this. That's not gonna cut it."

This went on for a while longer, until finally he gave up. He looked me in the eye, realized that I was serious, and that was it.

"Well, listen, Mike, I cannot guarantee you anything, but when it doesn't work out, you come to us and we'll try to get you another job here." I always thought it was funny that he said "when," and not "if." It wasn't malicious. He cared about me, that was all. But he didn't consider success a possibility for me.

I will never forget him for extending that offer though, because he was completely serious and way more generous than he should have been with me. I wasn't family, but he treated me like his own. He took the time to talk to me like a father would to his own son.

All the guys down at the port were the same way. About a year later, I went back there to say hello. I had lost a bunch of weight because I had started exercising, doing what I could to try to look good for head shots and auditions. The minute I walked in, I ran into Chick, the sixty-year-old Italian speed chess master, who stopped what he was doing and stared at me.

"What's the matter?" he said. "You sick? You're so thin." He probably thought I'd gotten AIDS from going on auditions.

"I'm not sick, Chick, I landed a role," I said. "I'm playing a starving actor now."

He looked at me, dead serious, and pointed his finger in my direction. "You listen to me," he said. "You come down here, you will always get a meal, you hear me? We will *always* feed you."

As it happened, I didn't starve and I didn't have to get another job before landing a paying gig in show business. It wasn't much at all, but I got a job right out of the fucking box in a dinner-theater play. A friend told me about the audition, and I got it, and it was a paid acting job, so I couldn't complain at all. The play was a murder mystery that was set in a catering hall, and I played a drunk priest with a Southern accent who actually turned out to be the murderer, which I thought was kind of cool. And for obvious reasons, since there was booze on the premises, it was great to have to play a drunk. It allowed me to be Method about it.

For the first three months of '92, we toured restaurants and catering halls in North, Central, and South Jersey. We'd perform a five-act show, and between acts we served the audience their courses of food, in character. That was cool, because I'd have to improv with these people as a Southern priest while serving them a salad. We got forty bucks a show, and since we were the waiters too, we kept the tips. On a good night, you could easily make an extra $100 that went right into your pocket.

One of my fellow actors in that production was this kid Jimmy Polumbo, who I'm still friends with today. Those of you who have seen *Beer League* will know him as Johnny Trino, the shortstop. We really got tight doing dinner theater—after three months it was like we'd known each other all our lives. So when that run ended, Jimmy and I figured that we'd try to make it in New York together, since it was better than going it alone. For the next three and a half years, we'd take the bus or Jimmy's shitty Honda or my shitty Chevy Citation into the city, chasing our dream.

I did stand-up wherever I could, Jimmy and I both wrote and did sketch comedy, and eventually we got an improv group together that we called Live on Tape. This kid Mike Stafford was in it with us and also produced it, and we did off-Broadway shows in a theater down on West Eighteenth Street. Our show was a revue of sketches and pretaped bits of material: We'd do two live sketches, then, while we changed costumes and set up for the next two, we'd show a taped sketch on a big screen so we didn't lose the audience—hence the name.

Those shows did well enough that we got to do gigs at Carolines, the famous comedy club. They let us do a "bring-your-own show," which meant that they gave us the place from 7 to 8 P.M., before the real show started for the evening, and we had to sell our own tickets. Four separate times we sold the place out. We did improv and sketches, and I did stand-up after. Those shows were really exciting: We invited friends down and we always killed. The fourth time, a guy from the William Morris Agency that Mike Stafford had met at a wedding came down—not because he was really impressed with Mike or anything, but because we'd bombarded his office with flyers. I have a feeling that if Carolines had been more than two blocks away from William Morris we'd have never seen the guy. But the show that night was great, and that's how we met a commercial agent named Peter Principato, who ended up signing five of us.

Jimmy and I were among the five that agency took on, and they started sending us out on auditions for commercials, which was a big, big step for us. Peter and I had a great working relationship for a while; he was my agent when I got *MADtv*, and after he left the agency to become a manager, I went with him. He became my manager for ten years, and even though we had a falling-out, I still love the guy. I really miss Pete in a lot of ways, but our relationship became dysfunctional and had to end.

It's too bad, because Pete stuck with me through everything. When I got arrested while on *MADtv*, which you will soon read about, he flew to Los Angeles the minute he heard about it and waited with my sister for hours at the L.A. County Jail. I couldn't believe he did that: He just left his desk at William Morris without a care for his job or his other clients and flew out to L.A. I feel terrible about how it ended with Pete. The truth is, years later it seemed like he wasn't doing much work for me after he'd moved to the West Coast. I guess it was too hard for him to be so far away and stay focused on my career.

In any case, I didn't handle it how I should have: I said some shit about him on the air after I'd been on the show for a couple of years and he wrote me a letter saying that maybe we shouldn't work together anymore. I responded by calling him and blowing my stack, and that's how we ended the relationship. I had my lawyer write a termination letter and that was it. I wish Pete nothing but the best, because he was there from the beginning and he really stuck by me. I blame myself for the unpleasantness; it's one of the things I really wanted to make clear in this book: I am sorry that I'm not with Pete anymore and I wish him the best. He's got a very successful management company in Beverly Hills now, so he's doing fine, but he was the guy who believed in me back in 1993, and he stuck by me and I miss him.

Show business is very bittersweet that way—always was and always will be. You meet so many people, and you grow so close to some of them for a while when you're working together toward a goal. Then some bullshit happens and you're enemies, or you end up not talking because there is some kind of weirdness between you, and it really sucks. In so many ways, show business *really* sucks. Being on stage or being on the radio or on TV or acting in a film is great. That's the high, that's the fun, that's what you do it for. But just about everything else—the business of it, most of all—is really fucked up, sad, and depressing.

And *that's* when you're successful. When you're not, there's a whole other level of hell piled on top. Luckily for me, it was only three and a half years between the day I quit working at Port Newark and the day I got cast on *MADtv*. Three and half years of struggling and being broke isn't bad at all, and I feel very thankful for that. I was only twenty-seven when I got my big break and ended up on a network show where I made good money. And I've never looked back. Unfortunately, there's always a downside to all of my upsides. During those three and a half years, I developed a terrible cocaine problem that I took on my back with me out to L.A. It ended up costing me my job and a lot more before I got it under control.

During my struggling years, the "Too Fat to Fish" story became legendary: The phrase was emblazoned in our memory from the day my mom first screamed it loud enough to wake the neighborhood. We laughed about that story at every holiday meal—it never got old. Even though I am the punch line in that story, I loved it when my mother or sister brought it up, because sharing laughter with them, cracking each other up around the dinner table, made me feel the way our family felt when my pop was still with us.

I had to commemorate that story somehow, because as time went on "Too Fat to Fish" became my mantra. I knew the outlet when I saw it. After my two years on *MADtv*, where I was making close to 200 grand a year, I got a development deal from Fox that paid me 750 grand, so I was doing very well. I had enough money to start a corporation, so my Uncle Tom, who is a financial planner, told me to take my first $250,000 development check and incorporate myself. I remember holding that check, showing it to my mother, and wondering how many roofs my old man would have had to climb to make that kind of money. We decided it would have been about 500,000.

Those were good times: I was able, all at once, to bail my mother out of every single financial debt she had. I was also finally able to do what I'd always wanted to do for her: buy her a house, a car, furniture, and anything else she wanted. I was finally able to be the man of the house for her, like I'd always wanted. Money isn't everything, but it sure helps when you have it. And since I've had it, my mother has

My Ma

been a lot less stressed, and I am very proud of that.

Anyway, I named my company Too Fat to Fish. I went to the bank, opened the account with that check, registered it all through a lawyer, and told my mother nothing. I did get my mother her own account in the corporation, though, with an official book of checks that had her name on it and "Too Fat to Fish, Inc." When she saw it, she burst out laughing.

"What did you do?" she said. "Why did you name your corporation that?"

"You named it, Ma."

The truth is, "Too Fat to Fish" is more than just that story to me. It represents all those times that I felt like a complete loser or was told I couldn't do something. But now that I've made something of myself on my own terms, the phrase is even funnier to me. It's a justification and an inside joke and a tribute to the mother who believed in me—except when it came to fishing—all at the same time. The only thing that matters is that I'm not too fat for comedy. And let's face it: Can anyone ever be too fat for comedy?

Driving
Miss
Wasted

7

In 1992, I willingly left a job working as a longshoreman in the Port of Newark and officially entered what I call "the struggling years." My only regular form of employment at this point was driving a cab. It wasn't all bad: Of the many ways I've wasted time, both mine and other people's, for money, driving a cab was absolutely the best job I've ever had. It was pretty enjoyable as far as struggling-for-a-very-meager-living part-time jobs go. It was fun. And I have to be honest here: There were so many fucking losers working that job, the fact that I had an IQ over 80 made me the company's most valuable player. Competition was not tough among a group of guys who were barely able to spell their names as an X on their employment forms.

Most people didn't carry cell phones in 1992, which in this particular field of employment really worked to my advantage. I spent most of my day making runs from Union Township to JFK Airport, a trip that involved crossing from our dispatcher's area into a huge Bermuda Triangle along the Belt Parkway where the company's CB radio was out of range. I think it took me exactly two days to figure out precisely where we drivers entered the Great Unknown: It was the moment you hit Randazzo's Clam Bar in Sheepshead Bay. You passed Randazzo's out there on the Belt and then you were off the map, completely incommunicado. Randazzo's was a beacon of freedom on the horizon. I knew Randazzo's from their classic low-budget commercials that ran during local Yankees television broadcasts. These ads featured a guy fanning his mouth in the worst acting job ever captured on film, saying, "That Randazzo's hot sauce, oh *boy* is that hot!"

Usually, I'd celebrate the fact that my boss could no longer track me for a while by stopping at Randazzo's for a meal on my way to or from JFK. I spent almost all of my tips on calamari and cheesecake, which made me think that cab driving was my kind of job. If you think I'm bullshitting, hear this: I once got my driver's license suspended for a DUI and the next day, when I dragged my ass into the office and told the owner of the company that I had to quit because I was no longer legally able to drive anyone anywhere, he looked at me and as seriously as he could said, "Well, you know what? I won't tell anybody about it if you want to keep driving." I've never been what anyone would call a strict observer of rules, so I was more than willing to stay on.

The truth? The truth is, I owe my life now to that guy and that dead-end job and the crap reception of that crap CB system, because if all of those factors weren't in place, I'd have never been able to drive myself into Manhattan, while "on the job," for stand-up sets every night. Each of those early open-mic experiences, as ugly as they were at the time, boosted me up (I don't know why) and got me one step closer to where I am now. If that shitty cab company weren't so fucked up, run by that loose-as-fuck system they had going, I'd never have developed as a comic, because it wasn't going to happen anywhere but in the clubs of Manhattan.

This cab job was the kind of gig where the hours were so unbelievably flexible that I could pull off an insane degree of bullshit. I was actually able to become a regular at the Comic Strip on the Upper East Side without losing my job: I got a twenty-minute set on any given night between Tuesday and Saturday. If I had a set from 9:30 to 9:50 at night, my dispatcher would let me drive the cab from 3:00 to 8:30. He'd be cool with me taking the car into New York, where I would double park in front of the Comic Strip and I'd get one of my comic friends to watch it while I went in to do my twenty-minute routine. Then I'd run back out, get in my cab, and drive back to New Jersey. As soon as I got through the Holland Tunnel, I'd call my dispatcher and say, "Hey, I'm back on." And then I'd work from 1 to 2 A.M. and make another $200 for the night.

I'll say it again: It was the perfect gig for a guy doing his best to make it in showbiz via comedy. It also left me free to do auditions during the day for commercials. I drove the cab to get to those too. The job was all cash too, so . . . you know, a cash gig never hurts either.

Now that we're talking about cab driving, I realize that for a very short, completely misled minute I made the mistake of thinking that taking a job waiting tables might be a better "career move." It's true—I thought being a waiter was a step up in showbiz. So for a millisecond I was basically a walking cliché: I was a guy who wanted to make it, who would also never be a good waiter. On every level, this short-lived endeavor had to go. And it did, in a manner that was swift, decisive, and awful.

My sister got me my one and only waiter job, at a Mexican restaurant in Hoboken, right across the street from the PATH train. It was an easy gig: lunch three days a week, with an arrival time of 10:30 A.M.

As I recall, my first day waitering went off without a hitch, though I really didn't like it at all. My second day was different; the night before, I went out drinking at a bar called the Rusty Scupper with my buddy Danny McGrath, who was a cop. I got ossified drunk, and for a reason I no longer recall I got into a fistfight. I swung at a bouncer, and in response to my aggression he took me by both sides of my hair and gave me what is commonly known among dickheads who get into fights in bars as "the stop sign"— you take someone by both sides of their head and introduce their nose to your kneecap.

That's what happened to me: My nose exploded. By the time the cops showed up, I was a mess and still drunk and ready to tussle. The officers were ready to arrest me, even though I hadn't done much more than get my nose rearranged. Luckily, my buddy Danny flashed his badge, after which his peers said to him, "Just get him the fuck out of here." Danny then drove me to Union Hospital, around the corner from where I grew up, and he waited with me for three hours while they patched up my nose. I was blacked out at that point.

When my sister called early the next morning, I was already late for the lunch shift. I remember realizing two things after I told her that I'd be there as soon as I could: I knew I was going to quit, and I also knew that my face looked like hamburger and I had two black eyes. I didn't want to embarrass my sister either. But what I still don't understand is how I figured that showing up in the condition I was in would be less of an embarrassment than not showing up at all.

So I got dressed and ran into the lunch rush at that restaurant.

The manager just stared at me the moment I crossed the doorway. He didn't say anything and he didn't get in my way, so I went about "doing lunch." The first couple I served were two yuppies who could have been on the cover of *Yuppie* magazine: khaki shorts, polo shirts, and a BMW parked outside. I went up to them, took their drink order, and quickly returned with their drinks. I cleared my throat and said, "Do you want to hear the specials?" The woman said, "Yes," and looked up at me as I began reciting them. I was in a trance, kind of wondering how I was even doing this at all, when I saw a look of horror come over her face. She started screaming— literally *screaming*—and I had no idea why.

"What!? *What?*" I said.

She looked like she'd just seen someone beheaded. She shrieked, "Your nose is *bleeding*!"

Sure enough, she was right. It was bleeding pretty good, flowing all over my shirt, nice and red. The sight of it had this woman in a complete panic. She was so out of her mind that the manager came running over before I could do anything about it. The manager was an intimidating middle-aged, Italian-American gentleman who hadn't, it seemed, gotten the memo informing everyone that carbs cause weight gain. He appeared at my side and dragged me into the back of the house and bitch-slapped me. He really got into it too: I remember him pushing me up against a wall and getting up into my face and hissing at me, "Get the *fuck* out of here. I never want to see you again." He also accused me of getting into a bar fight and getting coked up the night before. He had that completely wrong: I got coked up *before* the bar fight. I didn't care about being roughhoused like that; I was fucking pissed off that I'd been fired before I could quit.

Let me get back to my point here, which has to do with the worst experience I ever had at the best worst job I ever had. So I went back to the cab company after my brief interlude as a waiter and this one night I drove the cab from like 10 A.M. to 3 A.M., which was the longest shift I would ever work. On top of that, I had the Knicks getting five from the Bulls that night, so I was watching the game at the dispatch station. The Knicks lost to the Bulls, of course—fuck you, Michael Jordan. At 2:45 A.M., we got a call to pick up these two twits. It was a quiet night, but I was never what you might call ambitious at this job, so I still don't know why I agreed to take that last call. If there's one thing I learned driving cabs, and I learned it that night too, it's this: That one last call is always the strangest you will ever get.

Whatever. Then I didn't know. I took it on—I went out there. It was a pickup at the Holiday Inn in Kenilworth, New Jersey, a couple coming from a wedding. They needed to be taken up Route 22 West to Dunellen, which is about a half-hour drive. We all knew around the dispatch office that any wedding at the Holiday Inn at Kenilworth meant someone was ringing the white trash bell loudly.

So I get to the Holiday Inn and the couple drunkenly spills into the back of the cab. I get their address, and the good news was that I kind of knew where the street was so I would not have to bug them again—or so I thought. They were, as far as I could tell, a kid probably in a suit for the first time and his chick: a blonde in a black minidress—*really* hot. I'd say she was a nine or ten, and both of them were in their mid-twenties, but they were going on fifty-seven. As they came into my cab, I couldn't believe what I was seeing; I wanted to freeze-frame it. Being very very drunk is fine, but what I couldn't understand is why they were behaving like horribly old, extremely unhappy people. Not your run-of-the-mill unhappy people next door—they were unhappy like the people who live in trailers on *Cops*. From the outside they had no reason to fight, but when they got into the cab, they were about to start hurting each other.

I turned up the radio and listened to Allison Steele, the Nightbird, coming to me on 92.3, K-Rock. I focused on driving, thanking the stars above that I actually knew where we were going. About five minutes later, as we wound up Route 22, I started to hear some serious, clenched-teeth arguing going on in the backseat. It was fight night for these two, and it was *on*. Every other sentence was like, "Fuck you, motherfucker. No, fuck that, fuck you!" I took a look in my rearview mirror and saw the both of them red in the face, just really going at each other, each of them just inches away from the other, both flat-out yelling. I turned the radio up a little louder and I thought to myself, *Fuck it*.

Five minutes later, I heard it. *Slap!* Just a real solid slap, skin on skin. I hesitated again, then looked in the rearview and saw that my ears weren't lying: He'd fucking smacked her! Her lip was bleeding a little bit, and, to make matters worse, he had one arm around her shoulders, holding her, and with the other hand he was strangling her. I actually couldn't believe what the fuck I was seeing.

At this point, I thought what any decent man would: I figured, like my girlfriend, this bitch must have a listening problem. Just kidding—at that time I didn't even have a girlfriend. I pulled the car right over, leaned across the back of the cab, and grabbed the guy. He turned away from her and looked at me like I was the enemy. I said to him, "*Dude*, what are you *doing*? You are fucking killing this girl! If you keep this shit up, I am throwing you out of the cab, I am taking her home, and I am calling the cops."

I thought this was the obvious right thing to do, but I began to doubt myself as the girl looked at me blankly with a pair of drunken saucer eyes. She didn't seem to mind what was going on. And when the guy looked at me, I realized that I'd actually ruined some kind of a moment for them. I'll never forget what that guy said to me, because it was funny in a way that is so primal that there's no way at all that he could have possibly premeditated it. "All right, all right, man," he said. Then he put up his hand and waved me away. "All right, then, just *drive*, hero." Hero. *Hero?*

I started driving again. I put the radio up while I worried that this guy was going right back to killing her. A few minutes went by and I realized that it had been dead silent in the cab for some time. Fearing the worst, I took a look in the rearview and saw that it had been silent because these two idiots were making out in a crazy, sexy way. He had her skirt up over her top, and he was grabbing her ass. They were about two seconds from fucking. They went from the angry couple you see on *Cops* to the couple you see on *Cops* who get arrested for fucking in public.

Clearly, their problem had resolved itself, so I returned to listening to music. That didn't last long: A minute or so later, I found myself distracted, wondering whether I'd rather clean up her blood or his jizz at the end of the night. And I gotta tell you, man, it wasn't looking too good for her as that debate went on in my head. But at this point, something far more serious took over: I started to realize that I had a burning case of the shits coming on. I have never eaten well, and because of that this shits thing happens to me every once in a while. I don't know if it was simply that or if it was the sudden stress, but I can tell you this: It was fucking *happening*, all right. There was no doubt about that: These were the kind of shits where there was nothing to be done. These shits were coming, in a matter of minutes, no matter what, and they didn't care if my pants were on or not.

I looked up just then and thanked God that my passengers' exit was up ahead, because as I turned down the ramp, I was about a mile from their house and about a minute away from leaking all over the cab. This situation was no joke: They were making out like nobody's business and I was about to shit all over the front seat. And these two formerly fighting, now making-out fuckers were totally oblivious. They were sticking their tongues down each other's throat as I spread my legs and tried to hold my ass closed,

all while driving a car with the gas pedal pinned to the floor. I blasted through red light after red light, looking for their address.

It looked like I was going to make it until I realized, as I approached their house, that I had to ask this guy in back if I could use his bathroom. I figured it had been about twenty minutes tops since I'd almost punched him out and threatened him with police intervention. As I pulled into their driveway at around eighty miles an hour, I faced the fact that I had a pretty shitty chance at winning him over and not much time to do it. We came to a screeching halt and they were thrown all over the backseat.

They stumbled out, laughing, and fell over each other on their way up the walk to the front door. I followed them, not only because they hadn't paid me yet. "Dude," I said, trying to be at least a little bit cool, "I've got to use your bathroom."

"All right, all right," he said.

Then his girl looked at me crooked. "*You* cannot use our bathroom," she said.

"What?" I asked. "Why?"

"*You* are a stranger," she said. "We do not know who *you* are. We are not just going to let *you* in the house."

I looked at this girl, this same girl that I had tried to keep from being beaten up by the guy swaying next to her.

The guy looked at her too. Even he thought it was bullshit.

Honestly, at this point I wanted to hit her if this shithead wasn't going to do it again.

"Dude, man, I'm sorry," he said, all slurry. "She's a real cunt. She just fucking gets this way."

It was beyond the point of no return for me, so when the guy handed me a bill, I grabbed it without looking. I ran to the car as fast as I could without letting it all go, because my bowels were liquefying, I mean second by second, as I was standing there. I drove to the nearest place I could find: a 7-Eleven. I ran in, probably looking like I was about to hold up the place, and grabbed the guy behind the counter by his shirt. I demanded the bathroom key. He could tell that I wasn't fucking around, because I was so visibly uncomfortable and about to shit all over the room. No one in their right mind was going to keep me from doing what was obviously going to happen anyway.

Mr. Clerk did the sensible thing and allowed me to let it happen in the right place. And finally, for the first time in what seemed like an eternity, I enjoyed some fucking relief. And that's when I realized that I was still holding the bill the guy from the cab had given me. That's also when I realized that it was a $20 when it should have been a $50, which was the cost of the ride without a tip. So that little joyride from hell had cost me $30, which came out of my money at the end of the night, as well as whatever tip I would have hypothetically gotten. At that moment I felt a few things. I was relieved that my bowels had loosened themselves above a toilet when just a few minutes before I'd resigned myself to the worst-case scenario. I was also, after a moment's reflection, almost fine with the fact that I'd lost $30 to the negligence of those two model citizens. But what I really had a problem with—and the more I thought about it, the more I couldn't let it go—was the lack of tip. As far as I could tell, shits and speeding aside, I thought my service was impeccable.

Pig in Shit

8

It should be clear by now to everyone reading that I started abusing drugs and alcohol with particular gusto as a result of the sudden, tragic, and devastating accident that crippled my father and my family for four and a half years. My mother and sister could have easily gone down the same road or a similar one to cope with the heartache, the stress, and the financial burden of living as a family in the aftermath of that event. Thank God they did not; they stayed strong and they took care of me too, as I found my way through my own suffering along a pretty dark, winding route. For the record, my sister supported my decision to chase my dream as much as if not even more than my mother did.

After leaving the security of Port Newark and doing my first regular paying gig in show business—my stint in dinner theater—I dove into the New York City comedy club scene. I was cheered on by good friends like Jimmy Polumbo and Mike Stafford, as well as my mother's brothers and sisters, my younger cousin Frankie and my older cousin Jeff, who might have been my biggest comedic influence. Jeff gave me my first George Carlin album, *Class Clown*, and Woody Allen's *The Early Years*, an album of Woody's great stand-up from the sixties. Without these people, I would have been really miserable.

Drinking and drugs were, at first, a rebellious, knee-jerk reaction to cover the pain and get through my shitty everyday life. But it changed on me, like it does to anyone with tendencies like mine, so during that period I developed an addiction to cocaine and booze. It was easy to do: I spent as much time as I could, for nearly four years, in and around comedy clubs, which are hardly healthy, clean living environments. I met a lot of fellow dreamers in that world, and they introduced me to coke. I say "introduced me" because although I'd done it plenty of times before, I'd never experienced that drug the way I did then. Doing a bag of coke with your friends whenever some dealer was selling it in a bar was a universe away from doing gram after gram all night and into the next day and into the day after that with no end in sight to the supply. At that intensity, coke was a whole new drug to me, and I was happy to make its acquaintance.

Once I started to get regular stand-up slots around town, it was a no-brainer: There were three-day periods where I'd just stay up the whole time, chasing the dream and the high. I'd do a gig, score some coke at the club, and keep doing it until my next time slot later that night. I might go do another gig at another club and score some more coke there, then I'd go to after-hours places. I'd do more there, party into the morning, hit a few bars in the afternoon, and finish my coke, then go to another comedy club, score some more, and do another gig or two. Tuesday through Thursday, with proper planning, I could stay high nonstop without spending much money at all. That was great, because I didn't have much to spend. People in the audience at clubs always seemed to have coke and were eager to hang out with comedians. Believe me, if you were a regular comic there were plenty of ways to get coke for free or very inexpensively.

Cocaine makes fast friends, and one of my fastest, best buddies at the time was this party monster who worked at a big Wall Street firm, loved comedy clubs, and had a corporate Amex that he enjoyed throwing down to cover bar tabs all night long. I remember thinking I'd finally seen the face of the devil one night at an after-hours club on the East Side when he used his corporate card to buy us more coke. I thought it was a joke, but this place actually accepted credit cards for cocaine purchases: The guy behind the bar swiped it and handed us an eight ball as if it were a round of drinks. If that's not the embodiment of Satan in this day and age, I don't know what is. I looked at my buddy like he was Lucifer himself and decided right away that I was cool with hanging out with the devil as long as he could get me coke.

That was my struggling period, and as I've said before, I'm lucky it lasted only three and a half years, until the day God opened the heavens and shone a golden light down upon me. I got cast on *MADtv* as one of eight permanent cast members chosen from 8,000 comics who'd been screened. For any comic trying to make something of themselves, that was like hitting triple 7s—jackpot.

Landing a spot as a regular on a network sketch show in L.A. was specifically one of my dreams. Unlike a lot of comics, I didn't care about getting on *Saturday Night Live*. That show had such history and was so established that I didn't see the point. I wanted to be on an original show as an original cast member of a sketch comedy troupe, and I couldn't believe it when that exact scenario happened for me. In May 1995, I went to L.A. to shoot the pilot, which got picked up by Fox and put into the fall rotation, slated to debut on October 14, 1995. I was overjoyed that all of this was happening for me after wanting it for so long because finally I felt justified in my life choices just a bit. So in July I packed up and moved to L.A., ready to begin work on the show. I was twenty-seven years old and everything was great, except for the fact that along with a bunch of old concert T-shirts, I took my crazy drug problem with me to the West Coast.

I was now making huge money: $7,500 an episode plus a big signing bonus, all of which I intended to enjoy. I had my New York City drug dealer hook me up with a contact in L.A., and the second I got there I continued doing coke like it was going out of style. Everything had done nothing but get better for me, so I saw no problem with it. I figured that I could live like that for years! My rationale for the whole thing was that someday I'd quit, and the best time for that was my late thirties. But right now? It was party time.

Of course, I didn't realize at all how crazy and stressful shooting the show would be. I thought it would be sketch comedy as I'd done it in New York, which was creative and inspiring with some pressure involved, but it was mostly pressure we put on ourselves to be great. I had no idea how differently that would play out on a fully budgeted network program. For three straight weeks, six days a week, we'd rehearse sketches, then shoot them live in front of a studio audience on Fridays. Then we'd shoot commercial and movie parodies on location for two weeks—one week for rehearsal, one week for shooting. So there was no break for ages, and that's how it had to be. The format of the show was solid sketch comedy: We didn't have musical guests, so we needed eight solid hours of sketches, each with different characters, voices, and everything else that was involved. There were only eight cast members, so it was a lot of work, but I welcomed the challenge.

I got through the first eight episodes the way I'd been getting through everything in my life—by drinking and doing a lot of coke and working as hard as I could. That was fine in the stand-up world because I was the only one responsible for my act and getting to the gig on time. But on *MADtv*, there were eight other cast members to consider, plus a huge crew, call times, schedules, union rules—it was too complicated for the kind of one-man show I was running. It was bound to come to a head—and it did.

The last sketch we did before taking a break was called "Babewatch." We were shooting it way out in Malibu for two fifteen-hour days, so instead of having everyone drive home, they put us up in this little motel. "Babewatch" was a parody of *Baywatch* starring me as Babe the Pig, who becomes a lifeguard. If you had to equate me with a character on the real show, then I, as Babe the Pig, would have been David Hasselhoff. As you can see, the whole concept was ridiculous.

The first day of filming this monstrosity was the worst day of my life in show business. My call time was 4 A.M. because I had to endure three hours of prosthetic makeup application that left me looking exactly—and I mean *exactly*—like a pig. The *MADtv* makeup artist was as good as it got on TV. She had left *SNL* to work on *MADtv*, and she was great. Her name is Jen Aspinall. I love Jen—she had a real sweet way about her. She still works there, and I wish her the best and miss her very much.

Anyway, this mask was by far the most high-budget makeup effect I saw in the entire two years I worked on the show. After three hours in pig makeup, I had a snout, pig ears, a layer of white fuzz on my back and six teats, each of which was going to get its own bikini top. And I was like a grunge pig: I had to wear a dirty

flannel shirt, cutoff jean shorts, a wallet chain, and a backward baseball hat. They dressed me to look like a pig on his way to a Pearl Jam
concert. They did a great job too, because when Jen was done with
me I was disgusting—just a two-legged, talking man-pig. There's
no other way to describe it. The skit was horrible in every way, because there was way too much effort going into it. The whole thing
was a cheap sight gag that centered around me, the prosthetic pig.

It was strange to be up so early getting transformed into a pig
in a place that's as perfect as Malibu. It's that typical, ideal California coastline of nothing but beach and sun and beautiful ocean that
comes straight out of a Beach Boys song. The environment freaked
me out—it would have been easier to take if I were in a studio. By
the time my makeup was done, I was depressed and hungry, so I
went over to the catering area, got some breakfast, and took it into
my little trailer. I sat down and started to eat, but every time I went
to take a bite of my eggs, I'd catch a glimpse of myself in the mirror.
There I was, this pig, eating. I was hungry too, which made it
worse, because I was literally a fake pig who was eating like a pig.

"Ugh, Jesus," I said out loud to myself. "This is *not* why I signed
up for show business."

I finished the rest of my food, getting more and more annoyed
with every bite. There was only one thing to do: call my coke dealer.
I told him where I was and asked him to come meet me. I couldn't
have him show up at the set, so he told me to meet him at Duke's, a
seafood restaurant not too far away on the Pacific Coast Highway.
It's got a huge self-park parking lot, which in L.A. is fucking rare
because everywhere you go there's a valet dipshit waiting to park
your car and charge you anywhere from three to twenty bucks to do
it. I fucking hate that shit. Anyway, we decided to meet at Duke's.

"Can you get there, man?" he asked.

"Oh yeah," I said. There is no question that I'd get there. Without

The proud mother of a future
fat heroin addict.

My old man as a young man.

The best-looking hood ornament in Cadillac history.

Me and my dad around 1970, the first year we won *Life* magazine's award for Best Dressed Father and Son.

Me and my sister, ages five and four. I had just lost four teeth from meth abuse.

Fourth grade: I still had a shot at being good-looking.

My favorite picture of my mom and dad (circa 1979).

My maternal
grandparents, the great
Sal and Molly Caprio.

At the Crusader Motel in Wildwood Crest, New Jersey, summer of 1978—the last year I had an even tan.

Holding my own in a Little League All-Star game against nine seventeen-year-old black kids. Note the number 7—just like Mickey Mantle.

Tony Testa, Mike Testa, myself, and Joey Losito at the Jewish Community Center.

Union's Most Wanted: Bonnie and Clyde (Sue Pacardi and me) at the Union High School prom, 1985. I didn't get laid that night.

Cheesy mustache, Italian horn, and Curly Howard shirt—class personified.

Uncle Bruce, Grandma Caprio, Uncle Tommy, and me at my Aunt Dee's on Christmas Eve for the traditional Italian seven-fish meal.

Two of my favorite people in the whole world: my mother, Judy, and her sister, my godmother, Diane Niceforo.

I used to play a priest when I did dinner theater, and I'd leave the shirt on afterward to get out of public drunkenness tickets.

All coked up at Carolines (circa 1993) with Live on Tape, trying to forget I was in a gay improv group.

Nice teats: Like a pig on coke, I managed to gain weight *and* be addicted to cocaine.

David Herman, Orlando Jones, and me in a *MADtv* sketch in early 1996. Two great talents who saved my life. Thank you, Orlando and Dave.

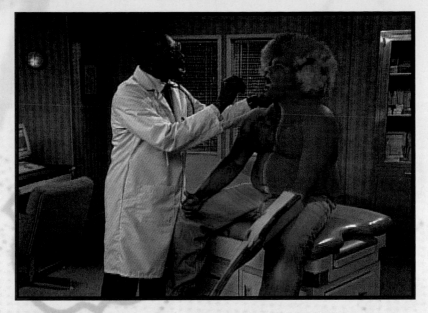

Orlando and me in one of my favorite sketches at *MADtv*, written by Blaine Capatch. As you can see, I play an obnoxious football fan who thinks he has an awful illness. Orlando, playing a doctor, informs me that I have something incurable: I'm an asshole.

Norm failing to keep a straight face after Don Rickles called me "Baby Gorilla" on the set of *Dirty Work*. The guy on Norm's right is Chris Farley's brother, Kevin.

I wanted this photo to be very prominent in the book, because it's significant to me for several reasons:

1. This pose—with the cigarette in my mouth, the lighter on my leg, and the huge glass of Jack Daniel's and water with ice and a straw—unfortunately sums up my existence for the last twenty years;

2. It was taken in the green room of one of my favorite clubs in the country, The Improv in Tempe, Arizona, which is owned by my friend Dan Mer, on April 24, 2004, the night I taped my stand-up concert DVD *It's the Whiskey Talkin'*; and

3. Dana took it.

The Reverend Bob Levy and me by the pool in Boca Raton. Dana took this after I went swimming in the ocean with all my clothes on. We were down there playing a club call Boca-nuts. What A-listers!

Stace and Mom at the Bel Age Hotel in Los Angeles, the day of the premiere of the 1999 film I did with David Spade, *Lost and Found*.

My favorite picture of Dana and me, at a loft party in New York City in 2002. She looks like Marisa Tomei.

On the set of the only movie ever shot in Rutherford, New Jersey, *Beer League*.

Showing off my abs during my famous 2004 Vegas blackout.

Doing stand-up in Wilmington, Delaware, Christmas of '04. This is the night I met my future heroin dealer for the first time.

A crazy fan brings me booze during the show. Goddamn peer pressure!

Chugging Jack through a straw. This caused me to miss a 9 A.M. spin class.

Thanking the crowd.

The surprise party Howard and Beth threw for my fortieth birthday.
They closed down John's Pizzeria on Bleecker Street in the Village
for me for the whole night. It's nice working for a generous guy who
dates a generous girl. (I also believe this is the only picture of me
and a model.)

This is me entertaining two radio legends at my Jersey Shore
house, August 2008. I fired my summer stylist shortly after this
picture was taken.

Jeff Anthony, Dave Attell, Nick DiPaolo, myself, and Gary Dell'Abate on a military flight from Kazakhstan to Kandahar, Afghanistan, during our 2008 USO Tour. My seat belt needed two extensions.

These guys were sitting directly behind us on the plane. I think even my closest friends and relatives would agree that you're looking at 500 people who, quite frankly, are better than me.

Me and Gary getting ready to board a Black Hawk helicopter. If Lou Costello and Chico Marx ever teamed up for a war picture, it would have looked a lot like this.

The Marx Brothers star in *A Day in Kandahar.*

Gary fucking up a manly activity like signing a bomb with a gay Mets hat.

Attell, Nick, Jim, and Gary with a bunch of heroes.

coke to pass the fifteen hours I had to spend in this pig getup, I would drown myself in the Pacific.

Because I was the lead of the sketch, two assistant directors had to be aware of my whereabouts because it was their responsibility to wrangle all the cast members when it was time to start shooting. I was going to have to find a way to give them the slip. Apparently, they were having problems getting the lighting right for the first shot, so I seized this opportunity and sprinted to my car in the the full pig outfit—teats, ears, everything. As I sped away off the lot, I saw one of the assistant directors waving his arms at me.

"Hey!" he shouted, his voice fading away behind me. "Where are you *going* . . . ?"

The Pacific Coast Highway is a winding four-lane strip right on the edge of the ocean, and I tore down that thing at about ninety miles an hour, just a pig who wanted his coke. My makeup was so good that the tone matched my skin perfectly, and every time I looked in the rearview it was just uncanny to see myself that way. When I'd catch people's eye at traffic lights, they did a double take: I think at first they thought I was deformed, but after a second look there was no mistaking that pig snout profile. If you were next to me, you would have said, "Look at that! It's a pig, driving."

I got to Duke's parking lot, went to the far end of it like my dealer said, and sat there waiting. I was so antsy to get my drugs, so focused on the moment his car would turn in to the parking lot, that after a while I forgot about the pig makeup, which was far from comfortable. When I finally saw my dealer drive in, it was like Jesus Christ appearing before me. I jumped out of the car and ran over to him. He was a black kid from inner-city L.A. and he was not prepared for what he saw.

"What the fuck is *wrong* with you, man?" he said, genuinely disgusted. "What the fuck kind of sick shit are you *into?*"

"Dude, I told you I was on TV," I said.

"What the fuck kind of show you on, man? That shit ain't *right*!"

"I'm on *MADtv*, man. We're doing some stupid skit and I have to be a pig," I said.

"No shit—you on *MADtv*?" he said. "That shit is funny! You didn't tell me you on *MADtv*! Who's that blond chick on that show, man?"

"Nicole Sullivan."

"Yeah, Nicole Sullivan. She's hot, man. You work with her? Damn, man, what's she like?"

I then had to have a fifteen-minute conversation about Nicole Sullivan with this guy, in my full pig face, standing outside in the parking lot of Duke's. After that, he wanted to know all about what it was like to work on a comedy show and how we came up with all the shit we did on the air. The concept of a team of writers was definitely new to him.

While this incredibly painful dialogue went on, I was on the verge of literally attacking the guy to get my fucking coke. I would have just told him I didn't have the time and thrown my money at him, but I didn't have the cash to cover the eight ball I'd ordered, so I felt like I had to hang out and endure this endless line of questioning. He was a great drug dealer, this guy—he came with a line of credit, so I could put the coke on my tab. I'm sure he didn't give everyone that treatment, but I was on a TV show, so he knew I was good for it. Besides, at the time I was what any drug dealer would call a very good customer. The only thing I feel incredibly guilty about is that back then Nicole Sullivan was single and I totally forgot to tell her that she could have dated this guy.

After I got my eight ball and my dealer took off, I started tearing through my backseat looking for something to do it with. That didn't take long; like a true coke addict, I had a nice selection of cut straws available. I was so focused on my drugs that I forgot, again, about the pig mask as I went to stick the straw in my nose. The thing hit my snout, bent in half, and got nowhere near my actual nostril. I tried it like three times, wanting to get the coke in me so bad that my brain did not compute why the hell the straw wasn't connecting my nose to the drugs. I pinched the end of the straw, got it in there good enough, and sniffed as hard as I could, expecting my snout to work just like my real nostril. Obviously, that failed miserably. I was on the verge of opening it all up on the passenger seat and just stuffing my whole snout in it in a desperate, piglike attempt to get high.

I hoped to do my drugs without disturbing Jen's work, but that wasn't happening, so I took the straw and started to dig with abandon into this expensive prosthetic stuff like I was tunneling out of prison. Finally, I managed to crack a hole in the bottom of the snout and get the straw up there and into my nose. I inhaled a line of coke as fast and hard as if it were my first drink of water after walking across the Sahara. At that moment, I didn't give a fuck about where I was, what I looked like, or what kind of shit I was gonna get for walking off the set. Those people could all fuck themselves as far as I was concerned. All I cared about was getting some relief.

Sure enough, once I was high, everything got a little better. So of course the obvious decision was to feel a whole lot better by doing a whole lot more coke before I went back to work. But since I was now high, I was also now paranoid that everyone on set would know I'd run out to get coke. I also worried that Jen would see that I'd poked a hole in the snout the size of a straw. I kept trying to look at the damage in the mirror in the sun visor to make sure I didn't have blow all over my face. I bent the thing every which way, but for the fucking life of me I couldn't see under the snout: Every time I lifted my head high enough, my big pig cheeks blocked the view.

My only option was to go into the restaurant bathroom to do my drugs as comfortably as possible.

As I walked through Duke's parking lot, cars driving by 200 feet away on the highway slowed down to honk at me like I was fucking Santa Claus, but I didn't care. I went inside, walked right by the hostess stand, through the bar and restaurant, directly into the bathroom. Nobody stopped me—I think they were much too freaked out for that. In L.A. there are always actors in costumes doing shit around town, so who knows, maybe they'd already seen a monkey and a donkey come through that day.

In the bathroom mirror I saw that I'd dug a gaping hole in this prosthetic snout that was covered, as I expected, with white powder. I tried to close it up and hide the damage, but it was fucked; there was a loose flap clinging by a thread. I was now a pig with a deviated septum. *Fuck it,* I thought and went into a stall, sat down on the toilet, and did more lines.

When I got back to my car, I realized that I'd been gone for over an hour and still had a twenty-minute drive back along the

Pacific Coast Highway. Faced with those odds, the only thing that made sense was to do a quick blast of coke for the ride. By now my straw was no longer necessary: I'd successfully fucked up the makeup to the degree that I could easily do a key hit, which is just what it sounds like—a small pile of coke on the end of a key. I did one of those and started making my way down the PCH.

Every time I hit a traffic light I stopped and did another key hit because I felt so shitty about both the skit and the fact that I was fucking up so bad by being so late. At one red light, as I maneuvered the key up my snout, I felt eyes on me. I turned to my left and saw this fucking hot Malibu chick with long blond hair and sunglasses— just smoking hot—driving some sort of Lamborghini convertible. She was there with her girlfriend, and the look on their faces was insane: They must have thought they were on an acid trip, sitting there looking at a pig, in broad daylight, doing cocaine.

I just stopped and stared back at them with the key in my hand. Then the driver leaned over so she could get a better look at me and said, kind of disorganized and pointing: "That's a pig . . . doing co- caine." She might have said that, I don't know. I'm going with the odds here and assuming she didn't say, "Hey, you're hot! Can I blow you?"

I just wanted to kill myself. I thought of my mother holding me in the hospital as a baby, staring into my face, never knowing that one day her baby boy would be in pig makeup at 10 in the morn- ing doing blow at a traffic light. I heard my mother's voice in my head, horrified, saying, "Look at my son! Look at him! What's hap- pened to my son?" I was miserable.

The light turned green, and I started driving with the hit of coke still balanced on the key in my hand. I started weaving in and out of lanes trying to get this thing in my nose and ended up cut- ting off this old lady and almost causing an accident.

I got back to the set and put on the rest of my costume: a red *Baywatch* bathing suit featuring twelve boob cups to hold my six sets of teats. I stashed my coke in one of them and made some excuse to Jen about what had happened to the snout. I told her I was drinking Coke from a can when it broke. Finally, six hours after waking up and three hours after my scheduled start time, I joined the cast on set. It was obvious from like 300 yards away that everyone from my fellow actors to the last crew guy wanted to fucking kill me. They were all just livid. My best friend on the show, David Herman, an amazingly talented actor, walked right up to me, looking more pissed than I'd ever seen him.

"Artie, you almost got the two assistant directors fired!" he said. "What the fuck? You have to let those guys know if you're going somewhere."

"Oh yeah? Well, *fuck you*, Dave!"

"*What?* What did I do?"

"You heard me. Fuck you. I don't give a fucking shit about you or those two fucking guys."

I gave him the finger and stormed off. We didn't speak for two weeks.

I then did the sensible thing: I went back to my trailer and did more coke until it was time to shoot. It was one of those times when cocaine wasn't at all fun, it just got me through the day, because that was the kind of user I'd become. The drugs did have the unwelcome side effect, however, of making the day more and more strange with each passing minute. Every time I bent over to do a line, I'd catch my reflection in the mirror out of the corner of my eye and I'd see me, as a pig, doing coke. I was a pig doing coke, it was as simple as that. It did wonders for my self-esteem and my growing self-loathing at being an addict. The monologue in my head was like a broken record: "I'm a pig! I'm a fucking *coke-addict* pig! I am a *fucking drug-addicted pig*!" The pig costume was more than a symbol to me. As high as I was, when I saw myself in the mirror, I had turned into a pig—a pig who over-ate and did coke.

When you did impressions on *MADtv*, the producers gave you a Walkman that played huge sections of whatever movie was being parodied, with your character's catchphrases recorded on a loop. You'd wear this thing around during rehearsals and for a week listen to the voice you had to impersonate over and over again. It drove all of us crazy. When David Herman had to do Pauly Shore, he almost quit. David is a really mellow, great guy who played "Michael Bolton" in the very funny movie *Office Space*. On his third day of rehearsals, walking around listening to the Pauly Shore tape and practicing saying, "What's uup, buuuuddy? What's uup?" he suddenly, out of nowhere, just tore the headphones off and smashed the Walkman on the floor.

"Fuck it! I can't take it anymore!" he screamed. "Fuck this! I fucking quit!"

Eventually, he calmed down. He didn't quit, and when it came time to shoot, David did the most amazing Pauly Shore impression ever. But who could blame him? The Wease is fucking annoying.

Anyway, the Walkman treatment made my coked-up pig reality so much harder to take. The rest of the cast were dressed as hot lifeguards. I walked around this beach in Malibu getting ready for my scene by listening to, and repeating over and over, lines like "Hey! I'm Babe! Hey, I'm *Baaabe*!" It was horrible. Then, when we shot, the cast and crew looked on while I did things like sit on a lifeguard stand eating a huge piece of chicken . . . like a pig. In another scene, I had to dig through a garbage can while the entire cast shouted, "You're a *pig*! You're a disgusting *pig*!" It was the most surreal day of my life.

By the end of it, I was a mess. I'd done so much coke and everything had been so weird that, in my mind, I was convinced that I'd been permanently transformed into a cocaine-snorting, binge-eating pig, which wasn't so far from the truth. When I got back into the makeup chair, I was so amped up and into my delusion that I didn't expect the stuff to come off. As Jen removed it, I could tell she was clearly terrified of me; if she hadn't guessed right away why this hole kept cracking in the base of my snout all day long, I'm sure soon enough she'd figure it out. My knee was bouncing at about a million miles an hour, and every twenty minutes I stopped her so I could go to the bathroom.

"Hey, listen, Jen," I'd say. "Sorry to do this to you, I really have to go to the bathroom again. I drank a lot of coffee out there today, you know?" Sure, *coffee*, that's what everyone drinks when they're on a hot beach for ten hours.

Anyway, I was overjoyed to discover how much easier it was to do coke once I'd gotten my God-given nose back. Which was good, because I was far from finished. I went back to the motel, this awful little dive on the side of the highway, knowing that everyone on the shoot completely hated my guts. All I wanted to do was go home, but we had one more day, so I kept doing coke and drinking Jack until I fell asleep around 3 A.M., about an hour before my 4 A.M. wake-up call.

When the phone rang, I felt like I'd arrived in hell. The only way to describe it is to picture the famous scene from *The Godfather* where Jack Woltz wakes up covered in blood with his prize-winning half-a-million-dollar racehorse's head in bed with him. As it dawns on him what's happened, he starts screaming, over and over and louder and louder, this really disturbing strangled yell: "Ahh! Ahhhhh! *Ahhhhhhh!*"

That was me, but instead of horse blood, my bed was full of my own shit. I kept shouting, "What *is* this? *What is this!?*" My body had had so much badness in it—so much coke and booze and bad food—that when I fell asleep all of it just fell out of me. I had lost all control in that one hour. It was so horrible and there was so much of it that it had filled my Jockey underwear, leaked out of every side, and spread all over the bed. And it was everywhere: on my arms, on my chest, up by my neck because I'd rolled around—exactly like a pig would do—and gotten it all over myself.

When I first saw it, though, I thought it was blood and I was convinced that someone had come into my room and done something violent to me. Cocaine paranoia is great, by the way, you should try it. Once I realized that in fact *I* was the only one who had done anything violent to me, I was even more horrified. I got up, took a good look at the mess, and it was just terrible. It looked like someone had filled a can of house paint with runny shit and dumped it in the vague shape of a human being on this fleabag bed. The room smelled, I smelled, it was awful. That had never happened to me before, and even though I was far from being done with excessive drug use, it's never happened since. Whenever I tell this story, I kid myself for a minute by telling myself that it's no big deal because everyone's got a story just like it. Unfortunately, reason wins out eventually. Unless I go to a Narcotics Anonymous meeting and make friends, I'm pretty sure I'll never find myself in a room full of people with stories like this.

Anyway, I was running late by this point and, judging by the carnage I was looking at, it was only going to get later. I felt cursed—there was just no way to keep every single person working on this shoot from fucking hating me. I was going to be late to makeup, which once again guaranteed that everything would be delayed. It was a miserable moment standing there in that dark little room in Malibu feeling this insane pressure.

I jumped into the shower and turned the hot water up until it steamed, then I scrubbed and scorched myself until my entire body was all red. I was clean, but I still felt disgusting. But that didn't matter, because by the time I got out, I was *really* late: There were people knocking at my door with a van waiting outside just for me, and they were definitely pissed off. I got into some clean clothes, I grabbed my coke, of course, and that's when I realized that I had no idea what the fuck to do about the huge mess on the bed.

"Artie! We've got to go, man, the van is waiting."

"Okay, sorry, I'm coming, one minute."

The only choice was to flee the scene of the crime. I grabbed the old crappy polyester bedspread, threw it over the horror show, and left. I had absolutely no cash at all, so I couldn't even leave the maid a tip. I had coke, though, and if I knew she partook I would have gladly left her some.

I got to the set, went to my trailer, and did some coke to steady my nerves enough to get me through the three-hour makeup process. The whole time I was freaking out, convinced that I still smelled like shit, as Jen once again turned my face into a pig. I got on set, hoping that maybe, somehow, my friends on the show had forgiven me for my behavior the day before. Not quite: My buddy, the great actor Orlando Jones, wouldn't even talk to me between scenes. It was too fucked up: I was there, dressed as a pig, with every other actor in the group turning their back on me, ignoring the pig between takes.

Somehow I got through that day and was overjoyed to be going home. As I drove back to L.A., feeling bad about the mess I'd left in the hotel, it hit me: Not only did I almost get the assistant directors fired, but my room had been registered in one of the guys' names! I had showered that place in feces and I wasn't even the one picking up the tab! What an asshole I was. I started to think of what I was going to say to explain it and how I would make it up to the guy.

Well, that never happened. No one ever said a word about it. I can only assume that they covered the damage—who knows if anyone ever said anything to anybody. I wouldn't be surprised if they didn't. As an eyewitness, I can say that finding that mess was like discovering a decaying corpse: It was so upsetting that they probably made a pact never to speak of it again.

After that skit, we had a break before going into another stretch of shooting, which would be the end of the first half of the season. During the time off, I went to San Diego to get my head straight. At the time I was casually dating a chick down there, so I went to see her. Once I cooled down off the blow, I did some damage control and got everyone talking to me again, though it wasn't easy. But I hadn't learned a thing and I was far from done with drugs in the workplace. You'd think that waking up in your own crap would be a wake-up call. Not for me; I looked at it as an occupational hazard. No, I kept on doing drugs at *MADtv* straight on until dawn. More awful shit was yet to come. Everyone knows that the darkest hour is the one right before the dawn. For me, this incident was just around midnight.

Wah! I'm Out of Cocaine! Wah!

9

The most important thing I've learned from working with the amazing Howard Stern for seven years is that the key to a great radio show and great comedy of any kind is honesty. Though I've tried to follow that philosophy as much as possible on *The Stern Show* and in my stand-up, it hasn't always happened 100 percent, but it's going to happen here. My goal is for this book to exist as the most honest piece of work I have ever done. The only way to do that is for me to put things on the page that I couldn't share on the air or in any public forum. The story contained here is the most personal revelation I can possibly make and not something that I see much comedy in. I suppose that's why it hasn't made it into my act.

The week before *The Stern Show* left terrestrial radio, each of us on the staff promised to reveal a surprising or highly personal story about ourselves when we got to satellite. That first week at Sirius, we told our shocking stories. I told one about an unfortunate incident I was involved in while attending a Hollywood orgy. But that wasn't the one I was intending to reveal—it was the runner-up. This is the story I'd have told if I'd have been strong enough to be completely honest that day:

When I was twenty-eight years old, I tried to commit suicide. It was no half-assed attempt, either. It came complete with a note addressed to my mother and sister. It didn't happen at a time when I was broke; it happened three months after my big break. In the fall of 1995, we'd completed the first shooting cycle of *MADtv*, the first nine episodes. Critics loved the show and the initial ratings were very promising—it looked as if this gig was going to last a while. I had my tenth high school reunion coming up, and I couldn't wait to be there and show off. I was a regular on a new, well-received network TV show, and there were more than a few people I was going to enjoy telling. But I never made it to the reunion. Instead, I was in a rehab center recovering.

My inability to deal with the stress of *MADtv* was a combination of the pressure I put on myself to deliver and my choice of diet. Cocaine was such a regular part of my day that I started doing things like pouring grams of it into glasses of Jack Daniel's and drinking it down four or five times a week because my nose was too sore. Not a good place to be. It didn't take long for me to develop an ulcer. I ignored it as long as I could; in fact, I made the mistake of thinking that drinking cocaine would numb the stomach pain that seemed to get worse every day. I held out until it became so unbearable that I had to be taken from the Fox lot to St. Joseph's Hospital in Burbank for a series of upper-gastrointestinal exams. I'll never forget the look on the doctor's face when he walked into the office with my test results. He looked like Lou Costello after he saw the werewolf in *Abbott and Costello Meet Frankenstein.*

"How old are you, Artie?" he asked.

"I'm twenty-seven."

"You're twenty-seven. Well, the kind of damage you've done to yourself is frightening," he said. "If you want to see thirty, you have to stop every bad thing you're doing—right now."

"Yeah, I know I don't really eat well."

"That's *not* what I'm talking about," he said, pausing to stare at me for a moment. "The booze and the drugs you're ingesting are tearing your digestive system apart. You have ulcers that will become fatal if you keep going like this. This is very serious. You have to stay off of that stuff, starting right now, for six months at least. There is no room to negotiate here."

"Oh," I said. "I forgot to tell you about all that."

"This is not a joke, Artie. You need to completely stop everything right now, for at least six months. It's not funny—you are slowly dying."

Whether he was exaggerating or not, he scared me shitless, so I decided to follow the doctor's orders. I'd had enough of that life anyway; the drugs had stopped being fun a while ago. I thought it would be easy: Half a year? No problem. I had my work to replace the drugs and booze, I thought. I'd dive into the show to keep myself busy and out of trouble. I'd probably do better than ever at work without all of that shit getting in the way.

All full of those optimistic thoughts, I quit drinking and doing drugs cold turkey in mid-September. I was okay for two or three days and started to think that addiction was bullshit. But the next day was a different story: After fourteen hours of work, the cast and writers decided to take the edge off with a few drinks and I realized there was no way I could go with them. Afraid that I would fall off the wagon, I went home alone to my apartment. I hear that when people with substance problems make decisions like that, it's empowering. Not for me—I felt like a kid who'd been grounded.

It didn't help at all that I hated my fucking apartment. Eventually, I would live with Orlando Jones in an amazing loft in downtown L.A., but I'd only just moved out west that summer and I'd decided to rent a place in the same housing complex where Fox put me when they flew me out to shoot the pilot. This place is famous for the number of celebrities who lived there when they were nobodies or in really fucked-up times in their lives. It's called the Oakwood Apartments in the North Hollywood section of the Valley on Barham Boulevard. I was in apartment Y108, a number I will never forget.

For those unfamiliar with the Oakwoods, they might be the single most depressing collection of structures ever built. The place is the epitome of corporate housing. It's bland and sterile, with fluorescent lighting and a fake cheerfulness to the whole thing, from the staff to the decor. To this day, whenever I drive by the Oakwoods, I get a feeling that must be similar to what a Jew feels when visiting Auschwitz. In spite of its misery, it was my only refuge, so every day after a rehearsal or a taping, I would retreat there alone to make sure I stayed clean and sober. It wasn't a good time: I was isolating myself from the world and suffering from sickening withdrawal symptoms and an alcohol-related hell called the DT's. I felt achy, feverish, and nauseous all the time, like I had the flu. My physical discomfort was not eased at all by my surroundings, and with each passing night I spent there alone, I slowly descended into madness.

I did my best to keep up appearances at work. I gave it all I had, and in general I think I kept it together. But privately, week after week, I was getting much worse. I'd go home and stare at the TV with no thoughts in my head—nothing but a dark gray cloud. I couldn't think, I couldn't sleep, I didn't want to eat; I just lay there in bed. I wouldn't talk to anyone on the phone and I wouldn't go anywhere. I started having trouble learning my lines, eating anything, or conducting a conversation when I didn't have to. It took every bit of strength I had to keep from missing work, because I knew if I let that happen, I was done for; I'd drown in a black hole inside apartment Y108 in the Oakwoods. So I made sure that I was never late and I did my best never to forget or stumble over a line in a sketch. I had some sort of angel on my shoulder—I hope it was Pop—because that is the only explanation I have for why I was able to keep up my obligation to the show. Thank God I did, because it's what saved my life.

The people at *MADtv* knew there was something really wrong, that I was severely depressed, and they could not have been cooler. They tried to reach out to me, but I didn't even know what to tell them. I was so alienated that I had no idea how to explain what I was feeling. At someone's suggestion I tried going to a shrink, but aside from a prescription for sleeping pills, I got nothing out of it really. It was my fault, I guess; I didn't have the ability to get to the bottom of why I felt so bad, even with the help of a trained professional.

On the first Friday in November 1995, after the last taping of a long week, I reached the end of my sanity. I could not deal with the physical illness and the feeling of emptiness—the loneliness and boredom and apathy. By midnight I started thinking about it, and at 2 A.M. I finally did it: I called my dealer and met him in the parking lot of the Cinerama Dome on Sunset near Cahuenga in Hollywood. I bought a little more than an eight ball, which would last me the entire weekend. I went back to apartment Y108 with the coke and two fifths of Jack Daniel's. I had some sleeping pills around to make sure I went to bed at some point. My plan was to get some relief, just do a little coke to feel better, but not jeopardize my health or my job.

It didn't quite work out that way: I stayed awake all weekend alone in that apartment, snorting blow and drinking whiskey. I sat in one spot on the couch with the TV on and all my coke and booze and cigarettes spread out on the coffee table in front of me. Next to all that stuff was a brand-new packet of fifteen sketches that had to be read for the network on Monday. I went through it as I started to get into the drugs and saw that I was going to be busy: I had more than a few scenes, many different characters to do, and a massive amount of lines.

I had to do an impression of Newt Gingrich on the show and I hated doing him each and every time. I thought all of my impressions sucked, but apparently that one went over well enough to keep bringing it back. Seeing that I had to do Newt again on Monday started the downward spiral, and this one never let up. Believe me, it wasn't a political issue for me at all—if it had been, I might have had more of an excuse for my behavior—I just hated doing impressions. By Saturday night, after having been awake for twenty-four hours doing line after line of cocaine, I was in such a state that Monday morning seemed like an impossible task. I had no idea how I could get my parts in those scenes ready for the network. The thought of Monday morning became so horrifying that I'd put it out of my mind by doing another line. It was a like a gigantic faraway wall that I knew I could never climb and hoped I'd never have to. But before I knew it, seemingly out of nowhere, it was suddenly 4 A.M. on Monday and there it was. And right on cue, as my own personal Armageddon was about to unfold, I ran out of coke.

I met a kid in rehab who said something very profound about cocaine in one of our group meetings. "The best part about cocaine," he said, "is going to get it." He couldn't be more right. When I started traveling to do stand-up earlier in my career, there was nothing as exciting as being in a strange city with someone you'd just met who knew how to get some coke and made the call. The

drive over to get it is always amazing; it's the anticipation of party-
ing that is so intoxicating. It's the best part of the night, before the
reality of doing it sets in.

If that's the best part about cocaine, the worst part is running
out of it. That moment can be devastating; it can bring on uncontrollable feelings of despair and suicide. That is what I was faced
with—on top of a network read-through in four hours that, to put
it mildly, I was unprepared for. I tried to gauge my mental state
and decided that if I went into work there was a very good chance
I would have some kind of crazy public breakdown and be hauled
off in a straitjacket. The panic I felt was out of control. I felt like I
was watching some guy who wasn't me and that guy had officially
lost it.

In that state, coked and drunk to the gills, I made the worst and
darkest decision in a life filled with embarrassing decisions. I came
to the conclusion that the only way out for me was suicide, and to
this day I still cannot believe what I did. I had turned twenty-eight
three weeks earlier and had lived to see one of my biggest dreams
come true. I was told the producers had booked a total of 8,000
people to audition for just eight regular slots. We'd done our first
nine episodes, they were well received, I was able to start really as-
sisting my mother financially—what else could I have wanted from
life? By anyone's estimates, I was doing very well, but cocaine had
reduced all of my achievements to nothing. Through the haze of
drugs, my life looked hopeless.

I went to the bathroom and got all thirty of my 10mg tablets
of Resterol, a powerful sleeping pill. I also took out a bottle of Excedrin PM and another pint of whiskey. I figured all of it together
would do the trick. I laid it all out in front of me, then I went and
changed my shorts, because after three days of sweating on the couch
the ones I had on stunk. I did not want to disgrace myself or my
family further by being discovered in dirty underwear. I considered

showering too. I began to worry more about the people who were going to find me than myself. I thought that those people didn't deserve to smell my foul BO. I debated taking a shower, but I never did in the end. I figured why bother, since I remembered hearing that your body lets everything go when you die anyway. I was going to be a mess no matter what I did.

It's hard to admit any of this, even all these years later, because when I think about it there is one thing that scares me most of all: I was 100 percent serious about dying. Once I'd crossed the bridge to killing myself, I didn't stop to rethink it once, I just barreled ahead. I had the drugs and booze laid out. Then I took some time to look in the mirror and clean up a bit. I would estimate that in my four years of high school, a time when everyone cares about how they look, I spent a total of three minutes on my clothes and hair. I couldn't have cared less then, but now that I was going to the Big Dance, I became very concerned with my appearance. I spent at least an hour cleaning up and getting into some nice clothes until I thought I looked okay. Then I sat down to write my note, because what suicide would be complete without a note?

I grabbed a legal pad and my complimentary Oakwoods pen and began to write. I addressed it to my mother and sister, the two women who had helped and supported me in every way possible. I was on the verge of ruining their lives, but that is how selfish and narcissistic that fucking drug cocaine makes you. I was so despondent that I could only think about ending my suffering; I couldn't think of theirs. I have not seen the note since I wrote it. It was eventually given to my mother, and I believe she destroyed it, which, to be honest with you, sort of offended me. Throughout high school my sister always got great grades on papers, which my mom would proudly display on the refrigerator. My grades always sucked, so for years I never had anything on the fridge, but I felt that my suicide note had excellent grammar and stellar penmanship. At the very least, it was worthy of a spot on the fridge. (That was a lame attempt at levity in a chapter that is nothing but a sea of depressing shit.)

In any case, I remember the note verbatim. It helps that it was also short and sweet and just how I wanted it:

> *Ma and Stace,*
>
> *I cannot deal with my life. None of this is your fault. Do me a favor and keep on living. Maybe we will see each other again someday.*
>
> > *Love,*
> > *Artie*

It took me only one draft, and when I was done I made sure it was easy to spot there on the coffee table next to all the drugs. Without further delay, I took all thirty Resterols and about twenty Excedrin PM and washed them down with the entire pint of Jack. My body was already in terrible shape from doing a mountain of coke all weekend, so I didn't think it would take long for all of that to do me in.

I have been told by psychiatrists and counselors that eighty percent of the time, people who try to commit suicide panic once they've taken the fatal dose of drugs or slash their wrists and start bleeding. Usually at this point they call for help—an undeniable sign that they really don't want to die. I was in the other twenty percent: I sat back on the couch, got comfortable, and waited. When I started to feel the effects of the drugs about two minutes later, my will to die did not change, but I had the weirdest emotional reaction: I was morbidly curious about what was going to happen and obsessively began going over the possibilities. This might be hard to understand, but I was actually excited and looking forward to whatever lay in store for me. I was about to learn the answer to the most-asked question in the history of mankind, the question that no great scientist, artist, scholar, theologian, or philosopher has ever been able to answer definitively: What happens when we die? I was about to learn if there was a heaven or a hell, whether I'd see my father again, or if I'd just go to sleep forever and slowly rot away. Discovering the truth made it seem like killing myself was the right thing to do, so I regretted nothing. I just sat there, smiling, as the drugs started to take over. My right arm started to shake while, in my head, I sang the opening line of the Sinatra song "My Way": *And now, the end is near, and so I face the final curtain.*

The trembling in my arm spread to my chest and then my entire body started convulsing. And then I passed out. I have very blurry memories of slipping in and out of consciousness in my friend David Herman's red Miata convertible. Even though I didn't meet him until I was twenty-seven, I've never known a better friend than Dave; he literally and figuratively saved my life. I have these vague images in my mind of him talking to me as we drove. He kept saying, "It's okay now, Artie. It's okay, it's over. You can go back to New York now and you can get better, okay? It's gonna be all right."

My next memory is of lying on a gurney in the Intensive Care Unit at St. Joe's Hospital in Burbank as they put a catheter in me. There is one thing I can tell you for sure: No matter how many drugs you have in your system, none of them can kill the pain of having a tube shoved up the hole in your cock. Once I was semi-conscious, they got me to drink this black, tarlike substance made of charcoal to save my liver. When I woke up again after that, they pumped my stomach, after which I went to sleep for a very long time. I woke up at about 4 o'clock the next morning and felt some-what normal. I heard someone reading, looked down, and saw that I was in bed with tubes coming out of me every which way. It sounded like someone was reading the Bible, and when I turned my head, I saw a 350-pound black woman in a chair next to my bed, reciting scripture.

"Excuse me," I said. "Am I in heaven?"

"Ha ha ha! No, baby, you are in Intensive Care at St. Joe's," she said. "What are you here for?"

"I tried to kill myself," I said. "I guess unsuccessfully."

"You tried to kill yourself?" she said. "Baby, you can*not* do that. If you kill yourself, you'll go straight to hell. Life is a precious gift— you can't take this gift we've been given for granted."

"Oh yeah?" I said. "Yeah, I know." I had nothing else positive to add to the conversation, so I went back to sleep.

The next time I woke up, it was early afternoon, thirty-six hours or more since I had tried to kill myself. David Herman and *MADtv*'s director, John Blanchard, were in the room and they cheered me up a bit. Then, later on, Orlando Jones and Nicole Sullivan came by to visit too, and they were really sensitive and gave me incredibly uplifting pep talks. The four of them then told me how I'd been saved.

When I did not show up for work, the two assistant directors, Josh Berger and Tara Passander, got worried. Josh was actually the guy that I'd left holding the bag in my motel room in Malibu. I can't imagine how sick of me he must have been: He'd literally dealt with my shit, and now he was dealing with my shit again—this time on a metaphysical level. Josh and Tara called my room and got no answer, so they decided to drive over to my place, which was just down the street, to investigate. They knocked on the door for a while and, just as they were ready to give up, I answered it in a stupor, unable to speak coherently and swaying all over the place. They didn't know what was wrong with me, so they grabbed me by the arms, led me back inside, and sat me down on the couch. That's when they saw the note. They immediately called the studio, and David Herman answered the call and rushed right over. They also called 911, but David beat the authorities there, so they put me in his car and drove me to the hospital. The producers then did all the right things: They got rid of the drugs, dealt with the EMTs when they showed up, and called my mom and sister back in Jersey, who flew out immediately.

This lovely occasion was my mother's first visit to California. When she entered the room, she looked great. She was strong, powerful, and classy through it all and she did not, for a minute, let me see her cry. She came over to the bed, gave me a hug, and said, "We've got to get you better, Artie. We've got to get you better." My sister was the same way, and their strength gave me hope. Some parents would have fallen apart, but not my mom. She is a special woman and she deserves every cent I earn in this life, not that she'd ever take it. It's the only way I can think to repay her for all that she's done for me.

Among the many reasons I've never before told this story publicly, the most important one is this: I was afraid that someone might think that my mother had failed in any way as a parent. Nothing could be further from the truth. My mother is the greatest person I have ever known. A better mother would be hard to imagine. I didn't learn any of my bad behavior from her; all of my tendencies were in me, they are a part of my personality. If anything, the values and knowledge that my mother passed on to me are the only things that have kept me alive.

Seeing my mother and sister there made me feel well enough to think about what I had to do in my life. After another night in the hospital, I went back to Jersey with them, entered rehab, and began counseling. For their part, everyone involved with *MADtv* was fantastic. The two guys who ran the show, Fax Bahr and Adam Small, never made me feel guilty or bad for what had happened; they were understanding and willing to give me all the time I needed to recover. Those two guys are the reason I lasted through that tough first year on *MADtv*, both before and after this incident, and they deserve so much credit for my achievements there. I will never forget their tolerance during the shittiest time in my life. I owe them a lot, and the same goes for the coolest guy I have ever met, John Blanchard. Quincy Jones and his partner, David Salzman, who owned the show, were amazing too. They treated my mother and sister and me with such respect. David is a good man, and Quincy is unbelievable—he's one of the most remarkable men I've ever met in my life.

I had about seven or eight conversations with Quincy in the two years I worked for him at *MADtv*, and they remain the greatest talks I've ever had about life with anybody. Anyone who has ever met Quincy knows why so many people thank him when they win awards: He is an extraordinary man. In January, after I got through rehab, I returned to the set. When Quincy saw me, he walked right over and gave me a big hug.

"Man, I've been thinking about you," he said in that smooth, calming voice of his. "I'm glad you're back, Artie. You're funny. We need you, and your job is still here."

"Thank you, Mr. Jones," I said, really embarrassed about what I'd done. "I'm doing a lot better, and I just want to say I'm sorry, you know. I let the drugs get ahold of me."

"Listen, man," he said. "The greatest talents in the world have drug problems. Miles Davis did too. It took him a while to beat his demons. Don't let that happen to you."

"No, I won't," I said. "I just want you to know that I thank you and I appreciate everything you've done for me."

"Listen, I love you, man. I want you to stay well."

Quincy was amazing. He'd even sent his private jet to fly me back out to Los Angeles. Talk about a thrill: Three and a half years before, I'd been unloading orange juice in Port Newark, and there I was, after having flown in on Quincy Jones's plane, being compared by Quincy to Miles Davis in a heart-to-heart conversation. That moment alone inspired me to give my all and keep it together. I wanted to work and I wanted to be back among my castmates. I moved in with Orlando Jones, which made the producers happy because they knew O. Jones would keep an eye on me. My pal David Herman gave me a hug and welcomed me back. I am still great friends with David, and knowing him has made me a better man.

I wish I could say the same for Orlando. He was an amazing friend to me and I love that kid, but for some reason we've not spoken to each other in twelve years, and I wish I knew why. I'm happy to see that he's gone on to be very successful. He deserves all of the good that comes to him, because he's a great talent and a special guy. I just hope that I see him again someday so that we can get a chance to reminisce about all the fun times we had. It doesn't matter to me that we haven't spoken; Orlando saved my life, and there's nothing I wouldn't do for him. If I found out that for any reason he wasn't happy, it would make me unhappy and I'd do whatever I could to help out. And just in case he's reading this, I'd like to say: *Mr. O. Jones, I miss you.*

After my stint in rehab, I returned to *MADtv* in a better place and with a clarity I'd never had before. My work on the second half of that first season was the best work I've ever done in sketch comedy by far. I wrote and cowrote sketches that made it to air, and I created a recurring character, White Mama, that became a favorite of fans of the show. When I was clean, my talent level was through the roof, but as often is the case when it comes to jerks like me, it didn't last. I wasn't comfortable having things too good for too long, so in time I fucked up again, and when I did, I did it big. I've never tried offing myself again, and thank God I didn't succeed, because I think that it's a terribly selfish act for anyone who has people that love them in their life.

This hasn't been easy for me to get out, and I'm still ashamed of my actions that night. I can't believe I'm putting this out into the world, but I made a promise to myself to do it and I'm going to keep it. I don't think admitting my suicide attempt publicly is going to help me as a talent or as a performer, and I don't want to be any kind of role model, but I do hope that this story helps somebody else. There is one thing I've learned the hard way in this life: If you can't help making stupid mistakes yourself, you can try to stop other people from making them. If I've accomplished that by sharing this, I'm glad. My confession is now yours; let it be my gift. If it's true that you're supposed to learn from your mistakes, I should be fucking Einstein by now. That's it. Take it easy, everybody. The end.

MAD Man Walking

10

During my first trip to rehab, which lasted only a few weeks, I said nothing. I was determined to say nothing for my entire sentence—that's how I thought of it: I'd committed a crime, and I was doing the time. I would sit there in group therapy, long-faced, feeling sorry for myself but knowing I was doing the right thing. I just hoped to get out without sharing. There was a Puerto Rican girl in my group who liked to fuck with me, and with each passing session she grew more and more angry that I wasn't participating. After a while she started to jab me in front of everyone.

"So, Artie, what's your problem, man?" she asked. "What drug you do?"

"Cocaine."

"Oh, so you're a cokehead?"

"Yeah."

"Well, you are the fattest cokehead I ever seen! What the fuck? How did you do cocaine and *gain* weight? Cokeheads are skinny! What did you do, put your coke on cheeseburgers?"

"Yeah, I put my coke on fucking cheeseburgers. You should try it."

That was the biggest rise she got out of me, and she wasn't satisfied. So she kept on saying shit whenever she saw me, but I remained silent in group therapy. Eventually I was forced into sharing, so I admitted that I was a comedian, and then, of course, this girl recognized me from *MADtv*, which seemed to make her even more determined to get a reaction from me. One day, as our group sat in a circle, she leaped out of her chair, got right in my face, and screamed.

"You never say *nothing,* man! You're a comedian," she said. "You're supposed to talk and make jokes. You don't do *shit*! You are not funny. *Fuck you*!" She was now pointing right at me. "My brother is funnier than you, you fat cokehead fuck!"

"So you really want me to talk?" I said. "I'm really that interesting to you? You really give a shit about what I have to say?"

"Yeah! You think you're fucking too good for us, you piece of shit. That's why you don't talk."

"Okay, fine. I'll talk. Are you gonna sit down or are you gonna stand here and scream at me the whole time?"

I'd had enough of this shit, so I figured I'd really show them who I was by sharing the story of how my dad fell off the roof. He'd put his ladder on top of a picnic table so that he could reach the top of this extra-high ledge and complete the job. While he was on top of the ladder, it began to wobble because it wasn't secure, and he fell thirty feet, directly onto his head and neck. At the end of the story,

I started to cry as I do whenever I think about what happened to my father.

And as if to confirm everything that I already suspected about group therapy, this kid sitting across from me blurted out, "Yeah that's too bad for you, man. Your old man was a selfish prick. He put himself at risk using that picnic table like that. Who the fuck would do that? He wasn't thinking of you or your family at all. He should have considered what he was doing before he did that. Fucking prick was reckless."

Now if any of you reading this agree with the guy and you ever meet me, I urge you to keep that opinion to your fucking self. I don't want to hear it from you, and I certainly didn't want to hear it from him. If you say it to me, there's a good chance that I'll do what I did then: I lunged at this kid and connected a solid punch right to his fucking face. He almost fell out of his chair, then he grabbed me by the shirt, and we started wrestling on the ground until the staff broke it up.

I got suspended from the rehab center for a week. It did wonders for my self-esteem to be such a big loser that I managed to get suspended from rehab. Think about it: I couldn't blame my behavior on drugs—I was just that big of a fuck-up. I don't care; it was worth it. I'm very protective of my father's memory and always will be.

Any fan of the show can tell you that I've not done too much in the way of anger management, considering that I've blown up at several staffers over the years, assaulting them with water, cups, and the worst insults I could think of. But once I was reinstated into rehab, I did take advantage of what it had to offer and got a lot out of the process in addition to just getting clean.

In that state, I returned to *MADtv* in August 1996 for the start of Season 2 without having taken so much as an aspirin for ten and a half weeks. I'd made a pledge to myself that I would try my very best to stay clean and sober. I was twenty-eight, and I hoped that the worst of my drug problems were behind me.

I'd spent the summer living in New York, doing a lot of sketch writing and doing stand-up every single night at clubs in the city and on the road. I worked on bits derived from my years at Port Newark and some of the quirky guys I'd met down there. Stand-up was my outlet for developing stuff that I intended to bring to *MADtv* in one form or another when I returned. It was easy for me to get headlining spots because of the success of the show, and I got together a forty-five-minute set that I was really proud of. I was even getting called to audition for films, and that summer I booked my first role, in an independent movie called *Puppet*. No, it was not a horror movie—at least not in the traditional sense.

I auditioned for this thing at the beginning of the summer when I was really hungry for work. The role required me to have a Russian accent, and I prepared for it by listening to tapes of someone speaking with that accent, just as I would have at *MADtv*, so I pulled it off. This film, which to this day I have never seen because I don't think it's possible to purchase a copy of it at any price, anywhere, starred Rebecca Gayheart and Fred Weller. The problem was, though, that the Russian accent part of my character grew tiresome, so as my summer got busier, the accent took a back seat. Basically, by the end of shooting, I was talking the way I normally do—like a loudmouth from New Jersey. I'm dying to see a copy of this thing, and if I ever get one, I will definitely screen it at my house for my friends so we can track the erosion of my Russian accent. I'm not worried about that performance resurfacing and ruining my future in Hollywood, because I don't know anyone who has ever seen or even heard of *Puppet*. All I can say is that it was screened in a theater at least once because my manager went to see it. My manager said it was funny, but he also admitted that if I'd have been in the Zapruder film he would have called it funny too.

I also booked a couple of voice-over commercials, so all in all I had a really productive summer. By the end of it I was good enough at stand-up to do a whole hour and I remember the feeling of crossing that threshold. An hour on stage was the goal I'd never felt confident enough to reach. So with movie experience under my belt and some commercials running that were making me money, I returned to L.A. for the second season of *MADtv* with everything looking up.

I managed to stay clean and sober for the first two months of the season, but after a taping one night, that went south fast. I have a lot of friends who have been on *Saturday Night Live* and after they do a show, they all jump into a big limousine and head to the after-party. *MADtv* did things a little differently. We'd tape a show, which was usually about fourteen sketches in front of a live audience, and wrap it up around 1 A.M. Then we'd go to a bar nearby in Hollywood to drink.

Usually we'd end up at the Cat and Fiddle pub on Sunset to get something to eat and hang out. I had gotten to the point where I could go to parties and not drink, and I'd spent the summer in comedy clubs and stayed strong, so I'd go along with them when they went and never had a problem. But after a couple of months I was tired of that routine, so all it took was one taping to go not quite right in my eyes. I did not particularly love what I did that show. I was pissed off at the writing in the sketches. I was aggravated by my performance and every other fucking thing that an erratic performer and an asshole like me could get aggravated about. I was already fuming when we left the show, so watching everybody kick back with a drink in their hands was too much.

"Fuck it," I said under my breath. "I'm getting a goddamned Jack and Coke. I'll say it's a fucking Coke."

That was how I dealt with it, and nobody knew any better. I put down three Jack and Cokes in no time and since I hadn't had a drink in six months, I had the tolerance of a Girl Scout. My bad mood just evaporated and I started joking around, laughing with everybody, loaded and happy.

I'd gotten the party started and I wasn't going to stop there. An old friend from Jersey had come by the bar to see me, and since I knew he did drugs, I asked him if he knew where we could go and grab some blow. We left the party and went to some spot in downtown L.A., got a little coke, and did something I'd never done before: Smoked it. He put some of it all over this weed he had and rolled us a joint. I went completely fucking out of my mind because after not doing any drugs, not even a fucking aspirin, I spent the whole night drinking, doing coke, and smoking weed.

"Fuck it," I told my buddy. "Fuck them, fuck sobriety. This feels too fucking good."

As the perfect example of my inability to do anything in moderation, the next afternoon I made an announcement to my roommate, Orlando Jones.

"Look, man, I'm drinking again, and I know people don't want me to," I said. "I'm fine, it's not going to be a problem. I just don't want to lie about it to everyone."

"You know, I have to tell the producers and everyone, right?" he said. "They can't stop you, you're an adult and everything, but I have to tell them."

"Yeah, I know. It's gonna be fine."

The producers didn't agree with my prediction and asked me to see a shrink again. But I'd learned one thing in rehab: The shrink they'd sent me to last season was fucking awful.

"Look," I said to Fax Bahr and Adam Small. "I can control myself. I don't need a shrink. The shrink will make it worse. I don't want that hell in my life, and I won't let it get to that point. I can go back to just drinking casually. I'm serious."

"Well, we can't stop you, Artie," Fax said. "But we can watch you, and we will be watching you."

After the next three tapings, I went out and drank at the after-parties. I got loaded a couple of other times too on my own with friends apart from the show. I wouldn't admit it to myself, but the signs were there: I was slowly becoming unhinged emotionally again and covering it all with lie after fucking lie.

———

One of the better things that happened during Season 2 for me is that I discovered Christina Applegate. She was a guest host for an episode, and one of the skits she was in was a spoof of the game show *Jeopardy*. She was really cute, so she could have just stood there and we would have created sketches around her just doing nothing. But she was so cool that she really got into it and gave great performances. I used to think she was okay when I saw her on TV, but I never considered her hot. Once she was there and really taking part in everything, I was shocked at how fucking hot she was. I found myself so insanely attracted to her that it was hard for me to be on set with her. There's only one thing to do when you see a girl that you're convinced you hate and then she turns out to be hot: You have to immediately jerk off. Christina Applegate became one of those people for me, but it got even better: I was lucky enough to jack off about two feet away from her.

It happened innocently enough. After we finished rehearsing a sketch, I was up in my dressing room doing nothing when I heard two girls next door in the wardrobe room having a conversation.

"You can wear this one," the wardrobe girl said.

"Hmmm, I don't know," the other voice said. "Do you have something else?" I recognized this voice as Christina Applegate's.

Like a moth to a flame, I got up and stood right behind the door. Just the sound of her talking about the most boring, everyday aspects of her wardrobe was too much for me—I had to jerk off, right there, right then, right up against the door. Between her comments I muttered things in response as if we were making small talk.

"Yeah, I don't know," Christina said. "Maybe you've got a skirt?"

"Oh yeahhh," I'd whisper. "Yeah, a skirt would be good. Wear a skirt."

"Or we could do a dress. Do you have a red one?"

"Yeah, red. I like red. Wear the red one. Yeah."

Thank God they didn't hear me because I know I was louder than they were and we were not far apart at all. But being that close and not being discovered was the whole point of doing it. I've never told Christina this. Christina, I'm sorry. In all seriousness, I haven't seen Christina since, and I'm sure she's forgotten me altogether. But if anyone connected to her life reads this, I'd like to apologize to her officially. I wish her the best after all she's been through with breast cancer. Going public was very brave, and her actions will help a lot of people. In a moment of rare sincerity, I'd like to wish her good health and a long and happy life.

———

In November, when we were almost halfway through the season, we were able to get tickets through Quincy Jones' company to the first Mike Tyson-Evander Holyfield fight in Las Vegas. The cast was going to do the show that week and then fly to Vegas for three days. We were getting rooms at The Mirage, and we were going to go and have a great Vegas weekend—gambling and seeing a boxing match, something I'd always wanted to do. I was really excited.

After our taping, we headed to Vegas, checked into The Mirage, and started gambling and hanging out. I gambled through the whole first night, drinking the whole time, and somehow avoiding doing any coke. The next day, I slept late, then got up and went to brunch at 3 o'clock, then sat at the blackjack tables until I'd lost about three thousand dollars. I was broke. A guy sitting next to me at the table noticed my ticket to the fight.

"Hey, buddy," he said. "I'll give you twice face value for your ticket. You interested?"

"I might be," I said.

I was playing with a couple of friends who weren't from the show and didn't have tickets to the fight, so I thought I'd just hang out with them and watch the fight on TV, suddenly willing to let go of my dream of seeing a major fight live in Las Vegas for another chance at winning some chips back. Like every asshole who ever lost his kid's college fund on a card game, I decided to sell the guy my ticket for $500 in chips, more than twice its $200 face value, which I then proceeded to lose in two seconds.

"Hey, Artie, you ready for the fight?" David Herman asked me when he found me at the bar. "It's almost time!"

"Uh, yeah, Dave?" I said. "About that fight, I'm not going."

"What? Why?"

"I sold my ticket. I'm going to gamble."

"What are you going to do?" he said, really shocked. "That's ridiculous. What are you doing, Artie?"

"Nothing, man, it's cool. I didn't really need to see it live."

"What are you talking about? That's all you've talked about all week."

I was going down a bad road and it only went one way.

As a favor to Fox and Quincy Jones, at fight time my buddy Jimmy Palumbo and I were taken by our liaison at The Mirage to a private party at the hotel for high rollers. I took that as a cue to act like a high roller, so I immediately went to a phone and called a bookie I'd bet with for years back east. Tyson had 3-to-1 odds to win, and I thought Tyson was going to absolutely kill Holyfield, so I bet Tyson for $15,000, which meant that if he won, I won $5,000. I had about $20,000 in my account, so I told the guy I was good for it once I got back home.

We watched the fight in the most amazing room. There were smoking hot cocktail waitresses, flat screens everywhere, and these Nerf footballs that you could throw at the screen when you got mad. I took full advantage of those. But the environment couldn't distract me from the rising panic in my soul when Holyfield got past the third round. Holyfield had figured out Tyson's Achilles' heel and started to chip away at him by jabbing him then moving away before Tyson could connect. Tyson wasn't as aggressive as he normally was. I was sweating like crazy, really starting to worry as Holyfield slowly but surely took Iron Mike apart. When I say starting to worry, I should clarify: I was drunkenly screaming like a maniac who was out of his fucking mind. As we already know, Tyson lost. It wasn't even close.

I had lost about $3,500 playing blackjack and $15,000 to a bookie in Staten Island who wasn't going to give me the type of pass that old Bobo did back in the day. This guy did not fuck around. There was only one way to make this day even better: Score some blow. When shit happens with me, it steamrolls, so I was going all the way with this. I called my dealer in L.A. and he gave me the number of a guy in Vegas. I went to an ATM, which are easier to find in a casino than an exit to the street, and I withdrew about $500. I bought two eight balls and then I disappeared for a few hours.

I told no one where I was going; I just locked myself in my room and did coke. Everybody else passed out at the end of the night, but not me: I stayed up all night and ended up back at the tables. By dawn I had won a little bit and lost a little bit. When my castmates came down to the casino the next day to get some breakfast, they found me, still up, playing roulette.

"Hey, Artie," Dave Herman said. "You're up early. Getting in a few more rounds before we head to the airport?"

"Yeah, Dave, whatever. Don't distract me."

"We've got to get going, man."

"I need to win one more time, man," I said, raising my voice. "Just hold the fuck on."

I had been playing the same number, over and over, for a couple of hours: 25 red. I will never forget that number. I don't know why, because neither red nor 25 has any meaning for me, but that's what I was playing, and I was so focused on winning that when I lost I started screaming at the top of my lungs. My friends tried to calm me down but I wasn't having any of it; I got so worked up that the pit boss came over.

"Excuse me, sir, you need to keep your voice down," he said. "I'm going to need to ask you to leave the table. You've had quite enough."

"I'm not done yet, buddy," I said, looking at the guy like I'd tear his head off. "Let me play one more, then I'll go."

"I can't do that, sir, you're causing a disturbance."

"Let me play red fucking 25 right now. Then I'll fucking leave," I said, getting up in his face. "One more fucking chance, that's it. You wanna see a disturbance? Try to keep me from playing red 25."

The guy spoke into his headset: "Security, two guards to the roulette tables."

The pit boss stepped in front of me and kept me from putting my chips on red 25 for the next spin of the wheel.

"Listen, buddy, let me play everything on that fucking number, you asshole!"

"Can't do that, sir."

Of course as I watched the wheel spin around that last time, it landed on red 25. I would have won thousands of dollars.

"You fucking PRICK SON OF A BITCH FUCK!"

I lunged at the guy and when I felt the hand of a security guard on my shoulder I spun around and swung as hard as I could, connecting pretty well too. The guards descended on me, pinning my arms behind my back and roughhousing me all the way to the exit. My friends followed along behind them, promising to get me off the property and out of town right away. They had to pull out all the stops, mentioning our Quincy Jones connection, every single contact we had in the hotel, everything.

"If you don't get this piece of shit out of here right now," one of the security guys said to Dave Herman, "he's going to get himself hurt."

"We are going to the airport right now," he said. "I promise you."

Dave promised, but I didn't. As soon as the goons were gone I made a plan to go back in there and get my money back. As my friends begged and pleaded with me to leave, I argued belligerently.

"I'm going to get it all back! You're all fucking idiots! You need to let me go in there and get my fucking money! I know what I'm doing, goddamn it! The casino *stole* it from me—you fucking *saw it*! That was *my* fucking money!"

My friends Orlando, David, and Jimmy literally formed a human wall and would not let me get anywhere near the entrance. They just kept talking to me until the hotel got us a car and then they pretty much forced me into it physically. They knew if they just said fuck it and let me go in there, there'd be a team of security waiting who would be more than happy to take me to some hallway without cameras and "talk to me" while we waited for the police to come. Once again, those guys saved my life.

Sitting in the airport at the gate waiting for the flight back to L.A. was as depressing as it ever is, especially when you're catching

that 1 A.M. last flight out. The gate is right next to a Burger King, and more times than I'm proud to admit, I've sat there drunk and broke, with just enough money to get a Double Whopper with cheese, fries, and a shake, the continuous sound of the slot machines nearby ringing in my ears, mocking me. If you are prone to depression, that setting will do you in, believe me. Why would you be happy if you're drunk, broke, mocked by slots, and on top of that flying back to *Los Angeles*? Even when I was flying back there to a job on a fucking network show where I was making money hand over fist every week, I was never happy sitting there. It's the ninth circle of Hell.

Anyway, we got to the airport long before that last flight, but I was such a fucking mess that we missed two planes until that last one was our only option. From what I've been told, the minute we got to our gate, I passed out cold on the floor. Dave, Orlando, and Jimmy had to roll me out of the main walkway because no one could get by with their carry-on luggage. Together they managed to maneuver me over to the side of the waiting area but they couldn't wake me up in time for that flight or the next one. I arose from slumber soon after that, and when I did I went directly to the airport bar and started drinking, and then, naturally, I went to the bathroom to do some coke. I was so fucked-up, so obnoxious, and attracting so much attention that my friends were afraid we'd all get arrested. Those three guys stayed close by, treating me like the time bomb I was. I nearly got into a few bar fights that they had to break up and I almost swung at some guy in the bathroom who gave me a dirty look for very obviously doing coke in the stall.

Somehow they calmed me down enough to get onto the plane without any trouble, but once we were in the air I kept ordering drinks and going to the bathroom to do coke, so I became a problem once again. All I kept thinking about, on top of the fact that I'd just blown every bit of savings I'd managed to sock away, was that I had a network read-through the next morning where I had about seven sketches to learn. Once again I hadn't even looked at the script and knew I was way too coked up and drunk to do so when I got home—if I even knew where my script was. And whenever any of those shitty realizations dawned on me, I'd lock myself in the airplane bathroom, sit on that tiny little fucking toilet and do lines of coke right off the filthy stainless steel sink with people constantly knocking on the door.

I was reckless and I didn't care if I got caught. "Fucking catch me," I said out loud. "Put me in jail, I'm better off." I owed a serious motherfucker fifteen grand back in New York. I made eight grand a week but lately I'd been cashing the checks I had formerly sent directly to my mother and had been running around L.A. like a fucking jerk-off. After a year and a half on the show, I'd saved over $20,000, and in one weekend of complete assholeness, I'd spent almost all of it.

When we landed, I got a ride back to the apartment, and Orlando was off to some girl's house for the night. I was on such a lucky streak that I should have predicted this one: I didn't have my apartment keys. That might not seem like such a big deal, but we were living in downtown L.A., which now is a very nice, hip, up-and-coming neighborhood, but back in 1996, it was the kind of place were you could shoot somebody with a bazooka at 3 A.M. and no one would know about it for three days. Living there had its perks, of course: For $1,200 a month, Orlando and I shared a 3,000-square-foot loft with beautiful hardwood floors that we could play full-court basketball on.

It was 3 A.M. on a Sunday night; I had a read-through in Hollywood at 9 A.M. I was coked up, drunk, and locked out. And as if on cue, it started to rain. Thank God that David hadn't driven away yet, because I was definitely too drunk to drive. He took me to my friend Andie's house, and she let me crash there and got me up in the morning in time to make it to my read-through.

My guardian angel was looking out for me again that morning. I did well enough that no one from the network knew what kind of shape I was in, but my castmates certainly did—the dead giveaway being that I was in the same clothes I'd worn since Saturday night, looking homeless and gross. The network gave major notes on the sketches and the producers wanted us to work with the writers to get the material up to speed, but I blew that right the fuck off. I had shit to do.

I went home and called my coke dealer and told him that I needed some coke on credit because I'd had a shitty week and I'd pay him when I got my next paycheck. I sat in my apartment thinking about taking a shower, which I never took, and changing my clothes, which I never changed. I just watched sports and made a few drinks and once the guy showed up with the coke, I was right back on the roller coaster.

I went bar-hopping all along Sunset until I settled in at the Rainbow, the legendary rock hangout on the Strip, where I found a lot of people sympathetic to my situation. I could just sit there, drink a nice whiskey, do blow all night, and bullshit with whoever I met there. I stayed there until closing time, then went down the street to Denny's by Sunset Plaza and got some breakfast. I ended up staying there, drinking a bottle of whiskey, until my 9 A.M. call time, when I went right back to work to rehearse my sketches wearing the same clothes for what was now the fourth consecutive day.

After I'd left the day before, the staff discussed the state of my sobriety and took me out of the three sketches I was in. They decided to limit my liability to one sketch with Nicole Sullivan in which I'd play an annoyed guy. Nicole was doing her popular recurring character Vancome Lady. My familiarity with those sketches plus Nicole's talent meant I could go on automatic pilot. Plus, at that point, portraying an annoyed angry guy came rather easily to me. I was able to wing it, but it was becoming obvious to everyone that something was very wrong.

To my mind, though, it was another successful day at the office, so after I was done, at about noon, it was Miller time. I went down to Sunset, scored more coke at a bar I can't remember, then, in yet another stroke of genius, decided to put $3,000 on a Houston Rockets–L.A. Lakers game that was being played in Houston. I called my guy in Staten Island, and he had the Lakers giving the Rockets five points. That was the Lakers' first year with Shaq and I fucking hated them, so I bet the Rockets. I'm an idiot, of course—the Lakers beat them easily. There was another $3,300 (with the vig) gone, which brought my grand total in gambling loses for the week to about $21,800—my entire savings. First thing I did the next morning was call my mother to ask her to send me more money.

"Ma, I need you to Western Union me $5,000 from the savings account," I said.

"Artie, why? What happened?" she asked. "Are you in trouble?"

"No, Ma, listen, I'll be honest with you. We went to Vegas this weekend and I gambled a little too much and I forgot that I owed Orlando for the rent and a bunch of other bills I haven't paid."

"Are you telling the truth, Artie? That money is savings that you were never to touch."

"I know, Ma, I know," I said. "I'm just dipping into it this once. I'll replace the money after my next paycheck, I promise."

"Okay. Just this once."

I used the money to pay off my coke dealer and pocketed the rest in anticipation of spending the weekend the same way I'd spent the whole week. I went off to rehearsal, again wearing clothes that reeked of coke and booze. That day we had Harry Connick, Jr., on as a musical guest. No offense to him, but at that point I could not have given less of a shit about meeting him. Throughout rehearsal, whenever he was around, my castmates would say things like "Straighten up, Artie!" under their breath because I wasn't being very cordial. If it had been Mel Brooks I would have gotten my act together, but for Harry Connick, Jr.?

After we wrapped rehearsal, I sought out a little sanctuary back at the Rainbow, where I stayed bullshitting and drinking until I ran out of coke at about 9 P.M. I had a feeling that the wolves would soon be at my door, because everybody at work now knew what I was up to. I figured I'd cool them down by not getting any more drugs for a night or two and sleeping this bender off. To help me chill out, I got good and loaded on Johnny Walker and decided that I'd sleep over at my friend Carol Sacone's apartment, which was right up the street from the Rainbow.

Carol was one of the first people I became friends with when I moved to L.A. She is a really sweet, kind, and generous girl. She was totally drug-free, so I knew if I went over there to get some rest, I'd get it. It seemed like the smart thing to do: I had a 10 A.M. call time to shoot my sketch with Nicole the next morning, and West Hollywood was much closer to the studio than my apartment. I was actually proud of myself for thinking it through, because by staying at Carol's I'd be able to get more sleep.

Little did I know that everyone I knew in L.A. had been calling each other all day long. My friends on the cast and production team at *MADtv* saw signs of trouble—I wonder how?—but they didn't want to alarm my family back east. They knew I'd had trouble the year before, but they also knew that I'd worked hard to get it together, so they thought that some kind of confrontation might do the trick. Their plan was to like kidnap me and take me to a hospital for a few days where I could dry out comfortably under constant surveillance. Carol had called Orlando when she'd heard from me and they'd made arrangements for him to meet us there and take me to get some help.

When I walked into Carol's place, she took one look at my homeless guy get-up and almost burst into tears.

"Artie, I'm sorry, but I'm so scared about what you're doing to yourself," she said. "Orlando is too. We all are."

"Listen, Carol, I'm fine," I said. "You've got nothing to worry about. I just had a bad week." And the understatement of the year award for 1996 goes to Artie Lange, Jr.

"Artie, I will not let you do coke in my apartment," she said, teary-eyed. "I am really scared for you."

"Carol, I'm not gonna do any coke. I don't even have any coke."

"Artie, I mean it, you can't do any coke here. You're killing yourself."

"I'm serious, I don't have any coke. I just finished it like an hour ago. That's it for today, I promise. Tomorrow of course is another story, but I promise I won't do any coke here."

"Artie, please, let's go to a hospital."

"Why are you sick? Because I don't need to go to a hospital."

"Yes, you do, Artie," she said, pleading with me. "Let's just get you to a rehab center right now. Everything will be okay. Orlando is on his way, but let's just go now."

"Wait, what?"

I ran out of there like I was being chased by the cops, which I guess I was since Carol ran down the stairs behind me, begging me not to leave. She lived at the end of a dead-end street and as I ran to my car, all I could think about was that any second Orlando and God knows who else would be pulling up to block my escape. I was driving a shitty Ford Taurus at the time and I wish that someone had caught this on film, because it was the greatest thing I'll ever do behind the wheel. I jumped into my car, turned it over, floored it in reverse back down her street at like eighty-five, then slammed on the brakes, spun a 180, and floored it out of there. It was some *Dukes of Hazzard* shit that I would have never been able to do sober, nor have I ever tried to do in any condition since. It was fucking cool. All the more so because I didn't kill anyone.

I went right back to the Rainbow, where everybody was starting to know my name, and sat at the bar a few seats down from Andy Dick, who was there with a handler. Andy was jumping up and down, off the wall and out of his fucking mind on something. He had done some stuff on *MADtv* and we had some L.A. comedy scene friends in common. I'd only met him briefly, but I knew through our common acquaintances that he had substance problems similar to mine.

As he was sitting there yelling out crazy shit and his handler tried to get him to leave, this platinum blond stripper-looking chick walked over to him and started talking to him.

"Hey, Andy, I've seen you on TV, you're really funny," she said.

"Yeah thanks."

"Hey, give me some cocaine. I know you have some."

That stopped Andy in his tracks. "Get away from me!" he shouted, real loud. "Fuck you, get away from me! Right now!"

The chick left, but Andy only got more insane until his handler, who was this big Italian guy, decided that it was really time to go. For some reason the guy came over to me and asked me to help him get Andy to the car.

"What?" I said with the utmost disgust. "No! Why would I do that? I don't care about him, and I don't care about you. I don't want to help you get him in the car, fuck that. I don't care if he gets hit by a fucking car tonight. You're on your own. I've got problems of my own here, pal."

"Oh, really?" the guy said, looking particularly intimidating and annoyed. "You really not gonna help me out here?"

"No, I'm not."

He clearly could have beaten me up, but I just did not give a fuck. Someone killing me or beating me up would have been doing me a favor at that point.

After the guy managed to get Andy to leave, the same blond chick slid over next to me.

"Hey," she said. "Can *you* get me some coke?"

I took a long sip of whiskey. "I got money for it, but I don't know where to get any."

"I can take care of that," she said. "There's a guy outside who can get us coke if you pay for it. Can I hang with you?"

I took a good look at her. She must have been about thirty-eight or thirty-nine, and she had really bad acne scars on her face. She had a nice body—fake tits, though, and even faker platinum hair. All topped off with a $4 pink mini-skirt.

"Yeah, whatever, you can hang with me."

Outside the bar in the parking lot, she called over a guy who had been hanging out around the corner in the alley. I don't know if he was a bouncer, but he looked like one: just a big fucking, 6'4" biker guy in a leather vest and long black hair. He looked like major trouble.

"There he is," she said. "He's got the coke. Give him the money and he'll go get it."

"Oh, really?" I said. "Is that how it works? How will I know that he's not just going to take my money and rip me off?"

"No, I promise you he won't. You stay here with me. I'll go nowhere while he goes to get it."

I literally had very little to lose at that point, so I gave the guy some money and then he left. In ten minutes he returned—with nothing.

"Listen, man, I have to go somewhere else to get it, in a car."

"Dude, what the fuck?" I shouted. "I was not born yesterday, Tonto. You think you're gonna just take my fucking money like that? Think again, motherfucker."

From the look on his face, the guy obviously felt he'd been insulted. "Dude, this is NOT New York," he said. "Do not be rude or loud with me, asshole!"

I'm going out on a limb here, but I assume he figured I was a New Yorker because of my accent. Clearly he'd never been to New York; if he had, he'd have known that people from New York and New Jersey shout at each other when we interact, and it's never considered rude. I found it hilarious, however, that a coke dealer was correcting my etiquette. But I didn't laugh—instead I said, "Listen, asshole, fuck you, I don't need a geography lesson from you."

That did it. He pulled a knife from his jeans and started marching toward me. Everything was happening in slow motion: I was watching that knife coming toward me, knowing it would be the end of me. I did nothing. I remember thinking, *This guy might just kill me* . . . and then what? How much worse could dead be than what I was doing to myself?

When he was about a foot away from me, the fucking coke whore stepped right in front of the knife.

"Listen, he's okay, baby," she said. "Please don't do anything. He's a good guy and a friend of mine. I can vouch for him. He's just fucked up right now and he's really sorry."

I didn't say anything. I just kept staring at the knife in his hand.

"You're sorry, right?" she said.

"Yes, I'm sorry. Sorry, man."

That was enough for the guy. That chick saved my life.

The guy went off to get our coke, and we went back into the bar to drink more. I fully expected the guy to never come back, but he did, and even though he overcharged me for the coke, what was I gonna do? It wasn't exactly a situation in which you can haggle.

This chick lit up like a Christmas tree once we had the coke, so we got in my car and drove to a parking lot and started doing it. I learned rather quickly that she was willing to do a lot of different things for more coke and I'm not saying it to brag because, really, any guy with a bag of blow could have gotten this chick. It didn't take long for me to get her to give me a blow job. Considering the week I was having, I expected it to be awful or cause me injury somehow, but the truth was, this girl gave an *incredible* blow job.

"Listen, honey," I said to her. "That is wonderful, really great, but I should warn you, there's no way I'm ever going to come. I've got way too much coke in me."

"Leave that to me."

That whore was right: She got me hard somehow and just kept at it until, after a while, she made me come in that mind-blowing way that anybody who has ever had sex on cocaine knows about. Sex on coke goes one of two ways, with no compromises: You do it for hours and never come at all, or you do it for hours and if you do come, you have the most incredible experience of your life. This blow job took a while, but I have to say, it was the best blow job I have ever gotten in my entire life. Between the drug binging and the gambling losses, I'd had so much badness around me for the last week that I'd started to feel my life literally slipping away from me. That blow job was the only bit of relief, the only good feeling, and the only gift I'd been given in a week that felt like a year.

Afterward, we drove out to the ocean and parked in a lot on the Pacific Coast Highway. We sat there with some coke and a bottle of Jack and talked about life with a nice breeze blowing through the car. At one point, I got quiet because it finally started to dawn on me that I was lucky to be alive considering how self-destructive I'd been. I made one of those drugged up promises to myself that I'd get it together the very next day. Before the sun started coming up, I drove the chick back to the Rainbow.

There I was, faced with the end of night. For better or worse, it's a lot easier to face in New York, where the bars are open until 4 A.M., and you can stay up all night until it's time to get breakfast and then sleep all day. In L.A., you have to go home eventually, usually much earlier than you'd like. I knew I had to be at work at 10 A.M. I also knew that Carol would have talked to Orlando, so I couldn't go home. I still had more coke in my pocket, so I did some and thought about where I could spend the night.

My skit the next morning was with Nicole Sullivan, a total sweetheart and one of my best friends in the business. She had a place in the Laurel Canyon area of the Hollywood Hills that I'd been to a few times, and I figured that she was so nice and passive she'd let me stay over and go to work with her in the morning. I also figured that she wasn't going to try to force me into rehab on the spot; she'd be too afraid to confront me about drugs right then and there.

By the time I found her place and started knocking on her door, very loudly, it was about 3:30 in the morning. She lived on the second floor of a three-family house with this cute ABC executive above her and Christa Miller, who was then on *The Drew Carey Show* and later on *Scrubs,* on the ground floor. Christa, who is really good-looking, heard me knocking right away.

"What the hell are you doing, Artie?" she said. "Get the fuck out of here. I have to work tomorrow."

"Oh, yeah?" I said. "Gotta get in there early to learn those complicated lines on *Drew Carey*, eh Christa? Good luck with that."

"You're being an asshole, Artie."

"I'm serious. Good luck, I know it must be tough. If the pressure ever gets to you, I'll be happy to take over."

I kept busting her chops, refusing to leave until she was screaming at me loud enough to wake up Nicole.

"Christa, it's okay," Nicole said, coming down the stairs. "I'll handle this."

"Hey, Nicole, didn't you get my phone call?" I said.

"What?" she said.

"Let me stay here. We've got the same call time tomorrow. It'll be easier if we drive over together."

She did not look like she wanted any part of me, and I couldn't blame her. But she has a big heart.

"All right, Artie, but you're going to sleep now, it's late."

"Oh yeah, definitely. I need my beauty rest."

Nicole set me up on her living room couch with a pillow and blanket and went back to sleep. I did not. I started looking through her CD collection, playing music critic. The ones I liked I put in her stereo and played; the ones I didn't like I did coke off of, scratching them all in the process. Nicole had a beautiful view of L.A., so I threw the living room window open and sat there singing along to every song I played. Her neighbors, one of whom I believe was

Jennifer Aniston, referred to this evening as the "Bobby McGee Night," because the track I put the most heart into was "Me and Bobby McGee" by Janis Joplin. I was so moved by it that I screamed along at the top of my lungs and woke up the entire block.

I didn't care about the awful position I'd put Nicole in either. By morning I'd done almost all of my coke and drunk all of my Jack, so I went to her liquor cabinet and took out a bottle and broke it open just as she was making herself some coffee.

"So, you ready to go, Artie?"

"Yep, sure am. Let's do this."

"Why don't I drive?" Nicole said. "You can just chill out and ride with me."

"Nah."

"I think you should. You're drinking."

"Nicole, I'll be fine. I need my car. I'm fine to drive. Follow me, you'll see."

"Okay." Being a petite girl, Nicole couldn't really tell me anything I didn't want to hear.

I got in my car and took off with Nicole behind me. At the first light, at Lookout Mountain, she got in front of me so she could see how I was driving and be a kind of buffer for me. I followed her all the way down Laurel Canyon, this long, winding road, to the corner of Crescent Heights and Sunset in Hollywood. At the stoplight, Nicole turned around to see how I was doing. I'd passed out cold behind the wheel: I was sitting at the red light with my head back against the seat, my mouth open, sucking air, with a bottle of Jack in my hand and a bag of coke up on the dashboard. She ran over to my car.

"Artie!" she yelled. "Wake up! You should not be driving. Please, Artie, just come in my car. Let me drive."

"I'm fine!" I said. "Fuck you!" And I sped off.

Nicole got back in her car and called ahead to the studio to let them know what was going on. She said that I was with her, had been at her house all night, was as coked up as a human being could possibly be, and was already drunk at ten in the morning.

"You've got to get somebody there," she told our producers. "You've got to have some sort of intervention. He needs to be taken away because he's dangerous. He's driving, for Christ's sake!"

Nicole has apologized to me since then for doing that, but thank God she did, because she obviously saved my life. If she had not made that decision, I have no idea how or when this run would have ended. Dying was definitely a possibility. Jail and rehab were a much better choice, though at the time, I didn't feel that way.

Nicole and I arrived at the studio at the same time. I walked in wearing the same clothes I'd had on for five days. I saw the usual people who'd been there since 8 A.M. preparing the sound stage and others who were rehearsing. I had to collect my script in the writers' room, which was at the top of a long flight of stairs, and as I approached I saw our two executive producers, Fax Bahr and Adam Small, and three agents from William Morris, as well as my manager at the time, Ken Treusch. All of them were on their cell phones and when they saw me, they immediately got shifty.

I took one look at all of them at the top of the steps, turned around, and bolted. The steps gave me a good head start, but they were right on my heels. I ran out of the Ren-Mar Studios on Cahuenga, which is just south of Melrose (and where at that time they shot *The Practice*), and took off down the street. This is another scene from my life that I wish someone had captured on film: me, fleeing from three agents, two executive producers, one manager, and Orlando Jones on a footrace through Hollywood. It must have looked like the last sequence in *Ferris Bueller's Day Off*.

I ducked down residential streets, I hid in backyards. I jumped fences, I avoided dogs, and I ran by people lounging at their swimming pools, all with this procession of fuckers behind me. It was L.A., so people didn't freak out the way they would elsewhere—they just must have thought we were filming a movie.

The chase ended, and my own personal Waterloo began when I turned the corner of Melrose and Vine and ran into the Pavilions Supermarket, right by Winchell's Donut House. I'd made the mistake of thinking I'd lost them and was trying to catch my breath in the parking lot when they caught up to me. There was no way out but into the market.

My manager confronted me in the produce section.

"Artie, you've got to stop this, man!" he said. "It's going to be okay, but you can't keep running."

"Fuck you, Ken!"

I punched Ken as hard as I could right in the face, and he went down, falling into a display of grapefruit. Ken, if you're reading this, I'm really sorry, man. I know you were just trying to help.

As the other guys closed in on me, I started pelting them with oranges and pears. At that point I started throwing fruit at everybody in the store—old ladies, soccer moms, no one escaped my rage. Everyone in the produce section started to freak out and there was a kind of mad rush to the door. The supermarket manager called the cops. In the hysteria and thanks to my expert aim with an orange, I managed to evade my tormentors and ran out of there . . . right into the welcoming arms of two LAPD officers.

They were not at all happy about my food fight. They grabbed me, turned me around, and threw me on the hood of their car.

"Calm the fuck down! Now!"

"Fuck you!" I screamed at them. "Shouldn't you cops be beating the shit out of some African-American for speeding?"

They turned me around and I took a full swing at the cop. Thank God in Heaven that it was the lamest, most floppy-handed, drunken, coked-out whiff of a punch and it missed him by a mile.

That didn't stop him from slamming me back on the hood with extra gusto. A minute later I was cuffed, stuffed into the back of the squad car, and totally busted.

They searched me, found the coke, and now had a nice list of charges on me: resisting arrest, public drunkenness, possession of cocaine, and aggravated assault if anyone in the store decided to press charges. Talk about leaving a network show the wrong way: How about doing it in the back of an LAPD drunk wagon after throwing fruit at everyone in a grocery store. I sure made an exit too. As the producers and a crowd looked on, they dragged me away while I continued to scream at Orlando Jones until they closed the doors of the paddy wagon on me. For whatever insane reason, I blamed him for the whole thing.

"You fucking sold me out, you fucking bastard!" I shouted. "I thought you were my friend, you two-faced piece of shit! Fuck you!" For the record, Orlando had done nothing but be a great friend.

Since I was so obviously high on drugs, the cops were required to take me to the infirmary at L.A. County Jail to figure out what kind of shape I was in before they booked me. I eventually realized that I was in deep shit, so I did my best to make friends with these guys, telling them stories, apologizing, and making jokes. Lucky for me it worked, because when you're in the care of law enforcement, as they like to say, you really don't want to make it any harder on yourself.

The cops handcuffed me to a bed in the ER, and a doctor took my blood pressure and a blood sample then left the room. When he returned he looked like he'd just seen a murder.

"I have never seen that much cocaine in a living human being in my entire career in the ER and I've been doing this for a decade," he told my executive producers. "The guy has enough coke in his body to kill a horse."

He gave me a sedative, and I passed out, while the team that had followed me there came up with a game plan. I woke up hours later to one of the cops who had returned to the hospital.

"Listen, buddy, you're going up to L.A. County Jail for a few days," he said, genuinely concerned. "But you don't have to stay here if you can post ten thousand dollars in bail. We can get you out of here tonight." The cop was really doing me favor, and I'd like to thank him here once again.

"Can I make a phone call?" I asked. "I can get the money."

It was a no-brainer—I was going to call David and Orlando and ask them each to put up five G's. I knew they'd do the right thing, and they did: They said no.

"Artie, I'm not going to do it," David said. "I don't care if you never talk to me again, I'm not helping you get out."

"Dude, what the fuck? I thought we were friends! How can you leave me in jail like this when you've got the money?"

"Everybody would rather have you in jail than dead," he said. "If you're in jail, at least we know where you are and what you're not doing. You're out of control, man."

"Fuck you, man. Fuck Orlando. Fuck all of you! I never want to hear from you again."

And so, later that night when the doctors informed the cops that my vital signs had stabilized to something that resembled a normal human being, I was taken from the prison hospital to the local precinct jail and booked. A few hours after that, I was put on a bus to the L.A. County Jail with eight of the fucking shadiest characters you've ever seen—all of them were Crips, Bloods, and Latino gangbangers. Who the fuck knows what they were in for.

I got processed in L.A. County, which takes a couple of hours. They took my picture, booked me, did the anal cavity search alongside these other eight guys who'd also just recently been arrested.

Without a doubt that was the single worst experience I'd ever had, far beyond every other bad thing that's ever happened to me: I was lined up with these gang members, all of us right next to each other, and we each had to bend over as the cops went down the line fucking checking our asses, one after the other. After that meet and greet, they took me into a waiting area, to get our cell assignments.

In the waiting area, I was handcuffed for six hours to a twenty-year-old Mexican kid who told me that there was a hit out on him by the Mexican mafia. He was in for murder but claimed he'd been framed. The kid was not a bad guy. I feel like I can say that to some degree because, let me tell you, there wasn't much else to do but get to know him, sitting there joined at the wrist for six hours. Someone had stabbed this kid in the ankle, and he was waiting to be admitted to the infirmary.

By the end of this kid's life story, I was totally rooting for him. He came from a really tough background and had definitely done some bad things, but he was pretty nice. The kid's entire back was covered with a huge tattoo of Speedy Gonzales, done really, really well. That was how I broke the ice.

"God, that tattoo is great," I said. "Who did that?"

"You want a tattoo man?" he said. "I call my buddy for you."

"Um, yeah, that'd be great. I've been thinking about getting one. Maybe I will if he's that good."

After six hours, we were ready to go. They gave us an awful meat sandwich for lunch and told us that when we were done they'd take us into the general population. And then, all of a sudden, this twenty-year-old Mexican kid recognizes me from *MADtv*.

"Hey, buddy, I know you!" he says. "You're that guy from *MADtv*!"

He'd been saying that he thought he knew me on and off for the past six hours, but he'd never made the connection.

"This guy is on TV, man!" the kid shouted loud, and stood up, so now the whole group of guys and the guards were looking at him. "You're White Mama!" He started doing an imitation of my most popular character on the show—he did it pretty well too.

"Don't make me break my foot off in your ass! You're White Mama!"

He'd aroused the guards' attention, although they clearly weren't *MADtv* fans.

"Who is this guy?" one guard asked the Mexican kid. "What do you mean he's on television?"

"He's on TV, man!"

"Are you on TV?" he asked me.

"Yes. I'm a comedian on a show called *MADtv*, and I also do stand-up, and I've been in a few films, and . . ."

"You're a comedian, huh?" the guard said.

"Yes."

"Get this, everybody, we've got a comedian! Why don't you tell us a joke, comedian? Come on, make us laugh, funny man."

I felt like I was in a shitty remake of *Cool Hand Luke*. The guards in L.A. County, in my opinion, could have used an attitude adjustment.

"I don't hear you. We're waiting to laugh here."

"Yeah, sorry, buddy, I'm not feeling too funny right now."

This guy was a real motherfucker. "Oh, you got to have something if you do stand-up and you're a big comedian on television," he said. "Stand up and tell all of us a joke, we could use a joke."

He'd made such a scene that everyone in the cell started shouting: "Make us laugh, fucker! You'd better be funny, you motherfucker! C'mon, make us laugh!"

The guard was right there glaring at me. "So, what's it gonna be, huh?"

"Listen, I wish I could tell you a joke," I said kind of under my breath. "I just don't have one, okay?"

"What is that? The funny man doesn't have a joke!" he said real loud to my fellow inmates. "What good is a funny man without a joke? Now why don't you tell your friends here what you just told me."

"Yeah, what the fuck, comedian! Tell us a joke!"

"Go ahead, pal," the guard said. "Tell 'em."

I stood up and tried to look as tough as I could in such a humiliating situation. "I really wish I could entertain you," I said, "but I don't have any jokes right now."

"You better think of one before I kick your ass, motherfucker!" someone shouted from somewhere behind me.

"Yeah, funny man, you better think of something quick," the guard said, grinning a real cocksucker, son-of-a-bitch grin at me.

I sat down and everyone booed.

"That's all right," the guard said. "We've got a lazy son-of-a-bitch funny man here tonight." Everyone started laughing, of course. "Now what kind of comedian is that? You bring a couch on stage with you?"

This guy was killing and I really didn't see why I needed to jump in, so I just sat there refusing to tell a joke and eventually they stopped fucking with me. I've never felt so mad about being recognized as a celebrity, but it turned out to be a blessing in disguise.

In jail, at least in L.A. County, every inmate gets a white wristband with their number and name. But if you are one of three things—a celebrity, a snitch for the police, or a murderer—you get a red wristband, which means that you're given your own cell, complete with your own personal shitter. If you have a red wristband, you don't have to deal with the general population at all. That is what my Mexican friend was trying to get for me, but the way it was going, it looked like the opposite was going to happen: Not only was I heading to general population, but now every single person knew me on sight and would definitely be fucking with me.

This one asshole guard, for one, showed no signs of letting up. "You heard of this show he's on?" It doesn't say a lot for *MADtv* that no one aside from the Mexican kid had heard of it. It says even less for the L.A. jail system that this guy was determining whether or not I qualified as a celebrity by polling the other inmates.

"Fuck that, man, I ain't heard of that show!"

"He ain't nobody! Fuck him! He ain't funny neither!"

"I never heard of that fucking show, man."

The Mexican kid kept telling the guards that I was definitely on TV, and he was apparently convincing: I got a red wristband when it was time for us to leave the holding tank and go to our individual cells.

"You got red, man," Speedy Gonzalez said. "That's good, man, you're going to get your own cell."

Before that could happen, though, it was time to shower as a group, which was monitored by the guards so nothing horrible happened. It didn't matter. I was convinced that my life was going to end at any second, but if you're expecting a lame "dropped the soap" joke here, you should go read a Wayne Brady book. The shower was uneventful, but my post-shower shit was not: All of the toilets were right next to each other, so while I was doing my business my knee touched my neighbor's, who was a very large, formidable black man. When he evacuated I could literally feel the shit tumbling out of him.

"I must have died today," I thought, "because now I am in Hell."

As romantic as it was when my knee grazed the knee of that heavyset black gentleman, it didn't last long. We were corralled out of there and divided up according to our bracelets. I was led into a waiting area as the rest of the inmates filed by.

A Hispanic kid gave me one hell of an evil eye as he walked past. "You got a red band, man? What does that mean, *jefe*?"

"It means I'm going to be in solitary," I said.

"Oh yeah? Well, you don't look like no celebrity I ever seen. And you sure don't look like no murderer. You too much of a pussy to be a murderer. So there's only one thing you could be then. You a fuckin snitch, ain't you?" He turned around to announce to the line of about thirty-five guys: "Hey! This pussy's a fuckin' snitch!"

"I'm not a snitch, man, I promise you," I said, but it was no use.

"Well you ain't Tom Cruise, is you, snitch?"

"Well, actually, I did do a scene with him in a movie called *Jerry Maguire* that's coming out," I said. "He was a dick." It's true, but let me finish this story before I get to that one.

"Oh yeah?" The kid eyeballed me, trying to figure out if I was lying. "So what kind of celebrity are you?"

I started reeling off my resume to this guy like I was trying to court him to be my agent. "Well, in addition to *MADtv*, I am also a regular at several comedy clubs in the New York area, and I have been on numerous television commercials."

A guard came over and broke that up, and finally I got to my cell, where I remained for the next three days and four nights. At some point, the guy in the cell next to me informed me that he was going to be in that small rectangle of a room for another nine years. I felt claustrophobic, but I couldn't begin to imagine what he was going through because he looked like he was about six foot nine. He didn't have much to say other than that he'd found Christ.

Make no mistake, the food in prison is truly awful. Lunch was usually unidentifiable cold cuts on mushy bread and dinner was usually some kind of nondescript pile of shit like soggy fucking noodles covered in brown gravy. I remember getting dinner that first night and not eating any simply because they dared to call that pasta. Like some kind of guinea Gandhi, I protested by refusing to eat it. In the morning, they served us a couple of eggs with grits that wasn't too bad.

The next day I asked the guard to let me make a phone call. I wanted to check my answering machine at home because it had been four days, and I was worried that the bookie in Staten Island might be wondering when he was gonna get all of his fucking money. I was scared that if he didn't hear from me he'd find out where my mom lived or hurt my sister. I filed out of my cell in my orange fucking jumpsuit and went down the hall to get on line to use the phone. I had a guard with a shotgun next to me and two gangbangers waiting behind me to use the phone.

There is one thing for sure in my life: When it rains, it fucking pours. As I sat there with just about nothing going right, I listened to the first message:

"Hey Artie, it's Cameron Crowe, your director on Jerry Maguire. *Long time no see, man! I hope everything is going really well. Listen, Artie, I'm really sorry, and I wanted to tell you this personally because you were really great and did such a great job, but we had to cut your scene from the movie. The movie is coming out in two weeks, and I didn't want you to wonder what had happened, so I had to call. It was nothing you did at all—you were great—the scene just didn't fit in the film in the end, so we had to cut it. I'm sorry, man. I just didn't want you to go to the film with friends and family and expect to see it and not know that it didn't make it in. But listen, I think you're great and you did a great job and I definitely think we will work together in the future. Take it easy, Artie. Bye bye."*

Eight months earlier, at the end of Season 1 of *MADtv*, I'd booked a small part in *Jerry Maguire* and shot a scene with Tom Cruise and Kelly Preston, both of whom were total douche bags. It was the scene in which their two characters break up and she punches him in the face. It's at the NFL Draft, and I play an annoying radio guy who interrupts this moment they're having and says, "Hey, Jerry, good to see you! Tom Jackson from WHDZ here. Are you going to the Big Tequila Volleyball Tournament later? It's gonna be great!" Then Tom Cruise gives me a fuck-off look, I pause, realize that I am being an asshole, and kind of creep away. It was a funny, awkward, jokey moment in that scene that didn't make it.

It probably would have been a forgettable moment, but what I'll never forget is how fucking insanely rude Tom Cruise and Kelly Preston were. This is before he started couch jumping, but let me tell you, that guy Cruise was already nuttier than a fruitcake. He had this thing about getting his energy to the perfect place before he did a scene, and he would ramp up by jumping rope. He had some guy, who was on the payroll for the film, standing there holding his jump rope off set. Cruise would jump rope with that insane grin of his until he was ready, then he'd signal to Cameron Crowe, toss his rope wrangler his jump rope, step in the scene, Crowe would yell, "Action," and Cruise would go right into it. It was incredibly distracting—and I only had two fucking lines to say to the guy! While I was standing there watching this nonsense, I kept wondering what the fuck he did to ramp up for a love scene.

Anyway, we did the scene maybe twenty times, and even though I was standing literally five feet from those two, once Cameron Crowe stopped the scene and the production guys went about moving the cameras and stuff, which could take anywhere from two to twenty minutes, neither of those fuckers would acknowledge my existence. No eye contact, nothing. I tried to make small talk, and Kelly Preston acted like she didn't hear me. And it's not like either of them was playing some difficult character where they couldn't break their focus. Please, they were reciting lines, that was it. Neither one is Laurence Olivier.

I did almost punch Tom Cruise, which I probably should have—it might have knocked some sense into that lunatic. I've always shown respect for my writers and their hard work by making sure that when I perform anything, I do the script as written. Particularly in a big-budget movie directed by a guy as cool as Cameron Crowe, I made damn fucking sure that I had my lines memorized correctly. Now, Cruise is the kind of guy who likes to change the dialogue that morning in the makeup chair with no regard for anyone, from the director to the screenwriter to anybody else in the world, who on average are probably a lot smarter than he is. So Cruise had changed what he was going to say and how he was going to play this scene and no one had informed me. Whatever I was doing by sticking to the script was severely going against his pacing, and judging by the whole jumping-rope bullshit, pacing was a big deal to that nutjob. We did a few takes and on each one he seemed to be getting more and more steamed, but he wouldn't look me in the eye or talk to me between takes to tell me what the problem was. He'd only talk to Cameron and say things like: "Cameron, that take was off, the timing was wrong."

Finally, he just exploded. He looked at me and screamed, "Can you come in quicker, please?!" Everyone got quiet and looked at me in disgust.

Cameron called for a break and pulled me aside.

"Listen, man, it's not you," he said. "You're doing it exactly as written. Let me go talk to him. He changed his part, so doing it according to the script is throwing him off. You're doing a great job. Just come in quicker, and it'll all be okay."

"Of course, no problem," I said. "I wish I'd known. I'm so sorry I upset him." Not too sorry to punch his fucking dumb grin into the back of his head, however.

Once Cameron got Tom back on set, we did the scene according to Tom's invisible pacing meter and that was it, I was done.

What a legendary moment in my acting career. To Cruise's credit, at the end of the take he yelled, "Thank you!" at me.

Kelly Preston wasn't any better. She chit-chatted with Tom between takes, but I might as well have been a tree with a pile of dogshit at the base of it. Her elitist attitude extended to every facet of her existence, by the way, which I'd found out the day before. I'd made friends with one of the P.A.'s, and we were playing catch outside the location. As anyone who has ever had anything to do with the production of a feature film can tell you, there is a hell of a lot of downtime. So me and this guy were tossing a baseball when this little dark-haired kid, probably about four years old, came running toward me, so I rolled the ball to him. He picked it up and was kind of staring at it and looking at us, when out of nowhere, like some kind of Aryan superhero, this insanely hot, tall blonde ran over.

"Vat are you doing?" she snapped at me. "You could have keelled him!"

"What are you talking about?" I said. "We just rolled the ball over to him. What's your problem?"

"You threw it at him!" As she was saying all of this she pulled the ball out of the kid's hands, tossed it on the ground like it was a stick of dynamite, and picked him up really fast. The kid got scared, more from her roughhousing than anything we did, and started to cry.

"See what you've done!" she said.

"What the fuck is wrong with you?" I said.

"We're really sorry, ma'am," my friend said. "It won't happen again." He gave me a look that said, *Shut up, now.*

"It had better not. No one is to speak to or touch Jett." Then she turned and stormed off with the now bawling kid in her arms.

"Jett?" I said, laughing. "Who the fuck names a kid *Jett*?"

"John Travolta and Kelly Preston do, man," my friend said.

Apparently all of the P.A.'s had been given very strict instructions on how to interact with Jett, Kelly, and, when he came to the set, John. Let me tell you, playing ball with any of them was definitely not on the rider. Treating them like outer-space royalty apparently was.

"You don't understand, man, this is really, really bad," the guy told me. "We are under strict orders not to talk to them, look at them, hand them anything. And their kid is so off-limits you have no idea. We'll be lucky if we last the day here." Turns out we were lucky.

In any event, one of the few things that got me through the hours alone in my jail cell was that bit part in *Jerry Maguire*. I figured that I was done for as far as employment by any major television network went, but at least I had a part in a legitimate, big-studio, big-budget, mainstream film—even if it was a bit part. I could keep doing that, I told myself, and build a film career.

I had expected an angry bookie threatening my life and my family, but hearing Cameron Crowe's nice, friendly message was much worse. The fact that he'd cared enough to remember to call me and tell me himself, two weeks before the film opened, when he was probably busier than I could imagine, touched me so much that it took all I had to fight back the tears. It wasn't just the bad news that made me want to cry, his kindness about it did too. Thank God I controlled myself, considering the setting.

"Hey, what's the matter?" the guard said when I hung up. I might not have cried but I couldn't hide how horribly disappointed I was.

"I'm just having a bad day," I said. "Make that a bad week."

"Hang in there," he said. He was one of the nice ones.

After a few days, I got myself a really good lawyer, Jerry Scotto, who got me out of prison. I got Scotto's name through an assistant director at *MADtv*, Tara Passander, who is beautiful and kind and another guardian angel for me out there in L.A. And even though

I had the biggest crush on her that you can imagine, she's another one I haven't seen or spoken to in twelve years. I hope she's doing well, whatever she's doing.

Once I got out of jail, I flew directly to New Jersey and entered rehab. I wasn't going to fuck around this time, so I did everything they said to do, including taking these antidepressants prescribed by the shrink. I was completely committed to the program and the course of action. As a result of that, my lawyer had me come back out to L.A., got my case moved to the front of the docket—all for a total of eight grand—and got me probation and time served. The guy was so good that in eighteen months he was able to wipe the arrest from my record. I was allowed to return to New Jersey for rehab and was scheduled to reappear the next January so the court could see how I was doing.

The cast at *MADtv* was told that I was back home in rehab and would be returning to the show when I could. That's what they said and that's what they told me, but behind the scenes they had other plans. It's okay—I owe them my life: the people at *MADtv* saved me from killing myself, without question. Fax Bahr and Adam Small, John Blanchard, Quincy and Salzman, the producers, the creators of the show, I respect them all, I love them all, I miss them all, and I appreciate everything they did for me. In rehab, I saw that Hollywood life as something in my past. I thought my professional career in showbiz was over and if I were lucky, I'd be taken back by the longshoremen at Port Newark again. I had my shot on a big network show, and after a couple of turbulent years, I'd blown it.

Little did I know that whatever angel had seen me through wasn't done with me yet. That guide was still on my shoulder, even though I'd put him to the test. He'd had to arrange for the whore to save me from the crazy drug dealer, for my castmates to stop my attempted suicide, and for some Chicano to recognize me in jail.

And he wasn't getting paid overtime. Some boss I am—he wasn't even going to get much of a vacation. I was far from out of the woods, so this guy had to come up with something. He's creative, so he goes big: The next thing he had in store involved a legendary major motion picture studio and the official beginning of my career on the big screen.

Baby Gorilla
in the Mist

'm not going to be all *wah! wah!* about it, but after my stay

in rehab in November 1996, following my suicide attempt

and then my arrest, I was deeply depressed. I'm sure what

contributed to that was my stay in the psych ward at Columbia

Presbyterian Hospital in Manhattan. If you've never been there

or never heard of it, trust me, it's a big deal. The fact that I'd

fucked up so badly right when I had so much going for me

really weighed heavily on my mind. Being sober and facing

things for the first time was incredibly hard for a guy who'd

buffered anything difficult that had ever happened in his life

with lots of alcohol and drugs.

I returned to my mom's house in New Jersey and immediately locked myself in the basement and became bedridden with depression. I slept about eighteen hours a day and felt like my life was over. The only thing I did regularly was go see the shrink that the *MADtv* producers and Quincy Jones had recommended: Dr. Hugh Butts, whose office is on the Upper West Side of Manhattan. He is a great, great doctor, and he did his best with me. I trusted him, so on his suggestion I checked into the psych ward and spent the Christmas season and the first few weeks of January 1997 there. It was, hands down, the most depressing period in my life. I had my own room and my own toilet, but I shared a common shower with the other people on the floor. My room actually had a great view of the George Washington Bridge, but I didn't care. The only thing I looked forward to was nighttime, when I was allowed to take a couple of Ambien to get to sleep. All I wanted was that little high I'd get from the pills before I crashed.

They woke us up at 7 A.M. The first person I'd see was an orderly, a black guy with a speech impediment. Every day he'd come into my room and say, "Artie! Breakfast." But the way he said it, it sounded like, "AR-IE! Breath-fresh." I always got a kick out of that. Mostly I played Scrabble with people who looked like they'd just committed mass murder, which was very intimidating. You try telling a kid from the South Bronx with severe anger issues that the word "mother" isn't spelled "mutha." If you find yourself in that situation, take my advice: Give him his triple word score, smile, and wait for group therapy to start.

I was in there for ten days with a one-day break for Christmas dinner when I was released into the custody of my mother and sister for three hours. We ate at my Uncle Tommy's, and that was *really* depressing. My mother and sister came to pick me up at the hospital, and they stood by the window trying to make the best of the situation by observing how nice and relaxing it was to look out at the water. But we weren't alone—a nurse and a doctor were required to be there to watch me as I shaved. I'd once tried to commit suicide, so I was on suicide watch and could not be left unattended with so much as a safety razor in my hand. That was too much for my mother, and who could blame her: It was Christmas, and she was picking up her son from the psych ward. My mom is stoic, and she'd been strong through a lot over the years, but this was too much. She burst out crying, and a second later so did I.

In January, I was returned to my family's custody. I locked myself back in the basement, crippled with clinical depression. Anyone who has suffered from it or is familiar with it knows that it can incapacitate you mentally and even physically. In my case, I literally could not move. My depression felt like a wet blanket over me, keeping me from getting out of bed. This was the second time I'd been through this in two years, the first time being the period leading up to my suicide attempt. Looking back a year later, I could see that I was definitely clinically depressed—I'd just self-medicated with mountains of coke. This time I had nothing holding the depression in check and I couldn't handle it at all.

For the next two months, I gave my mother every excuse in the world about why I could not get out of bed, could not get to the shrink, could not go back to rehab or do a stay in the psych ward. I couldn't cope with any contact, however small, with the outside world. Some friends who had known me forever tried to see me because, like my family, they were worried about me. I told my mother to send them all away. I wasn't doing much to help myself because I also refused to take my prescribed medication. I'd taken the antidepressant Paxil during my last few weeks with Dr. Butts; I'd taken it the year before, and it had helped me. But like everything else in my life, I just dropped it.

After a few weeks of lying there in a stupor, I finally just got sick of being that way. Without drugs or anything else helping me, I woke up one day and suddenly I'd fucking had it. All the things I berated myself for—the suicide attempt, ruining my career, hurting my family—none of it was going to be made better by staying in bed. I had to make it better through action. The line from *The Shawshank Redemption* came to mind that day and never left: "Either get busy living or get busy dying." I picked the first one.

I got myself into New York City to see my manager, Peter Principato, after I'd rejoined the living. He had been my commercial agent at William Morris for a couple of years in the early nineties. Unfortunately, drugs destroyed my relationship with him, but Peter always believed in me, and years later when I left *MADtv*, Peter asked me to be his first client after he left the agency to become a manager. I will always be grateful to Peter for that. We're not together anymore, but Peter is a good guy and there's nothing I wouldn't do for him.

Sitting in Peter's office back in March 1997, I got the bright idea that we should call *MADtv* producers Fax Bahr and Adam Small and beg them to let me come back to the show. I was in no condition to attend a matinee of *Bambi*, let alone get back to work doing sketch comedy. But Peter was wise enough and knew me well enough to let me make that call. It was a bridge I had to cross. We got on a conference call with them and he sat there listening as I shamelessly begged them to let me come back to finish the last episodes of Season 2. I promised them that I'd kick ass like I'd done before. I promised them that my drug problems were behind me, and I swore up and down that they'd never have to worry about my mental health again. I told them all the things I'd been doing to get back on track, I told them about the psych ward, and I assured them that all I needed to do to get on my feet was to work again.

"Art, we love you," Fax said. "And for that reason we have to insist that you go through formal rehab. You've gotten through the depression, but you've got to put your demons behind you."

They were right of course, and they stayed on the phone with me for hours until I finally agreed with them. Once we hung up, I had Peter make arrangements to get me into rehab. We settled on a place my mother knew of in New Jersey called Honesty House, which boasted a very high success rate and handled a lot of celebrity clients. My mother's boss of twenty years, Joel Goldberg, ran a company that did psychological profiles for large corporations including the New Jersey Nets and the New York Giants. He was always a great help to our family and very, very generous with us after my father fell. Joel made some calls and got me into Honesty House right away. I was much more open to the process than I'd been before, but my goal still wasn't getting well. I was just hoping that after a few weeks I'd get a good report card from these people and I'd be able to take it to *MADtv* and get my job back.

Coming out of that deep depression made me feel like a bear coming out of hibernation. It was early spring and starting to warm up and I felt like I was emerging from a long, dark sleep. My schedule at Honesty House was group therapy for four nights a week from 6 P.M. to 9 P.M. and one-on-one therapy once a week with Kevin, our group leader. Kevin was an older guy who'd been clean and sober for thirty-five years and believed completely in the Alcoholics Anonymous 12-Step Program.

I followed the steps diligently for two straight months and did all of the group sessions. All in all, I got a lot out of it. Then I got to the step where you have to write a note to your drug of choice that ruined your life and basically tell it good-bye. You are supposed to think of it as another human being you have wronged. This is where the process broke down for me because I couldn't keep a straight face, sitting there writing a letter to cocaine. In the end, here's what I came up with:

Dear Cocaine,

*You are a guy that I loved to hang with, and we had a
lot of fun together, but you lied to me quite a bit. You told
me that I could stay up for five straight days with no
problem, you told me that I was way more interesting when
I hung with you, and that everyone around me liked to hear
me talk incessantly for hours on end. You also lied to me
on several occasions when you told me that I could beat up
several bouncers at bars. That was completely untrue, and
I got stitches and now have scars on my head to prove it.
So good-bye, cocaine. Take it easy.*

Artie

When I handed it in, Kevin said, "Well, obviously you are being funny and not taking it seriously. This is not great, Artie. Do it over."

It took me about three drafts to come up with something sincere enough so Kevin wouldn't think I was making fun of the exercise. I still was, of course, because I still think it's a silly way to make a point, but if it works for some people, I'm not going to fault it. I would have written anything at all at that moment, because I was desperate as hell to get back on TV.

Group therapy was a pretty interesting mix of about fifteen people. There were girls and guys, older and younger, with one or two hot chicks in the mix. No matter who was talking, you heard amazing stories. I do a joke in my stand-up based on that, because all I kept thinking as I listened to them was, "God, a year ago, this would have been a great fucking party. Now, it's just a bunch of self-righteous people telling each other not to do drugs or drink." That's the truth. One of the hot chicks, this beautiful girl with a really nice set of tits, told us how six months earlier she used to get so out-of-her-mind drunk that she'd jump on tables, rip her shirt off, and yell and scream for no reason whatsoever. She ended her story by saying, "I'm glad those times are behind me, and I wish all of you keep from drinking or doing drugs as I have." All I kept thinking was, "Really? I wish it was six months ago." I made the mistake of whispering that to the guy sitting next to me, and we both laughed and got in trouble. I felt like I was back in school, trying to get laughs and getting yelled at for it.

At the end of my two months of rehab, I got the official word from *MADtv* that they weren't going to pick up my contract for the next season. I'm convinced it was because of the report they got from Honesty House, because truth be told, I fooled around here and there and didn't finish a few of the steps. Unless it's baseball or comedy, I've never really been much of a team player. But it meant that the *MADtv* chapter of my life was officially over.

I had gotten fired from *MADtv* for my coke problem, and now I had a reputation in Hollywood. But in those two years on television, I'd managed to do enough decent work to make a five-minute reel of tape that featured the full range of my sketch material. As I finished up my therapy and got myself back together, my agent and manager started sending it out to people so I could get booked for stand-up and other work.

Once again someone was looking out for me because the tape got hits right away. I got called to screen-test for two network sitcoms. I couldn't really believe it: Being offered screen tests is a big deal because it means you don't have to do preliminary auditions. I did five auditions for *MADtv* and was lucky to get that far. Screen tests bypassed all of that. It was a message saying that I was good enough to be flown out to L.A. to audition directly for the casting director, director, producers, and everyone important. Those calls boosted my confidence astronomically.

I started doing a lot more stand-up at all of the New York City clubs—The Comic Strip, Stand-up NY, Catch a Rising Star, New

York Comedy Club, and Carolines. Between the comedy and the therapy, I felt like I was getting all of my issues out there and dealing with the shit. I felt ready to screen test for those two shows, and I was completely excited about it. I remember sitting down with my mother one day, feeling like I'd crossed a bridge.

"Ma, I think I might be back quicker than I thought."

She looked at me for a long minute.

"You are back, Artie," she said. "But go slowly this time."

The therapist in my group sessions thought I was moving along much too quickly, but I thought he was full of shit. In my mind, the only thing keeping me from being me again was staying out of the game. I felt rested and ready to get back into show business. And considering the interest, show business was ready for me.

While my agent negotiated my deal for the screen tests, my manager got a call from Norm MacDonald. I had never met Norm before, but I was a big fan of his. I loved his stand-up, and while I was at *MADtv* David Herman and I used to imitate all of his best jokes from *SNL*'s "Weekend Update." His style and delivery were perfect. In 1997, Norm was the biggest star on *Saturday Night Live*, literally the face of the show. So when my manager told me that I was asked to audition as the second lead in a buddy comedy starring Norm, I was ecstatic.

The script was written by Frank Sebastiano, a brilliant writer who would become my collaborator on *Beer League*, Norm MacDonald, and the great Fred Wolf, a former head writer for *Saturday Night Live* and one of the funniest guys I have ever met in my life. I belly-laughed at a lot of the jokes when I read the script. Norm's voice came right through, and I totally loved his best-friend character, Sam McKenna. When I finished it, I called my manager and told him I had to do this movie. It was called *Dirty Work*.

It was a big deal—an MGM feature, produced by Robert Simonds. For those who don't know, Bobby Simonds produced

Problem Child, which made a lot of money, as well as all of Adam Sandler's films: *Billy Madison*, *Happy Gilmore*, and *The Wedding Singer*. On top of having a huge producer involved, a major studio, plus Norm, the biggest star on *SNL*, I found out that the guy who'd signed on to play my character's father in the film was Jack Warden. Hands down, Jack is one of my heroes. Chris Farley was also signed on to play a supporting role, and Don Rickles had a cameo. Chevy Chase had a cameo too. There was even talk that Adam Sandler and Howard Stern might also do cameos. To top it all off, Bob Saget, a guy I'd admired but had never met, was directing. It was a major project, no doubt about it.

"They want to test you," Peter, my manager, told me. "We've got to get you on a plane immediately. You're going to fly out there and screen-test with Norm in the room. Possibly Bob Simonds and Bob Saget too. They're going to videotape you to show you to the powers that be at MGM. You are going to do it in Bob Saget's offices in Santa Monica." He paused for a moment. "Artie, you need to tell me if you can do this, and you need to be very honest with me and with yourself."

"Peter," I said. "Look at me. I *promise* you, I can do this. There is nothing else I want to do in the world but this." I meant it 100 percent. He could see it in my eyes.

"Okay, Artie. Then let's do it."

When I walked into the *Dirty Work* audition, I wanted that job more than a hobo wants a steak. If I got it, as far as I was concerned, I would be getting back into the business in the best possible way. This film was going to feature just about all of my heroes in comedy—working with them was my dream homecoming.

I was nervous as hell when I got out to L.A. because the last time I'd been there, aside from my court appearance, I'd been arrested, high out of my mind, and throwing produce at my agents and producers at a supermarket. So that was on my mind, but I made up for it by preparing well. Bob Saget, Norm MacDonald, and Norm's assistant Laurie Joe, who became one of my favorite people in the whole world, were in the room for my audition. They taped my performance, and I thought I did well, except for the fact that during the whole thing Norm never got up from the couch. He just lay there the entire time saying things like, "Hey man, thank you for coming out, good to see you." What was even more confusing was that Saget was like a hyper kid—jumpy, happy, and enthusiastic the whole time. He was probably as excited as I was because a chance to direct a talented group like that was a big opportunity for him.

The next day Saget, Norm, and Bob Simonds called me on a conference call in my hotel room.

"So?" I said. "How was it?"

"Well," Norm said, taking this dramatic pause, "it was great!"

Then Saget chimed in: "Yes, it was, Artie. You were great!"

To be honest with you, I had no idea what that meant at all. Maybe they liked it, and they were trying to let me down easy. Maybe they knew about my past and didn't want some kind of freak-out on their hands. That was all they told me, then they hung up.

I sat there staring at the wall wondering what the hell they'd just told me when the phone rang again.

"Hey man, it's Norm," he said. "Listen, we have to see some other people, but you did an amazing job."

"Well, thanks, man, that means a lot."

"We can't say anything for sure yet, but let's just go shoot some pool in Hollywood tonight."

We were all in Santa Monica, so they picked me up, and we drove to the pool hall, which was about thirty minutes away on Fairfax and Sunset. Once I got in the car with Norm and Bob, the real meaning of the outing became crystal clear.

"So Artie, we want you to know that we want you in this movie," Norm said.

"You were great today, man, and we think you're perfect for the part," Saget said.

"Well, I want to do it, there's no question of that," I said.

"That's great," Norm said. "There's just one thing. You don't have the greatest track record."

"Guys, I will be as good as a second-grade ballerina," I said. "You will not see me doing drugs, and there is nothing I won't do to make sure that if I get this part, I won't lose it."

"That's great, Artie," Norm said. "That's what we want to hear. And I think you really mean it."

In typical me fashion, I was feeling so good that by the time we got to our destination I was ready to ruin it. What I'm about to tell you is so embarrassing, but it is the reality of being an addict. We got to the pool hall, we started shooting pool, we had a few drinks, and here's how stupid I got.

"So Artie, we know about the drugs," Saget said, eyeing me and my third Jack and Coke, "but how are you with the booze?"

"Oh man, fine," I said. "That was never the problem. Just coke, man. I can drink, it's totally fine. It never got in the way."

I'm not sure if they were comforted by that—I doubt it—but as if to prove my retarded point, I started drinking and I started winning at pool and because of that, after a while I felt like I had the part, no problem. I got happy. I did about seven shots of tequila in front of them. There was no one there to come out of the corner and smack me on the head to remind me that I was one step away from getting or losing the part in the movie, so maybe getting brazenly drunk in front of these guys wasn't the best idea. No, I was feeling so confident about my position with them that after I slammed my last shot, I didn't think twice about very obviously asking one of the four Mexican guys playing pool next to us if he could get me some cocaine. I'd been kind of talking to the guy for a minute because he'd recognized me from *MADtv*, which in my drunk logic made me think that I was even more valuable in Norm's and Saget's eyes. The coke transaction wouldn't matter to them—besides, I was so slick they wouldn't even know.

"Hey, man," I whispered drunkenly to this kid, "so you know me, right? Can you get me some coke? I got money, man."

"What?" this kid said. "No, no, man. I don't sell coke, man."

"Oh yeah? Well, no problem." One look back at Saget and Norm proved to me that we hadn't been whispering. It didn't help that after he talked to his buddies for a minute, this guy came back to me.

"It's cool, man," the guy said. "I'll give you my number. We'll score for you tomorrow, okay?"

I was already aware that my drug trafficking wasn't going down unnoticed, but I didn't care. I got the guy's number as Norm and Saget watched. They didn't say anything, but they wrapped things up. Norm went home to his place in West Hollywood, and Saget drove me back to Santa Monica to my hotel. I was definitely drunk, and they definitely weren't. I got to my room, I ordered myself a cheeseburger from room service, and the next morning I woke up with a beef patty on my chest, half eaten. I looked over at the clock—it was 9 A.M. In about ten seconds, the entire evening came back to me.

Anyone who's ever been drunk, been dumb, and remembered it the next morning in bed knows what I'm talking about. The depression and disappointment I felt when I realized what I'd done washed over me and it was as overwhelming as my harshest drug withdrawals. I couldn't understand myself at all: I'd told myself not to act that way, and then I'd done it. And there I was waking up to my own actions once more. There was a terrace visible through the window, and I thought about jumping off of it, but I'd promised myself that I'd never do that or even try to do that again, so I just sat there feeling helpless. I wasn't going to go against two promises I'd made to myself back to back. I started to cry, thinking there was nothing else in the world that I could possibly fuck up in this life.

By 11 A.M. I'd been pacing around my hotel room with the shades drawn for two hours wondering whether I should just go for broke and start drinking and doing drugs again until I died, or if I had a chance to rescue this thing. Then the phone rang. I put it on speaker: It was Norm, Saget, Bobby Simonds, and Laurie Joe.

"So . . . Artie," Norm said. "We've been thinking about this. And we've talked and we've got to tell you. You got the part."

I didn't believe them at all. "Come on, man, this isn't cool," I said. "Don't bullshit me."

"No bullshit, man. Really. We start shooting in two weeks. Congratulations!"

I was already pretty wound up, so once my mood changed from anxiety to celebration, I started jumping up and down, all by myself in my hotel room. My thoughts and emotions were so conflicted in so many ways. I was in L.A., a city I had a love-hate relationship with. I'd nailed a screen test for the biggest thing I'd ever done, yet all of my demons had reared their heads the very same night and almost caused me to lose it. I had not, until that night, even *thought* about doing coke—it was the last thing I wanted to reintroduce myself to on my road back to show business. I looked at this as a victory that I'd won by luck: I was convinced that those guys hadn't seen me try to score coke, and that they'd believed me when I told them I could hold my liquor.

The first day we started shooting the movie, Norm set me straight.

"Hey," he said. "Saget and I knew you were trying to score coke that night."

"Really?"

"It's not like you were quiet about it, man."

"It was pretty loud in there and you know, we could have been talking about anything, I thought," I said. Norm just stared at me. "Okay, fine. But you still hired me."

"Look, dude," he said. "I don't judge anybody. You're funny. We need you, and I figure that I can keep you in line. I'd never fire you just for that. I felt bad for you that night. But you have to know that I know. You didn't get one past me at all, okay?"

Thank God Norm is who he is. I owe that man so much. He was so understanding at a time when so many others would have been judgmental hypocrites who wouldn't have dealt with me at all. Everything I have ever done in my career following *MADtv* I owe to Norm MacDonald. He is a great man and a great friend, and I love him. The same goes for Saget. He had the patience of a saint with me, and without those two motherfuckers you would not be reading this book, that's for sure.

Once I'd officially gotten my role in *Dirty Work*, my agent turned down my screen test for the network sitcom and used it to my advantage: He told them that I'd booked an enormous movie with Norm MacDonald, Chris Farley, and Chevy Chase for MGM and I was going to play Norm's buddy in the film. Hollywood logic is absurd, so of course the very same day he turned the network down, my manager, Peter, got a call from the same network and two others who had heard of my rejection of the screen test and were suddenly interested in offering me development deals. They wanted to have meetings as soon as I was done shooting the film. Now, for all those who think that there's still easy money to be made in Hollywood, let me be the guy who saves you the effort and rejection—those days are done. This was the tail end of a period in TVland when everyone was feeling good because the economy in general was strong, so studio executives were handing out very lucrative development deals to everyone. Even to people like me.

Two weeks later I showed up to the *Dirty Work* set in Toronto walking on air because I knew that I was fucking back: After we were done shooting the movie, I was set to fly back to L.A. and meet every single network that mattered. They'd all probably try to outbid each other and in the end I'd walk away with several hundred thousand dollars for a development deal from one of them. All because I'd said no to a TV-show screen test, which I'd been able to reject because of this movie—a movie that starred everyone I could ever hope to work with. Damn, my life was good—so good that I forgot about the month and a half I had left in my program back at Honesty House. Once I'd gotten a degree of affirmation in the show-business world, suddenly my work there was meaningless. I told them that I'd booked a movie and had to leave in a week. I said it as if it made complete sense: Getting work again meant I was well. My group leader, Kevin, wasn't buying that at all.

"So what? You think you can walk out of here and you'll be fine just because you have a job?" he said, right up in my face. "No way, Artie. I'm not gonna give my consent. You think you're ready for that?"

"Yeah, I do," I said. "I'm ready to work. What do you want me to do? Fucking stay around here forever? This is bullshit. I'm gonna go work."

"You're not ready for that at all!"

I was ready to scream at the guy all day, until he believed that I was fit for society and ready to work. Unfortunately for me, there was a loophole in my MGM contract that said if I didn't get a bill of approval from rehab they could turn me down without question. I was looking at freedom, I was looking at my rebirth, and this guy Kevin was keeping it from me. There was only one thing to do: It was time for a little New Jersey hand-greasing. I got myself a meeting with the president of the place.

"Listen," I said. "What can I do here? I have to do this movie."

"Well, Artie, we want you to do well, we have nothing but your best interests in mind," the president said. "We love you, and we want to give you a good report and a chance to get back to work."

"Yeah, I know," I said. "And I've learned about myself and all that. And you know what, all I want is to stay clean and sober. But the thing is, I really need to do this movie or else I really won't reach my potential."

"Well, you've been good so far and you've come a long way."

"I know I have. And I know I'm not exactly done yet, but I've got to do this now and I could use your support."

"I know, and we have confidence in you, and a donation would not hurt your case at all."

"Really?"

"Really. We can always use funds from private donors."

I called my mother and asked her how much I had left in my savings account. There wasn't much, just a few grand. So I made out a check to Honesty House for $1,500 and swore to them that I'd plug them on every talk show I'd ever get on. They went for it, and the next day they sent a letter to the powers that be at MGM that Artie had completed rehab with a clean bill of health. Yeah, it's all true, and you know what? *Salud!* Fuck it all! I can say all of this without threat of litigation because Honesty House closed down years ago. Too bad—there's more than a few celebrities who could use a rehab facility where it's possible to buy a clean slate on the way out.

I had a few days at home in Union before I flew out to Toronto. The night before I left, Bob Saget called and was beyond honest with me.

"Listen, man, we're all excited to have you on board," he said. "But I'm the one who's been elected to say this to you."

"Um . . . okay."

"Whatever you do, if you're doing coke, pot, anything . . . if you're doing coke, don't bring it up there to Toronto. Okay? Because if you do, and you get caught, you'll throw all of this away."

"Bob, I'm not gonna . . ."

"Listen, you don't have to tell me, okay? I just want to be really clear. We have given you a second chance. Don't try to take drugs across the border. And don't try to score drugs in Canada. If you are caught, Artie, you don't get it. You won't be the only one in trouble. If you fuck up, you'll shut down the whole fucking movie."

"Bob, that's the last thing I want to do, believe me."

"Yeah, I believe you, but we know you've had your trouble with the authorities, and we know you like drugs. If you shut down this fucking movie because you go across the border to score drugs, we will all be *fucked*. Do you understand?"

"Yeah, I understand."

"If you don't do that, we'll be fine. We'll make a great movie, okay?"

"I promise you, I will never do that." I told him so with the same conviction I'd expressed ten minutes before I'd tried to score coke off those Mexican kids. In any case, he believed me.

"Okay, Artie. We'll see you up in Toronto."

The cast did rehearsals for five days at The Four Seasons hotel, and the first night after we were done, me and Norm and his assistant Laurie Joe went to shoot pool at a place on Yonge Street. When you sign on to do a movie for two months where you'll play a second lead alongside someone, it's like going away to boot camp with them: You're either going to end up loving your co-star or hating them. From the beginning, I knew that me and Norm were going to love each other like brothers because we had at least one of the same vices: we both loved gambling. I found that out the very first night as I shot pool with the guy who technically had given me the job and could definitely have gotten me fired in a heartbeat. No one but a healthy gambler would be totally fine with his lesser-billed co-star walking away with $2,500 of his money after a game of nine ball. He eventually paid up—in Canadian dollars.

The thing about Canadian money is that, to an American, it doesn't look like real money. I felt that way during the entire *Dirty Work* shoot. We'd get our per diems, which are supposed to cover your "daily expenses," and we'd go hang out in all the bars and strip clubs on Yonge Street, and it made whatever we did much more fun, because in my mind I wasn't spending real money so none of what we did meant anything. I'd go get blow jobs from strippers when I felt like it, I'd buy drinks for everyone in sight, and when I got back to my room whatever I had left was play money for tomorrow.

Toronto is a funny place. One night I got this chick back to my room. I thought I'd been smooth and she'd responded to my charm, but that wasn't the case. She was a hooker. She'd caught me off guard, and once we had done it she asked me for money. I was so embarrassed that I acted like I knew she was a hooker the whole time. I gave her a wad of that Canadian funny money and when I did the math I realized that I had given her the equivalent of about $1,000. Essentially I got a hooker who I thought just liked me to give me an unbelievably overpriced blow job. But you know what? She was hot. She really was. So fuck you. It was Canadian money anyway: There were no pictures of presidents to stare you down. There was shit like geese and bacon looking back at you from a backdrop of weird Monopoly paper. It didn't matter anyway because I'd won $2,500 off Norm that night. This all happened the first night I was there, by the way.

My agent called me the next morning. "So, how's it going?"

"Pretty good, man," I said. "I won $2,500 off Norm playing pool."

"What!? You're going to get fired!" he said. "Listen to me. You *lose* to him from now on. You *lose* shooting pool."

"Fuck that, man," I said. "When I win, I win. And Norm is not that kind of guy. He'll be more mad if I lose on purpose."

"Fuck you, Artie. Lose to him from now on, you hear me?"

The two months it took us to shoot *Dirty Work* were arguably two of the most enjoyable months of my life. I was back: Coke was out of my life for good, I just knew it. My mother and sister came to visit me over Labor Day weekend, and everyone treated them really nicely. It seemed like every week, a new actor showed up to shoot their part, and I loved all of it. Chevy Chase came up the first week, and one night, me, Norm, Laurie Joe, and Chevy Chase went to shoot pool. We were drinking, doing shots, and everyone but Chevy and I left early, so I got to hang out with him for two hours, shooting pool. He could not have been a cooler guy, and I'm so glad, because I'd idolized him for years. Plenty of people have told me that Chevy is a pain in the ass, but he was unbelievably nice to me. We had an in-depth conversation, and I learned stuff from him about how to do physical comedy that no one else could have taught me. He told me what he had planned for the supporting role, and none of the physical stuff he had in mind was in the script at all. He'd come up with it, and that was what made his appearance so good. Unfortunately, everything he did didn't actually make it into the movie. That's another story altogether, but trust me when I tell you that he was amazing to watch in rehearsal.

More important to me as a comic, I got to grill Chevy about John Belushi and the early *Saturday Night Live* days, and he answered my questions with not a stitch of attitude. He was brutally honest about all of it, and as a fan and a comedian, I have to say there's no greater gift the guy could have given me. At the end of the night we walked back to our hotel like two high school buddies. I couldn't believe that I was lucky enough to live that moment.

After Chevy left, Jack Warden came up to do his ten days of shooting. Jack fucking Warden is from Newark, New Jersey, like my family; he played my father in the movie, and on set he became a father figure to me. When I told him my father was from Newark, he said, "I bet your father was a fighter. Guys from Newark are fighters." He couldn't have been more right.

And then, as if things couldn't get better, Don Rickles showed up for his one day of shooting—one of my great, unforgettable moments in show business. Don's first day shooting was my first day shooting too, and at that moment, I wasn't sure I was going to make it to the end of this movie. I'd heard that if you're going to get fired, it usually happens in the first two weeks because there will still be time to reshoot everything. After the first two weeks, you're home free; it costs more to get rid of you than keep you.

So my first take on a film that I'd gotten despite my solicitation of cocaine from Mexicans at a pool hall involved Don Rickles berating me. Norm and I played loser ushers at a movie theater, and Don's character was our boss. The scene opens with him telling us just how awful we are.

Besides how great it was just to meet a fucking legend like Rickles, he also happened to be incredibly nice. (I even got him to insult me on camera and then say hi to my mother.) He showed up at 6 A.M. for an eighteen-hour day. I think they were paying him something like $100,000 a day, so obviously they wanted to get his scenes done in one long day. And that's what we did, from 6 A.M. until midnight, and the whole time Don was on fire. The man is a ball of energy.

Norm, Saget, and I were standing around the food service table early in the morning when Don walked up.

"You know, before I left Hollywood the other day I saw Marty Scorsese," he said. "I told him, 'Marty, I'm going to Toronto. Bob Saget is directing a film.' And the man grabbed his chest!"

We all started to laugh, but Don wasn't done. "What are you

doing here, Saget? Go back to L.A.! A cat pissed itself on *America's Funniest Home Videos*, they need you to direct him!"

Rolling into our first scene, Bob didn't even try to ask Don to follow the lines in the script; he just asked him to insult Norm and me. The two of us were dressed like goofy movie theater employees in stiff shirts and stupid bow ties, standing next to each other like prisoners in front of a firing squad. Saget said, "Action," and Rickles came right up to me and said: "Look at *you*. Look at you, you *baby gorilla*."

I cracked up, out loud, as if that was the first and best joke I'd ever heard in my life. Because you know what? It kind of was. Everyone else on the set laughed too, and the take was blown, as they like to say on movie sets.

"That was great, Don," Saget said, trying to control himself. "Okay, let's do it again."

Rickles came up to me again and said it again: "Look at *you*. Look at *you*, you *baby gorilla*." And once again, I died laughing. As I lost it, again, I decided that I was probably getting fired, but I was having so much fun that I didn't give a shit. If laughing at Rickles got me kicked off this picture I'd be happy to go out like that.

Saget came up to me. "Artie, you've got to get it together."

"Get it *together*?" I was still gasping for air. "The man is a legend. He is in my face, two inches from me, saying the funniest shit ever! I may never stop laughing for the rest of my life!"

It took about twenty takes to get those two lines on film, I'm not kidding. Eventually I was able to get through a take with Rickles calling me a Baby Gorilla, but if you watch *Dirty Work*, you'll see that Norm is laughing. They did what they could to cut around it, but it was hopeless. So once we got that first line, Rickles moved on—because he was far from done with me.

"You know," he said, "Baskin-Robbins called me and he said

you ate them down to only five flavors. You fat pig." He then put his face by my stomach and said, "Having a good time in there, ice cream? You dancing around?"

None of us knew that was coming either, and we couldn't do anything but laugh. Ten or twenty takes later—again—we finally got one take where we managed to stifle our hysteria long enough for him to deliver that second bit.

Finally, Rickles was done with my half of his insult tirade. We had probably two usable takes—and I'm using the word *usable* loosely. Then he moved on to Norm, and those insults were even funnier, mostly because for the first ten takes Rickles insulted him not as his character Mitch but as Norm MacDonald.

"So tell me, how did you get a movie?" Rickles said.

"Cut!" Saget said. "Don! Very funny, but you cannot insult Norm as Norm. His name is Mitch in the movie. We can't use the take if you insult him as Norm MacDonald."

"Fine," Rickles said, eyeballing Saget with that shifty look of his. "Okay, Bob. That's fine. I understand what you're saying to me."

"Okay!" Saget said. "From the top! Action!"

Rickles walked right up to Norm and said, "Uh, Norm? Who wrote these jokes? This script is awful."

"Cut!" Saget was laughing hysterically. "Don . . . do not insult the script either. We can't use takes where you insult the script."

"Okay, Bob, sorry about that. I must have gotten ahead of myself."

This went on for what felt like two of the best days in my life, until finally we got through the scene, which is probably the funniest scene in the whole fucking movie. And so a Baby Gorilla was born.

After Rickles graced us with his insults, Chris Farley showed up for a week. Now *that* guy—I'd heard everything there was to hear about him. I thought he was just the most hilariously funny man alive. And meeting him changed nothing: Chris Farley remains one of the funniest comics ever to have lived as far as I'm concerned. I'm lucky to have had that one week to get to know him. I only saw him once more after the shoot in October 1997, a month and a half before he died, when he hosted *Saturday Night Live*. I went to the taping, and then I went to the after-party, and it was obvious that Chris was hurting. He was back on blow, drinking, and doing everything else in sight. I didn't know him very well, but Norm loved him dearly and was very concerned about him.

For that week of the shoot, though, I got to sit there and piss myself laughing at him every day on set. *Dirty Work* is Chris's last movie. In it he plays a guy called Jimmy No Nose whose nose was bitten off by a Saigon whore. That was his entire storyline. It wasn't much, but Chris made it shine.

Every day that week I had lunch in Norm's trailer, where all of the famous guys coming through to do cameos would hang out. From Chevy Chase to Adam Sandler to Jack Warden to the great John Goodman, we'd all have lunch together and just bullshit. I was in fucking *heaven*. The week that Farley was up there, man, I don't think I've ever laughed so hard in my life. He would come in with his lunch and just start telling stories, acting stuff out while eating lunch just like the rest of us. Doing something simple like eating ice cream became an opportunity for Chris—anything he did was a chance to do all these different characters. You could just tell that he truly loved making people laugh. The fucking guy had such a kind way about him too; he treated me very nicely because I think he could tell just how intimidated and in awe of him I was. It's not like it was hard for me to hang out with him; what was hard was not being able to tell him everything I wanted to say.

It didn't take much for me to see that Chris was fucked up. At that point his management, Brillstein-Grey, had hired a guy to watch him and keep him out of trouble, like Belushi used to have. The guy's specific job was to keep Chris Farley off dope. From what

I saw, that guy shouldn't have gotten a recommendation letter because it was clear that Farley knew how to ditch him. That's pure speculation of course because I never actually saw Chris take drugs. To this day I can only dream of being as funny as Chris fucking Farley. Rest in fucking *peace*, my brother.

If you get the chance to see *Dirty Work*, see it for Chris; you need no other reason: Every time he's on screen, every line, every joke out of his mouth is hit out of the park. And there are outtakes running over the end credits that are priceless. There's a great one with Norm and Farley doing this one scene that took them like half a day to shoot because Norm could not stop laughing. It was hopeless. In the outtakes you can see just how much Chris and Norm liked each other and how much joy Chris was getting out of making Norm laugh like that. It's touching and sad and it's very real.

When he died in December 1997, I was out in L.A., running late, trying to catch my plane back to Jersey for Christmas, when my manager called to tell me the news. I barely even knew Chris, but it felt like a punch in the stomach.

"Are you kidding me?" I said.

"I wish I was," my manager said. "You can guess what it was. He was with a hooker, and they found him dead of a coke and heroin overdose in his condo in Chicago."

I was really affected by it, not only because of the eerie similarities to the death of his hero, John Belushi. Both of them died in the company of a shady woman and from the same style of overdose—a speedball. They both died at thirty-three. It was an awful turn of events, and it was a huge wake-up call to me. I had just turned thirty. Let me tell you, more than therapy, more than rehab, more than almost losing everything I'd worked for, Chris Farley's death kept me off coke. I remember wandering into the airport bar to catch the announcement on the news and staring at the years 1964–1997 listed under his face. I couldn't believe it; I'd just done a movie with him, and he was so vibrant and so alive. And drugs took all that away from him. I got the message all right. I stayed clean and enjoyed a very productive period in my life after that.

The other great I got to meet on the *Dirty Work* set was Adam Sandler, who was only up for one day. Because of that, I didn't get to spend as much time as I would have liked with Rebecca Romijn. She hadn't yet added the Stamos to that name of hers, but he was there too because they were already dating. Anyway, Sandler was someone I'd wanted to meet ever since his early bits on *SNL*. He was always great in a sketch, and his comedy albums were amazing. I'd seen *Billy Madison* multiple times: it was what I did between walking around to commercial auditions in New York City and doing stand-up that night. I'd kill time in theaters and watch his movie. Adam was really very cool and it was fun to meet him.

I learned an important lesson doing *Dirty Work*: If you are ever given the chance to work with someone who is smarter and funnier than you, without question, do it. It will make you better at whatever you do. Just about everyone involved with *Dirty Work* was smarter and funnier than me, so it was like fucking comedy school for me. Frank Sebastiano is younger, smarter, and funnier than me. Norm is very obviously smarter and funnier than me. The comedy writer Fred Wolf is smarter and funnier too. Chris Farley was much funnier and, okay, I'll give you smarter too. And Adam Sandler is definitely smarter and funnier. So if you look at it constructively, there was no way I wasn't coming out of that experience better at my job.

Another treat for me on *Dirty Work* was meeting the legendary comedy writer Jim Downey, who did a bit part in *Dirty Work* as he had in *Billy Madison*. After *Dirty Work*, I became good friends with Jim, and we would have dinner from time to time. One night the following April, he invited me to watch the NCAA semifinals with him and one of his friends. This friend was staying in a brand-new hip hotel called the Soho Grand. I had no idea until we got to the room that Jim's friend was Bill Murray.

Bill was in town shooting a film and was staying there with two of his sons. Bill is one of my absolute heroes, so I couldn't even believe I was watching basketball with him. There were a couple of impressions and things I would do that made Downey laugh, which was thrilling to me, to get a great comic writer like Jim to laugh. Jim asked me to do them for Bill Murray that night and I blew it. I completely bombed in front of Bill Murray. Downey enjoys bringing that up.

On *Dirty Work*, I felt like I'd been juicing: In just two months, I'd gotten funnier than I deserved to be. I'd learned a ton of stuff about jokes and how to write them, and I got a more enlightened sense of what was an obvious, hacky joke and what wasn't. I took that stuff seriously, and it inspired me to get out there and write and perform new material.

When *Dirty Work* wrapped, a great time in my life began. The networks and tons of production companies wanted to meet me. God bless them and God bless my agents, Jennifer Craig and James Dixon at William Morris, and my manager, Peter Principato, all of whom worked it perfectly. Right from the film set, I flew to L.A. for meetings with Fox, NBC, ABC, UPN, WB, and loads of production companies those corporations owned, as well as a few others. I was full of amazing stories from the set about working with all these comedy legends, so I destroyed in every fucking meeting. I met with Warren Littlefield, the head of NBC at that time, Peter Roth, then the president of Fox, and other power players. Those meetings were tough because there was pressure to perform. My representatives discussed business, but I was there to shine.

The story that came in most handy about the star-studded set I'd just flown in from was the Baby Gorilla story. I repeated it to every network executive I hoped would give me money. By the time it surfaced on the *Stern* show, it was road-tested and in great shape.

In the end, I got a development deal that resulted from a bidding war. Every single network—all five of them—made offers. William Morris and my manager played them against each other brilliantly, working them up from an offer of $250,000 to $750,000. I signed a development deal with the Fox TV Network and the film production company 20th Century Fox and my first check was for $250,000. It arrived just before Christmas 1997, and I immediately took it home and started up my corporation, Too Fat to Fish, Inc. I paid every one of my mother's bills, I paid off the mortgage on our family house, I got her out of debt, and we finally started to breathe easy for a change. I put the rest in the bank and began to meet writers to start developing things. In eight months, I'd gone from a deep depression, living in my mother's basement, preparing myself to start driving a cab again to having shot a movie for MGM and having a development deal to come up with a film or TV show of my own on a major network. I got a new car, my mom got a new car, and it was finally happy times once more. It had been ages.

That Christmas, I was so grateful for everything that had happened. I'd made some permanent changes. I wasn't done with drugs, but I was done with coke, thank God, because that guy Cocaine, take it from me, is the biggest devil out there. I'm not mad at him anymore. He was a fun guy to hang with aside from the part where he almost killed me and made my life complete chaos.

My development deal was very lucrative because I got paid the whole $750,000. Normally, you have three chances to accept a show runner or executive producer the studio offers you to help develop an idea; if you turn them down, you only get half the money. If you agree on a show runner or executive producer and you shoot a pilot, whether or not the pilot gets picked up, you get paid all the money. There's a time limit on all of this, of course, and toward the end of my deal, around February 1998, Fox started to panic because they'd given me all this money and hadn't made an offer on one thing I'd pitched. I wasn't submitting scripts and didn't have too much that I was working on, but I was cashing multiple six-figure checks. I was so antsy to get something moving that I went out to L.A. for the first couple of months of '98 just so I wouldn't miss any emergency meetings with my writer.

For two and a half months I lived at the Bel Age Hotel in Hollywood, right off Sunset. I hung out at the Viper Room every night and saw some cool bands. I walked over to Duke's on Sunset, stopped by the Whiskey A Go Go. I drove around in a rented Mustang convertible and lived in the hotel and spent 10 G's in two months. Typical me. It was important for me to be happy in L.A. trying to make stuff happen. I also spent that time doing stand-up and got familiar with L.A. venues like The Laugh Factory and The Comedy Store.

I hung out a lot with Norm MacDonald, who by then had been famously fired from *Saturday Night Live*. Norm had been doing "Weekend Update" for four years, and without warning was fired by executive Don Ohlmeyer because he "wasn't funny." The rumor was that Ohlmeyer didn't like how much Norm made fun of his good friend O. J. Simpson, but that's probably not true because when Norm was replaced by Colin Quinn, Colin laid into O. J. just as hard. Lorne Michaels never went to bat for Norm, and for a while it looked like NBC was going to boycott any promotion of *Dirty Work* on the network. Even if they had, the appearances Norm got on shows like *Letterman* made up for all of that. Letterman is legendary for hating television executives, so he sided with Norm. He said on the air that he'd met Ohlmeyer, who claimed to be a creative type, but Ohlmeyer wasn't even creative enough to create gas. Norm then told Dave about how he got fired: He walked in and Don said, "Norm, I've got some bad news. You're fired."

"Oh wow. That *is* bad news," Norm said. "That's horrible! Why am I fired?"

"Because you're not funny."

"Oh my God. That's worse! I'm not funny? I'm in comedy! I'll never get another job!"

Letterman, of course, loved that story. And when Norm and I went in to promote the movie on the *Stern* show, he told the story again. It's a classic.

Anyway, after a few months of cashing checks and not getting any ideas to the network, they finally hooked me up with this writer Sam Cass, who used to work on *Seinfeld*. He had a script where I'd play a doorman at a hotel, and I liked it a lot. But the network made the poor guy rewrite the script practically overnight since pilot season was almost over. The script was not ready to be shot, but the network execs were afraid they were going to lose the money they were giving me. They rushed it through, we rushed casting, we rushed everything. The week we actually shot the pilot, I knew it was going to be a disaster. I didn't know what I would do if the network actually picked it up. I hated the result and hated my performance in it so much that the prospect of doing it for any length of time made me want to leap off a building. I'd be back into the frying pan with another show I didn't like and I was afraid that I was going to relapse.

The night we shot this thing could not have gone worse. The taping went from 7 P.M. to 4 in the morning. The cast turned out to be really good. Luis Guzman, a great character actor who's been in a lot of Paul Thomas Anderson movies, played a fellow doorman. Luis really wanted the show to get picked up and, despite my reservations, in a way so did I because I would have been making 55 grand a week with a couple of points on the back end, but there was no way it was going to get picked up.

It wasn't Sam Cass's fault; it wasn't anyone who worked on its fault. It was a mess because the network let it go too long and then rushed it through. This was April 1998, and the pilot was called *The King of New York*. I played a doorman who worked at a hotel like the Plaza—the kind of doorman who can get you anything: tickets to a show or a game, whatever the hell you need. I was a fast-talking guy, which I liked. The script was just not there. We shot our pilot the very same season that they shot *The King of Queens*, which was coincidental because that show has a similar premise. That year one *King* went on to major success and the other *King* did not. But you know what? I got the whole $750,000 because I had shot a pilot. Once again, someone upstairs was looking out for me.

In the end, I learned a ton about what not to do with a development deal. I had said yes to the script even though I knew it was not ready because I felt guilty taking money from these network people for doing nothing. But that was stupid; if the network couldn't get the script up to par in time, it was their problem, not mine. My mistake was agreeing to something I didn't really believe in.

I got my last check for 250 grand a few weeks after that, and I still couldn't believe it.

As is the case with my life, when stuff goes good, it goes *great*. When I got out of that first development deal, my agents immediately got me a holding deal about a week later with NBC. NBC wanted to cast me in something, so they paid me $350,000 to keep me from being picked up by another network. The first check from them was for $150,000.

"Artie, what do you have to do for this money?" my mother, being old-fashioned, asked me when I handed it to her to deposit in the corporate account. "What do you do for them? Do you have to run drugs from Mexico or guns to Cuba?"

"No, Ma, even worse," I said. "I have to be on TV. This is showbiz."

The terms of the holding deal stated that NBC intended to cast me in a supporting role in a script that they had under development, and until they did I couldn't take on any other TV acting work. Like I said, when it rains it pours: I also got an audition for a romantic comedy called *Lost and Found* starring David Spade and Martin Sheen and this gorgeous French actress Sophie Marceau. I had two great auditions for the director Jeff Pollack and then I met Spade at the screen test and killed it. Norm is a friend of Spade's so he put in a good word, and in the end that's probably what got me the part, which was like the third lead of the film. Spade was hilarious, and Martin Sheen was great. I enjoyed another two months with a ton of per diem money. Plus we shot in L.A., so I was able to do stand-up here and there when I had time. I opened for Norm on the road too.

Immediately following *Lost and Found*, I got cast in *The Bachelor*, a $30 million New Line Cinema movie, with Chris O'Donnell, and Renée Zellweger. I played the third lead and got to pal around in that movie with Hal Holbrook, Ed Asner, James Cromwell, and Brooke Shields. Then I shot *The 4th Floor*, which I got because the director, Josh Klausner, was a major *MADtv* fan and loved the White Mama character. Even though it was a drama, he offered me the part. I did scenes with Juliette Lewis, William Hurt, Shelley Duval, and the great character actor Austin Pendleton. These were major dramatic scenes where I play the superintendent of an apartment building who kind of grunts all the time. It's a murder mystery and you're supposed to think I'm the murderer. Guess what? I'm not.

I couldn't believe that Josh Klausner had enough confidence in my abilities to offer me the role without an audition. God bless him! I hope he wasn't disappointed, because I gave it my all and I think it all worked out in the end. Unfortunately that movie never got a theatrical release; it went straight to HBO. That's fine with me.

Dirty Work was my re-entry into show business, but it didn't get its due. It opened on June 12, 1998, and for all intents and purposes, it made about 4 million bucks. The critics panned it, but fuck them, that movie is funny. Adam Sandler loved it, and that really meant a lot to Norm and me because the approval of someone you respect is more valuable than the approval of a bunch of faceless critics. Sandler was right too—*Dirty Work* has become a cult hit. I have signed more *Dirty Work* DVDs than anything else, hands down. I've had more than a few younger kids tell me it's their favorite movie of all time. When they say that, I tell them, "You know what? You should really rent *The Sting*."

MGM is the reason why *Dirty Work* didn't do better. I remember talking to Chevy Chase, who knows the business better than anybody, about how the studio was going to fuck it all up.

"Look," he said, "this movie is funny. It's politically incorrect and it's hilarious. Do not let those motherfuckers make it PG-13. For business, after a couple of test screenings, they might beg you to do that. Do not let it happen. Stand firm, do not let these cocksuckers fuck up what you're doing here. If they make it rated PG-13 they will tear the guts out of it. At least keep the movie funny. Keep it rated R."

He knew what he was talking about all right, because that is exactly what the studio did. Despite our protests, they made it PG-13, and PG-13 movies are, by nature, bland. The R-rated version of *Dirty Work* was two million times funnier. It's totally unfortunate, because just a few months later, the Farrelly brothers released *There's Something About Mary*, which was rated R, and that changed everything.

MGM also fucked up the release. They were going to bring out *Dirty Work* in February, which is where they initially put Sandler's movies. But they kept delaying and delaying it until it came out the same fucking weekend as *The Truman Show* and a week after *Godzilla*. To say it was buried is being kind.

Fuck it, who cares. Watch it now. You'll see how it would have been so much better and you'll still like it. As far as my life goes, I became friends with the great Norm MacDonald, Frank Sebastiano, Fred Wolf, Jim Downey, Bob Saget, and a bunch of guys I love. I got to be in the last movie Chris Farley ever made. It was an honor just to meet the guy for a little while, and I would have done it just for that. *Dirty Work* also got me a couple more movies in a row and $1.1 million worth of development deals. It led to everything for me, that movie.

If you are fan of mine, you already know that when Norm was out promoting *Dirty Work*, he brought me along with him to the *Howard Stern Show* in 1998. Here's how he introduced me.

"You will love Artie, Howard," Norm said on the air as I sat next to him in the studio. "He got kicked off of *MADtv* for co-caine."

I was so pissed at him; I thought he'd fucked me over. What did I know? That was the biggest favor he could have done for me. I had no choice but to tell the whole story of how I got arrested and fired from the show in all its glory and Howard, of course, loved it. Two years later, when I did *The Norm Show*, Norm and I did the *Stern* show a few more times. Four appearances in all.

When Jackie Martling left the *Stern* show in 2001, a bunch of comics descended like a pack of hyenas, trying to get his seat while the thing was still warm. I'm a lucky motherfucker: I got in there only because they remembered me coming in with Norm. Tell you the truth, I don't know what Howard saw in me. Yeah, sure, whatever, I know I'm funny. If I weren't funny, Norm and Saget wouldn't have given me a chance. But Howard saw something else in me. Some days I think he saw the biggest fuck-up he'd ever taken under his wing—and that's saying a lot. Other days, I think he saw the right guy to round out that perfect chemistry that he and Freddy and Robin and Gary have made into the most unlikely, undeniable success story in broadcasting history. In the end, on whatever day, however he feels, I just hope Howard sees me for what I am—the fan who won the lottery.

Roselle

13

95

Toll

GOETHALS
BRIDGE

Ma
Ha
6

4

Grasselli

440

2

Heroin: It's Better for Your Liver!

12

Let me tell you, living your life on the air in front of eight million listeners who pay attention to every single thing you do every single day is pretty fucking strange. I mean, I'm a comic, I'm all for using things from my fucked-up life to get laughs and, I hope, make people feel better in the process, but being under the microscope for five hours each morning—and I hate the morning—on *The Howard Stern Show* is something that no one but Howard, Fred, Robin, Gary, and everyone else who has ever been a regular understands. It's strange, because the fans really do care in their way, they're really a part of your life. They're like relatives who keep tabs on you, but for someone like me who also likes his privacy, that's both a blessing and a curse. I don't need a bunch of people, let alone an audience, inserting themselves into my life. My mother and sister are enough. Fuck, *I* am enough. I drive myself pretty crazy worrying about my life all on my own. Not to mention that nothing gets by Howard.

This story was not part of the original plan for this book, but I don't like to disappoint, and this whole period of my life seems to fascinate fans of the show. So this one is for anyone who could easily hold their own at a Superfan Roundtable. This is the story about the time in my life when I was lying to everyone: my family, myself, everyone at *Howard*. I'd been doing heroin behind everyone's back for a while. I wanted to kick it, but I was on some powerful drugs and I wasn't acting right. I told everyone on the air that I was drunk; I made it sound as if I was on a bender. But there was much more going on than that.

I got into this mess innocently enough. I got addicted to prescription pills, just like any honest, average, hard-working American. And like the average health-insurance-enabled pill-popper in this country, I got into that shit because I worked too hard.

In December 2004, I put out a DVD of my stand-up called *It's the Whiskey Talkin'*, and sold it on my Web site. A distributor put it out for general release in stores in February 2005. That DVD was the result of a long year and a half of gigs during which time I'd perfected my act, taking it to a whole new level. To support the DVD release, I committed to six more months of gigs and signings in cities all around the country. That was ambitious: I'd do *The Stern Show* from Monday to Friday, then do Friday- and Saturday-night stand-up shows, with an afternoon signing on Saturday. If we were in, say, Buffalo, I'd go to a Coconuts, FYE, or Tower in the late afternoon, stay there until they closed or ran out of DVDs, do a gig that night, then fly back on Sunday. The next morning, I'd be back on the air for another week. It was an insane schedule, but I figured that I could handle it for six months. At the end of it, I would have sold as many DVDs as I could and then I'd be able to relax all summer. It didn't work out that way. Another blessing turned into a sort of curse.

Back in 2001, I'd started writing a script called *Beer League* with Frank Sebastiano, who wrote *Dirty Work* and was a writer on *The Norm Show*. He'd also won a couple of Emmys for *SNL* and *The Chris Rock Show*. It felt like a perfect match—he's a really funny Italian kid from New Jersey who'd also played softball. I had a vision for this film, so in 2000 I put fifty grand into making a seventeen-minute short that was brilliantly directed by my friend Michael Ruane. I wrote it myself and called it *Game Day*, and we put it on the *It's the Whiskey Talkin'* DVD as an extra. We shot it on 35mm film, and it looked really good. It showcased my abilities as an actor, and I was really happy about that. I got Frank interested in the short, and we worked on it together over time and had a full-length script by 2002. Once it was done, we made a pledge: We promised each other that should the movie ever get made, we would compromise nothing, no matter what. We agreed to stay true to our original vision and swore that if we couldn't find the right investors we wouldn't do it at all. Most important, after the mess the studio made of *Dirty Work*, we were filming it as an R-rated comedy, no questions asked. If there was one single joke that we loved but the investors or the studio wanted to take out of the script, then fuck it—the deal was off. Down to the joke, that's how we agreed to do this thing. It was a passion project, not a necessity, because we both had jobs that paid well and we didn't need the money.

We met with a lot of money people between 2002 and 2004 and no one was the right fit. Finally, a company called Crush came to us promising to deliver $2.5 million. They were the first to say they wouldn't change a thing and would grant us, without question, full creative control. All that they cared about was getting me to agree in writing that I'd promote the movie on the air. In the blink of an eye, *Beer League* was set up to be made, and soon enough it was scheduled to be shot in July of 2005, just when I'd hoped to be relaxing after that six-month DVD promotional tour. I'd do my last gig and signing in Chicago on June 4, and we'd start shooting *Beer League* on the July 4 weekend. I wasn't happy about the situation, but I was getting to make the movie I wanted. What could I do? I looked at it this way: I'd kill myself this one year, just break my ass, live through it, and have a fuck of a lot to show for it afterward.

This whole *Beer League* thing came with a lot of stress for me, aside from the pressure of starring in a film that I wanted to make. First off, the company who secured the money was getting millions from hedge funds all over the place and just handing it to us. It wasn't a studio full of experienced movie-industry veterans behind the funding; it was just a group of guys and us. I didn't want to let anybody down.

The second difficult thing was asking Howard for a few weeks off. I knew he wasn't going to like it, because Howard values loyalty to the show above all. He's not a total dictator about it, but the show has to come first. The filming of *Private Parts* was designed entirely around his radio schedule. They built an entire fucking apartment for Howard at Silvercup Studios in Long Island City so he could live there, shoot all night, and get to the show on time. Obviously, that was fucking impossible on our budget unless I planned to sleep on a cement block in a parking lot. I had a clause in my contract with the show that said I could take time off whenever I wanted, and I'd done it before to shoot films like *Old School* and *Elf* and to take some meetings in L.A. A couple of days here and there were fine with Howard, but a shooting schedule that called for three weeks off since I was in every scene was something else.

I kept putting off that conversation, because I was worried that Howard would say no. If he did, we had real problems, because from the minute the guys at Crush said it was a go, Frank and I got right into preproduction and casting meetings and working on the script, all while fulfilling our commitments. At the time Frank was a writer on *Letterman*, so it's not like he was sitting at home playing solitaire. That Frank had done it the right way and had already gotten clearance for a three-week break from *Letterman* failed to inspire confidence in me. If you've read this far, you already know that's not one of my strengths.

I'd been drinking heavily on the road, trying to stay away from the coke, but I was always able to get myself back to work on Monday to do the show. Usually, I'd sleep off the weekend on Monday night and by Tuesday morning I'd be fine. I've always had trouble getting to sleep early for *The Stern Show*, and doing gigs on weekends with the late hours and travel really fucked me up. After a gig I found it almost impossible to get to sleep, even when I went right back to my hotel room. I'm not one for travel and hotels anyway—some people love the road; I really don't. So to get to sleep and to make the experience more pleasurable overall, I started to take a lot of painkillers. Stress loves painkillers, take it from me. Comedy clubs are just one big medicine chest too—there's always a lot of Vicodin, Percodan, Percocet, Valium, and whatever else going around. I gave myself a pill allowance to get through the plane rides and sleeping in shitty hotels and that's how it started, but with my addictive personality, it quickly got crazier and crazier. Soon I was washing down whatever I could get my hands on with Jack Daniel's, thinking it was under control and that there was a reason for doing it. After a month or so, I started taking pills during the regular workweek, which led me right into the weekend again, until before I knew it I was taking like twenty painkillers a day. The most that I ever took is probably about fifty 10mg Vicodin in one day. They were my daily vitamins. With the drinking on top of that, my liver was walking wounded like a Civil War soldier. I knew that I would have to take a blood test to get insurance for *Beer League*, and I figured the results were going to be as toxic as Chernobyl. I had to get a complete physical too, and I couldn't imagine that a doctor was going to find me fit enough to carry my own bags through an airport.

I put all of it off until finally, in early March, when my back was against the wall, I went for it at the end of a Friday show. Howard was not happy. As always, though, he was cool about it.

"Art, you mean a lot to the show and I'd rather have you here for those three weeks," he said. "But you do whatever you have to do and I'll support it."

The fact that he was being so nice about it meant that of course I was going to continue to do the show—there was no way I couldn't after that. I was distraught. I didn't think there was a chance we could get the filming done, and I felt like a fucking asshole for waiting so long to get that answer. I called the producers thinking it was the last time I'd ever talk to them.

"Listen, guys," I said. "I hate to have to make this call, but there's no way I can get three weeks off from the show. I just can't do it. I can't quit the show to do the movie, and all that time off is out of the question. So I guess we can't do it."

They were quiet. I figured they were getting ready to fire me, but they weren't. They didn't want me to leave the show—the show was what they had banked on to promote the film and make it profitable.

"Well, here's what we're going to do," they said. "It's going to be a lot of hard work, but you're going to do it. You'll do the show in the morning, and in the afternoon, you'll be shooting."

They rearranged a five-week shoot, with the first two weeks falling during my vacation from *Stern* in July. I'd have to work two six-day weeks and then spend the last three weeks shooting every day after the show. They redid the budget and the schedule, did everything to accommodate me and have me home most nights to get enough sleep to be functional on the air at 6 A.M. Three weeks of eighteen-hour days was going to be tough, but as long as I was healthy I knew I could do it.

At first I was angry with Howard for not saying, "Just go do it," but I realized that I had to suck it up. That was the only time I've ever had negative feelings toward him in the seven years I've been at the show. What I wasn't seeing was that he was also being supportive. After that conversation, it was kind of chilly between us, and I know I walked around with a bit of an attitude.

"Look, Artie," he said to me one day. "I need you here at the show. I want you here. We need you here every day."

"I know, Howard, but you know I want to do this. This movie means a lot to me, and now it's going to be really hard. I can't give it my all if I'm burning the candle at both ends like this."

"Listen. Ultimately, if you do it that way it will be the best thing for the movie, because you'll be talking about it every single day while you shoot it. That's more airtime than you'd get if you just went off and shot it and weren't on the show for three weeks." He was right in every way.

So we were all set to shoot in July. I looked at the calendar and circled June 4; it was the last day of my DVD tour and the last day I'd let myself take pills. I planned to start kicking one month before, taking less and less so that by June 4 I'd be able to stop altogether and be clean. I'd have a full month of regular, sober living, then I'd show up and make the movie. That never happened, so I had to go with my backup plan: quitting cold turkey. Of course, that didn't work out so well either, because I had no idea how terrible painkiller withdrawal would be. Every time I tried to cut back, I felt horrible physically and so anxious that I never really put a dent in how many I was taking. Pretty soon, June 4 was the mountain looming up ahead, and I was definitely going to crash into it. It was terrible. The only good thing that came from the stress, worry, and pills was that I lost a lot of weight.

I remember being on tour and running out of pills at a club on a Friday and having to do a signing the next day and thinking that there was no way I'd be able to get up in the morning and sit there for three hours meeting fans. I asked a guy in the club if he knew where I could get some pills, and he hooked me up with a dealer who could get just about anything. I told this kid I needed a hundred Vicodin if he could get them. The kid looked at me like my head had just turned around.

"You want how much?"

"A hundred," I said. "A hundred Vicodin."

"You selling them or something?"

"No, they're for me."

He looked confused. "Listen, man, that's a lot of Vicodin for one guy. How many you taking?"

"You know, like ten, maybe more, a day."

"What? Holy shit, man, that's a lot. All that Vicodin is bad for your liver. Do you know what that shit does to your liver?"

"Yeah, I know, but what am I going to do?"

"What are you going to do? There's a lot of things you could take that are better than that. You could use some heroin, man. Let me get you a couple of dime bags. You just snort it and you'll get the same effect. Forget taking all those pills. Take heroin, man, I'm telling you. It's better for your liver."

That seemed perfectly logical to me.

"Right," I said. "Okay. I'll just snort some heroin instead."

The guy brought me two dime bags after my set that night, and I went back to my hotel room wondering what was going to happen. In my life I'd done tons of coke, but even in my biggest coke phase, I'd stayed away from heroin. Back in my room, I had about a million things to think over and discuss with the *Beer League* crew. We wanted to get Ralph Macchio involved, we had to cast the actress who was going to play my girlfriend, and we had to talk about a bunch of other auditions. I wanted nothing to do with any of it—not that night. I laid down a couple of lines, snorted them up, and a great euphoria washed over me. I remember hitting the couch and nothing more. All was quiet. But just before I passed out, I heard my own voice as if from across the room saying, "I am in . . . trouble."

Overnight, scoring pills became a thing of the past. Scoring heroin became my new hobby. In typical paranoid druggie logic, I decided that I'd be able to keep things together, or at least undercover, if I didn't score too close to home. I found a dealer who put me in touch with another dealer in Wilmington, Delaware, and that guy became my supplier. And so my life very quickly became ruled by chaos.

From March to June, a regular week for me went like this: I'd be on the road all weekend, doing the heroin I'd brought along. I'd do the gig, I'd do the signing, I'd get myself through Sunday night and to the show Monday morning. The withdrawals would start to kick in for me around 11 A.M., just as we wrapped it up. I'd make a quick exit, get into my car and drive three hours to Wilmington, sweating and feeling sicker with each passing minute. I'd try to buy as little as possible, hoping to cut down how much I was doing. That didn't happen, so I'd end up driving down there three days a week.

I hate to be judgmental, but heroin dealers aren't the most reliable guys. Sometimes I'd drive all the way to Wilmington and the kid would never show up. I'd sit in my car in a deserted alley behind a factory, desperately calling his cell phone, the withdrawal symptoms coming on strong. More than once I waited all night for him, too desperate to risk missing him. I'd have to bail before I got too sick to make the drive back and miss work the next day. On those nights, I'd call a different guy on the way home who could always get me pills. I'd take enough to stop the shakes so I could make it through the show. Then I'd drive back down to Wilmington to score again. Usually, the kid never had what he said he would. Sometimes it would be a big score, and sometimes it was barely enough to scrape by and not nearly enough to justify the trip. But the worst thing were his voice mails.

"Hey, man, where were you yesterday?" he'd say. "I waited for you, man. You weren't here. I got your stuff, so you better get here today."

He didn't have to tell me twice; I knew I had a matter of hours and a handful of pills before I'd be in bad shape.

While this "commute" was going on, the *Beer League* crew expected me to be part of all aspects of preproduction. I blew it all off: script reads, auditions, wardrobe meetings. I always had something to do, which was true—just nothing constructive and nothing I was going to tell them about.

At the time, I was getting $20,000 or so for stand-up gigs, so I had the cash to support my habit. I'd ask for half of it in cash from the promoter so the people who kept track of my finances wouldn't see that there was all this money being spent. It was such a crazy time in my life, I'm amazed that so many things that could have happened didn't: I could have been pulled over at any time driving back and forth to Wilmington high. When I was either high or coming down, I speeded. I drove like a reckless, desperate drug addict trying to fend off paralyzing withdrawals. I could have gotten into a car accident, I could have killed someone, I could have gotten arrested. I didn't exactly meet my dealer in the most scenic section of Wilmington. I could have gotten shot or killed, sitting there in my car for hours in the middle of the night. And even when I did score, I could have died from getting shit drugs, or I could have thrown up and passed out on the air. The possibilities were endless.

None of it happened, so I kept at it, thinking I was on top of things. I had a girlfriend at the time, Dana, and I was keeping all of this from her too. In the same way that I blew off the movie stuff, which had been so important to me, I blew off Dana. We'd have Saturday night plans to go to dinner, and I'd be unable to leave the house. I'd come up with some excuse about why I couldn't make it. It drove a spike into our relationship, and slowly we grew apart.

And I was getting into heroin deeper and deeper. I was in Dallas with Dana when I contemplated shooting it for the first time, and thank God I didn't. I also never smoked coke or crack, even though both were within reach many times. There's no doubt in my mind that if I'd started shooting or smoking the drugs I'd be dead by now. I just kept snorting more and more as everything I had to accomplish in just a few short months seemed increasingly impossible. The movie was being set up and my schedule had been decided. I walked around resenting Howard for not giving me time off. It wasn't that it was such a tough schedule; it was that it was a schedule I couldn't manage on drugs. That's what I wish I could have told Howard.

With just over a month to go before shooting was to begin, my goal was to do whatever I needed to do to get through the movie. I had no idea how I would do it on drugs, since I was in every scene. I had to carry the picture, and my fear and paranoia didn't help me shoulder that responsibility. I started to feel trapped: I couldn't back out of it, but I didn't think I could do it either. Our money came from guys from New Jersey, and that was enough to start my wheels spinning. I had fantasies of pulling out of the movie and finding out that the mafia had put up the money, which, God knows, might still be the case. You don't want to go back on your word with guys like that when they hold up their end of the bargain. In my head I was convinced that this would end one of two ways: I'd either get fired from *Howard* or be killed by Jersey goodfellas. If I didn't die,

I'd lose my career and be broke in two years, so a grave at the bottom of the Hudson River didn't sound so bad.

By June 4, I wasn't off drugs, but everything was moving along. Frank had gotten the script in shape all by himself, and he did a great job. The producer, my friend Anthony Mastromauro, kept it all together. He'd gotten a lot of decent names to be in it, like Ralph Macchio. My friend Laurie Metcalf from *The Norm Show* agreed to play my mom, and she was great. Exciting stuff was happening. And then, in the biggest coup ever, we got Seymour Cassel, and that brought the whole thing up to another level.

It didn't matter to me. I was depressed. I knew that it was the end of the party. I barely got through my signing at the Virgin Megastore in downtown Chicago. Not many people showed up, which is good, because I was rude and belligerent and the signing was awful. The gig that followed was a bad one too. It was at the Arie Crown Theater in Chicago, and it's the single worst stand-up performance I've ever done aside from my first open-mic attempt. I drank and did more drugs than usual that night, and it was weird to be on stage. I was so out of my mind that I started to hallucinate. I don't know if it was depression, booze, heroin, or all of the above, but standing there, all of a sudden I realized that people were yelling at me. Not in the usual way the audience yells during stand-up shows—they were yelling at me because I was repeating jokes. It took me a while to make out what they were saying, because everything was blurry and moving very slowly for me.

"You just told that one, you fucking drunk prick!"

They called me a drug addict, a drunk; they told me they wanted their money back. They were right—they deserved it. I was in another dimension of high. At one point, I stood there waving my hand back and forth in front of my face, seeing two of them and enjoying that immensely. It was the most surreal moment I've ever had on stage. I was contracted to do forty-five minutes and I did them, so they had to pay me. I had arranged to get fifteen grand by check and five in cash. And as I sat in the promoter's office while he got it together, I could hear the crowd in the alley behind the stage door going crazy. The guys out there were pissed, banging on the door, yelling, "Fuck that guy! He ripped us off, that show sucked!" I was still high and really paranoid. I was convinced that I was about to get the shit kicked out of me.

"Hey, man," I said to the promoter. "Can you get me a ride back to the hotel?"

I got back to my room, where I had one bag of heroin left in my suitcase. I planned to do it Sunday when I got off the plane, which would last me through that night and *The Stern Show* the next morning. I don't know what made me think I could just kick heroin like it was Twinkies, but it was the same type of logic that convinced me it was okay to cut up a few lines from that bag.

"Fuck it. I've gotten through this tour, and the movie guys are happy. Howard hasn't fired me. We're making a movie . . . fuck it . . . I'm going to sleep. . . ."

When my alarm went off Monday morning, June 6, 2005, at 4:45 A.M., the contents of that bag had passed entirely through my system and were long gone. I was at Defcon 5. I was sweating, panicked, paranoid, and controlled by a deep chemical need. I made it to the show, but I was like a corpse. I barely said anything. I tried to eat, I tried to drink, but nothing went down. I was thin and sweaty. I thought about driving to get more heroin once we were done, but as every minute ticked by I realized that I couldn't go anywhere. I finished the show, slipped away before anyone could talk to me, went home, and curled up in a ball. After an hour or two, I called the *Beer League* production office, which was just three blocks from my apartment, and told them I couldn't make it today. I said I was sick but I'd be there tomorrow. They were pissed: They'd set all of this up with no help from me and I couldn't make a meeting three blocks away? They had no idea how much more pissed they were going to get. I spent the rest of that day going through utter drug withdrawal hell.

I called Gary at 4:30 the next morning and began a hide-and-seek game I played for the next four days on the show. I just kept mysteriously calling in sick and refused to answer my phone. By Thursday, my mother and sister, who were getting their information from listening to the show, really started to worry. As I've said, those two are the strongest women in my life, and they proved themselves that day once more. My girlfriend, Dana, was unbelievably strong too. She knew that something was wrong—everyone close to me did, I guess. The three of them came to my apartment on Thursday morning while the show was still on and kept banging on the door, demanding to be let in. When I answered it I had a beard, I was shivering, and I hadn't changed my clothes in days.

"Listen," I said. "I've been taking heroin, and I'm trying to kick it here."

They had no experience with heroin detox, and neither did I. I knew enough to tell them that I needed some sleeping pills and some whiskey to hold off the real sickness because at that point I was green. That didn't do much; it gave me a few hours of relief before the withdrawal symptoms started all over again. We talked about how I could get myself in shape without having to drop out of the movie and without going back on heroin.

I'd consider that a pretty big problem to solve, but I had a bigger one that I had to address immediately. When I missed work for the fourth consecutive day and blew off all the movie meetings, the two main money guys started calling, demanding to hear from me. The theories being aired on the show didn't ease their minds any: Was Artie back on coke? Was he holed up in Vegas with a hooker? Was he on a gambling bender somewhere? They needed the truth, so I came clean to Frank Sebastiano, who'd signed on to direct, and Anthony Mastromauro, the producer.

Frank was the first one I let up to my apartment, then Jimmy Palumbo, who'd been my friend for years. All I had to do was open the door for them to see how I was. Frank had put more blood, sweat, and tears into the project than anybody. He wanted it to get made every bit as much as I did. But he took one look at me and that went out the window.

"Art, I've known you a long time," he said. "And I never thought I'd see you looking like this."

"Yeah, I know, Frank. I've been doing a lot of shit and it caught up with me, but I'm going to get through it."

"Art, nobody else has the balls to do this, but I'm going to call off the movie."

Frank is a real tough kid from Jersey, so when I saw him start crying, I knew it was serious. I started crying too.

"Frank, you know how much this means to us."

"I do, Art, but we've got to pull the plug," he said. "The only thing that matters is that you get better. I'd rather have you alive than have this movie."

Frank's sincerity and compassion moved me as much as Quincy Jones's had back at *MADtv*. Frank put things in perspective for me.

"Art, fuck it," he said. "Fuck the movie, fuck the money. So people lose money, so maybe you never go back to *The Stern Show*. If what you've been doing for work has gotten you to this place, none of it's worth it. Don't go back to *The Stern Show*. Don't do anything. You just do whatever you need to do to be happy. Because if you're not happy, you're going to do this to yourself and you're going to die."

"Frank, no, I can't do this. I want to make the movie. I'm not going to do this to anyone involved. I'm not going to do this to you."

"Don't worry about me, just take care of yourself. I'm going to pull the plug."

"Please don't do that yet, Frank," I said. "Just give me the weekend."

He talked to our investors and they called me up the next day, a Friday afternoon.

"Listen, Art. We are about to write a check for this thing, you understand," they said. "We're about to write a check for five hundred thousand dollars to set up the production office for the shoot. You've got to tell us what the fuck is going on. We've put three hundred and fifty thousand dollars into this already, we need to know what's going on."

"I'm really sorry, guys. Listen, I'm going through some shit, but I'll get it together."

"You're going through some shit? What kind of shit are you going through, Artie?" They were not pleased at all. "This isn't a joke, man. We need straight answers."

"I'll be okay—I'm going to get clean, okay? I've been taking some pills and that got out of control, and I thought I could get off them on my own, but I can't. I tried and I got myself sick, but I'm going to do this the right way. Don't worry."

There was a painful and long silence after that. "Artie, we're sorry that you're having drug problems and we're glad that you're getting yourself together. But this is serious and so are we. Part of this deal is that you have to be on the show. If you're not back to normal on the show Monday morning, we're pulling the plug."

"Listen, man, don't do that. I'm feeling sick, but give me till Monday. I will get back to work," I said. "If I don't do that, whatever money that you've put into this I will personally pay you back. I promise you."

"Artie, we can't wait until Monday to see how you're feeling. If you'd come to these meetings, you'd know that we have a schedule to keep. We have to know right now if you're going to be able to do this. We need to give Anthony a check today for half a million dollars, because he's got to pay people and get everything set up or else we lose our shooting window. You don't understand, Artie—we need you to answer us right now."

I paced back and forth in my bedroom wondering what to do. I was sweating, I was shaky, and I felt like saying no. It seemed impossible to me. But something inside me told me I was wrong. I knew I'd never get over the disappointment. Frank and I had our chance to make the movie we wanted, starring me. The pussy thing to do was to say no. Fuck that, I'd been in tough spots before. I'd find a way out by Monday.

I took a deep breath. "Write the check," I said. "Give it to Anthony. I'm doing this. I will be there Monday morning."

"Are you sure, Artie?"

"I'm sure."

"We hope you are," they said. "Because if you're not, it's done. The plug will be pulled and we will cut our losses."

"I understand. I'll be there Monday."

I had no choice but to get it together right away. My mother and sister and I called a few rehab centers to find me a bed where I could detox properly over the weekend. I tried a rehab center in Summit where I'd gone to kick coke ten years before and I left a message with the receptionist.

"Uh, hi, my name is Artie Lange, I'm a comedian who stayed with you a while ago to kick coke and I'm wondering if you could help me out this weekend."

"Sure, what's the problem?"

"I've got to detox from heroin right away."

"Okay. I'll have someone call you back."

The doctor who did, in my opinion, is the hero of this story. He was a huge Stern fan who'd taped the show every day for years.

He's also the singer in a power metal band. His name is Thomaso Skorupski, and when he called me back he wasn't surprised: He'd known from listening to the show that I'd been out for four days and figured there was a good chance it had to do with drugs.

"Listen, Artie, there is a drug called Subutex—have you heard about it?"

"No."

"It's a miracle drug. It will get you through the withdrawals and make you feel like a human being again. I am going to get you six eight-milligram tablets. Cut the eight-milligram tablets in half so you have four milligrams, because you don't need the full amount. Do not have anything to drink ten minutes before you take it; put it under your tongue and let it dissolve. And once it dissolves, in twenty-five minutes, you will feel completely normal and all of the withdrawal pains will go away."

"Does it get you high?"

"No, craving the high is a whole other problem, and we'll get to that. This won't make you high, it will make you normal. We use this to take away the physical addiction, to get people straight enough to start putting their life together. That is where we start."

"Okay."

"You'll stay on it for six months. You'll get your life together. And then, under my care, we will get you off it." He called in the prescription and made a plan to come to my house in two days to give me a full physical.

My mother and sister were skeptical about allowing me to put more drugs in my body, but I was going to do anything at all to get myself to work on Monday. My sister picked up the Subutex, we cut the tablets in half with a cigar cutter, and I put one under my tongue. It's scary, but twenty minutes later, I felt like I could build a house. The sweating stopped, the shaking stopped. I didn't just feel well, I felt great. I felt like I was flying, completely normal, and high too. If this was detox, I was all for it. I went and shaved for the first time in what felt like four months.

What a guy—in the year 2005 this fucker made a house call. Skorupski came over Sunday night at 7 P.M. to give me my physical, and he asked me how I felt. I really did feel fine—probably too fine. I suppose knowing that I had that option of detoxing made it seem like less of a big deal than it was.

Monday morning, I strolled in to the show fresh as a daisy. Thanks to Subutex and Thomaso, my life was saved. But I had a lot of explaining to do. We signed on and Howard started right in.

"All right, Artie, do you want to explain what happened?"

"Look. I had a bad few months on the road. I started drinking too much. I was drinking too much, way too much," I said. "I wasn't doing drugs, just drinking. But I was drinking a lot."

"You were out for a week."

"I had a really bad hangover. I had to clean myself up for a few days."

No one believed me, and who could blame them? Gary said it himself: "I think someday we'll get the whole story, but if that's what you're saying, that's fine."

I got a week of solid ball-breaking from every fan who called in, from Howard, from everybody. And then finally it went away, just like another chapter on the show and in my fucked-up existence. I moved on to do what I had to do for the movie: I went to every meeting, met the wardrobe people, all of it. I signed off on all the decisions I needed to as producer and star and cowriter. And on the Fourth of July, we started shooting. I never missed a mark or line or day at *The Howard Stern Show*. We finished the film on time and under budget. On the last day of shooting, I was still not quite sure how we did it. Within a month, my life had turned around from complete darkness to amazing light.

Dana was such a big part of getting me through the shooting

that even mentioning it here makes me feel guilty that we're not together anymore. She was there every step of the way, holding my hand after every tough scene. She was around the days when I had to shoot for ten hours and then go to *The Stern Show* the next morning. I had three insane weeks and she was with me constantly, massaging my shoulders, talking me through what was worrying me, whatever I wanted. She was off work for the summer, and I got the producers to pay her as one of my assistants. I remember one day I looked at the amount of lines I had to memorize and just started crying in the makeup chair. Dana calmed me down, got everyone out of the room, and helped me get through it. Dana was so essential to the success of the film that we gave her a small part in the movie. She plays a friend of my girl-friend's at the diner, and she looks beautiful in it. It's hard for me to see the scenes she's in today. I just start crying.

If it weren't for Dana, I wouldn't have been able to do my job. But if it weren't for Frank, Anthony, the cinematographer Dave Phillips, and pros like Ralph Macchio, my buddies Jimmy and Mike Deeg, Jerry Minor, Joe Lo Truglio, Seymour Cassel, and Cara Buono, who played my girlfriend, the movie wouldn't have shined at all. They were fucking great. Not a weak link in the bunch. I dedicated *It's the Whiskey Talkin'* to Dana and I should have done the same with *Beer League*.

When we premiered the film at the Ziegfeld Theater in August 2006, we got a distributor deal immediately. Comedy Central saw it and bought it that same night. That's when I felt like we'd really done something—walking the red carpet at that legendary theater for a film I'd starred in and had total creative control over. The fact that the movie destroyed was icing on the cake for me. Everybody from *The Stern Show* loved it, and so did a lot of people I respect. Colin Quinn called me and said it was the funniest movie he'd seen in ten years. He said he hadn't laughed that hard in a long time, and I could tell he was genuine. Hey, Richard Roeper even gave it a thumbs-up. I wasn't expecting that.

Beer League is something I'll always be proud of for so many reasons. I might have taken myself to the edge and almost lost it all, but in the ninth inning, I pulled it out. I couldn't have done it alone, and what I learned most of all was that I'm surrounded by people who care about me. I'm lucky that way, and I know not everyone is. I'm the kind of guy who keeps things in, who likes to go it alone, and who doesn't like to ask anyone for help. I like to take care of everything myself, because I think I know best. My "best" may not be a good idea, but it's mine. But this episode in my life changed that point of view, because I couldn't bullshit myself anymore. My way wasn't working. I needed help from the people in my life. I had to ask for it. And they were there for me. Sometimes your guardian angels aren't just in Heaven. They're all around you if you know where to look.

When I see a guy on the streets of Manhattan who appears to be a homeless junkie, I never see him as just some bum loser; I see him as a reflection of myself, because I could easily be him. The only difference between us is that I have a great family and friends around me and most likely he does not. Now, if I were to find out that he ended up that way in spite of having a great family and friends around him, I'd be the first to throw a lit M-80 at him, which I'd follow up with the following soliloquy: "Fuck you, you lazy junkie, bum LOSER. Why don't you fuck off and die!" The next time I see a guy like that, I may actually go ask him a little bit about his life, and if I get that chance I'll definitely take it. Compassion is fine, but I have to admit, judging and making fun of people who are less fortunate than me is a lot more fun.

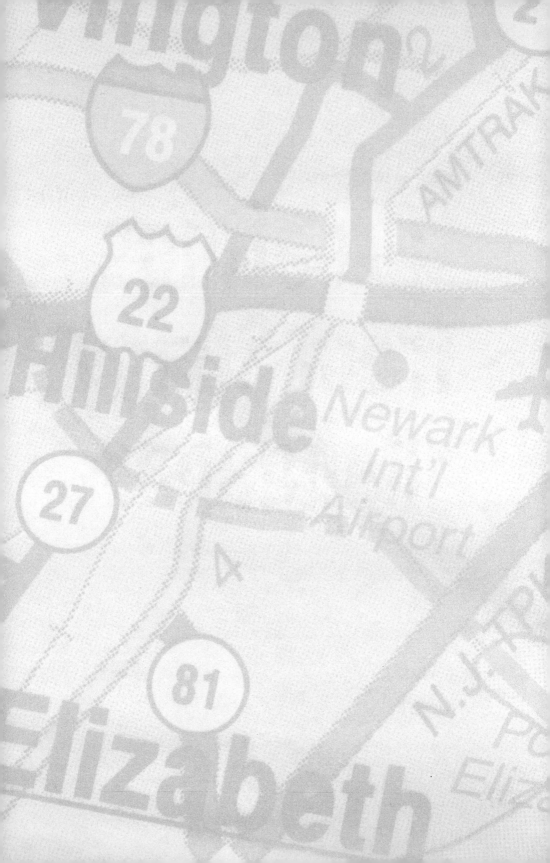

Greetings from Sunny Kandahar

N ot too long ago, I caught a documentary on cable called *Patriot Act* that was made by Jeff Ross, a comedian I've known for about fifteen years. Most people probably know him from the brilliant job he's done on Comedy Central's roasts. I've worked with him on the roasts of Hugh Hefner and William Shatner for Comedy Central as well as the roasts of Donald Trump and Pat Cooper at the Friars Club in New York City. Jeff is always great in that atmosphere, but this documentary showed a whole different side of him.

The filmmakers followed Jeff on a trip to Iraq to do stand-up for the troops with a group that was headlined by Drew

Carey. It was really well done and it brought you right there. It got me thinking about the many things we tend to forget living in a country as great as ours. One of those is the simple fact that we are at war, and for the past five years thousands of brave American men and women have been risking their lives in the Middle East, fighting for the good old U.S. of A. Whether you agree with the war or not, as a citizen of this country you've got to support our soldiers. By now I think most people would agree that we shouldn't have gone into Iraq, but we did, and now that we're there we have to support the troops and their efforts, otherwise our soldiers are dying for nothing. Personally, I think we've got to pray as hard as we can that we can get this thing in Iraq done as quickly as possible so our troops in Afghanistan can get the help they desperately need.

Winning in Afghanistan is the only thing that can ensure that something like 9/11 never happens again here or anywhere else in the West. Afghanistan is where the terrorists are, not Iraq. Of course, that sounds like the naive ramblings of a schoolboy, but there's one fact that no one can deny: It's a fucking mess over there, and our brave countrymen are in the thick of it. The only thing that makes me feel better about that fact is the knowledge that if anyone is capable of figuring out the best course of action, it's the men and women in our armed forces that I met over there. They amazed me every single day. (Excuse my brief political rant. I promise that's all you're going to hear from me as far as politics goes. I'm not exactly qualified to run for office, so believe me, I know when to keep shit to myself.)

Anyway, getting back to how I ended up in a desert in 120-degree heat during wartime, Ross's documentary really affected me to the point that I became obsessed with the idea of going over there to entertain the troops in one way or another. These are extraordinary times, much like any time of war is, and I wanted to do my part as so many people do. I feel privileged to possess a talent

for comedy, which is badly needed over there, believe me. I know it sounds like show business bullshit, but my desire to go really had nothing to do with good PR—I just wanted to help.

I know exactly why too. My grandfather, Sal Caprio, fought in the Army in World War II and was a true war hero, although he was very humble about it. He never made a lot of money in his life, but that doesn't mean a thing; if I'm lucky, one day I'll be half the man Sal Caprio was. The worst shrink in the world could deduce that my desire to serve my country by doing stand-up for the troops was my attempt to make him proud of me. Sal's been dead for fourteen years, but believe me, that is the correct assessment, no doubt about it.

I was determined to do it, so the next step was figuring out how to do it. In September 2007, I called my stand-up agent at the time, Conan Smith, to get the ball rolling. Conan is a rare creature in the agent world: He is both very bright and he understands how to deal with someone of my unique mind-set. In other words, he knows how to handle comedians with unbelievably self-destructive, loser tendencies. Conan foresaw some trouble with this scheme of mine.

"Well, Art, I know who to call because I've done this before," he said. "But you might be what I'd call a risk. Your record isn't exactly clean."

After a few weeks with no word from Conan, I called him to check in and heard the news I expected: It didn't look good. It seemed that the people at the USO did something that has become my kryptonite in recent years: They Googled me. People Googling Artie Lange has cost me jobs, health insurance, and that first time, the chance to fulfill my dream of entertaining the troops. Not to get all Unabomber on you (and I did promise I was done with politics), but to me certain types of technology are the fucking devil. One simple Web search provided the USO with my history with drugs and the law in startling detail, and they told Conan all about it. What a wacko time we're living in! Twenty years ago, if you wanted to run a background check on someone, you had to hire a talented, well-connected private investigator. Now all you need are parents who make enough money to buy their shithead kid a fucking computer. For a guy with a background like mine, "Google" is the worst noun that can also be used as a verb (besides "Jew").

The USO knew that I had a history as a drug addict and that I'd been arrested before, and they felt that I wasn't exactly the ideal candidate to head up one of their comedy tours. Conan put it to me this way: "Art, they're pretty skeptical about you."

My personal history and mistakes weren't my only problem. I'd heard a rumor that Sirius Satellite Radio had wanted to bring the entire *Howard Stern Show* cast to Iraq to do a few weeks of live shows. It would have been amazing—now, that's what I call a huge publicity stunt. To say that *The Howard Stern Show* is beloved by a lot of our troops is one of the understatements of the century. Having the show broadcast live from Iraq would definitely bring a lot of cheer, but it didn't happen because the USO had its reservations about the show and were particularly concerned with Howard's tendency to be completely honest. Honesty in wartime is not always considered the best policy by those in charge. Add to that the show's usual subject matter and regular list of taboos that are broken on a daily basis and you have a clear reason why *The Stern Show* was turned down. Unfortunately, as a representative of the show, I probably would have been turned down too even without my fucked-up background. The strikes against me were just too big.

But I wasn't going to leave it at that. I was determined to turn the situation around, and the irony was I figured I could use *The Stern Show,* the biggest strike against me, to help me resurrect my dream. I went on the air and told Howard how I'd been turned down to entertain the troops because of the show and my sketchy background. I hadn't wanted to make a big deal about it at all—I just wanted to go and quietly do a tour during one of our vacations. But now I had no choice.

"I'm a little aggravated," I said. "I think that I probably have some fans over there in the military who would enjoy the show I'd put together, so if there's anybody out there who can help the situation, I'm putting it out there. I'm annoyed."

"You know what? That is really horrible," Howard said. "I know a lot of soldiers love the show, they love Artie, and hey, if Artie wants to do his part, I don't see any reason why this shouldn't happen."

Sure enough, about a month later, my agent, Conan, called me and said that the USO had called. After I'd brought it up on the air, quite a few soldiers had expressed an interest in seeing me perform. The USO did the right thing—they came back to us and okayed it, but they were going to pay strict attention to who I wanted to bring over with me. They also were going to require that I get a note from a doctor saying that I was healthy and drug-free. The last thing they wanted, and who could blame them, was for me to go through heroin withdrawal over there.

This was great news. I had a physical, and the doctor sent them a note saying that I was in good enough shape to make the trip. He assured them that I was not doing heroin. I promised them that if I wasn't clean, I wouldn't get on the plane.

A woman named Tracy Thede at the USO, who is a very big deal over there as well as being a very professional, nice, and confident woman, got on the phone with me in April 2008 and in no uncertain terms laid out what I was getting myself into. By that time, my agent had left the world of stand-up agenting, much to my chagrin. Like a lot of the bright agents, Conan Smith went to work as an executive at a production company to produce TV shows and short films. I hope to work with him in the future. Even though Conan had made this move, he graciously agreed to remain the point man on the tour as one of the last things he would do as an agent.

"We got the note from your doctor and that's great," Tracy said. "The conditions are hotter and rougher than you can imagine, so as long as you are confident that it won't be a problem we are fine on that requirement."

"No, that won't be a problem at all. I expect that," I said.

"Now, tell me who you intend to take over," she said.

I began to lay out my dream team for her: Jimmy Florentine and Nick DePaolo, who are both great friends and greater comedians, were first on the list. The rest I was going to have to think about.

One of the USO's stipulations was their right to censor certain material. We weren't to talk about anything homosexual or obviously offensive to women, or disparaging of marriage or relationships, or do drug-related humor. Not even anything on masturbation. I yessed my way through that speech, figuring that we could probably get away with it once we were over there. I figured it would be hard to take the mic out of my hand if I was able to get a crowd of guys laughing who'd just taken fire from the enemy. Even if it was a fag joke. But on one point there was absolutely no uncertainty: We could not make fun of President Bush.

"He is the Commander-in-Chief," Tracy said. "He leads the armed forces. This will not be tolerated at all."

"That will not be a problem. I completely understand."

"This is serious. Other comics have wavered from this, and they were not welcomed back."

"Okay, I will be sure that everyone involved is well aware of this."

I wasn't surprised. I figured that politics and religion were going to be huge no-no's. Religion and politics were two of the reasons we were at war. Who could expect to take that stuff lightly?

Jimmy Florentine and Nick DePaolo, besides being great talents, are guys' guys and not very political in their comedy, so I didn't see a problem. They're the kind of guys soldiers—both men and women—would love. And I don't think they'd mind me saying that they're not known by anyone to be ultraliberals. Neither am I, for that matter. The chances of any of us doing a lot of political, anti-Bush stuff was nil.

They were okayed, and they signed on immediately, eager to help out their country, as I was. I needed one more guy, and I wanted it to be a friend of mine. My dream guy at that point was Colin Quinn, who is one of my heroes as a comedian. He really wanted to go, but the USO had an issue with him. I never got an official reason. He had done several USO tours before and the soldiers loved him, but the USO must have felt he'd crossed a line. It could have been a president joke, but I don't know for sure. Anyway, Conan Smith tried his best, but the USO wasn't going to budge, so I had to give up on that idea.

While I was trying to decide which comedian friend I'd take, Gary Dell'Abate—Baba Booey from *The Stern Show*—stepped up and said he wanted to come.

"I realize I don't do stand-up, but I'd like to come and introduce you guys," he said. "I'd like to be kind of a host."

Gary is really good at this; I'd seen him do it on the road: He tells a couple of minutes of jokes, he emcees, and he's good at introducing the show to the crowd. He really wanted to give back to the soldiers in any way he could. I thought it was wonderful—the only issue I had was that he didn't fit one of the criteria I'd set for every member of this tour: Gary had children. He's got a beautiful wife, a beautiful house in Connecticut, and two great little boys, one twelve and one ten. I really had an issue with this, because I would not be able to live with myself if something happened to him over there. Especially if something happened to all of us and I lived, that is. Gary understood this, so he went home one day and talked it over with his wife, who said it was cool. He explained to his kids that their father was going to go help the country, so they thought it was cool too, and since he really wanted to do it, that was it.

Now, let me just state for the record that I love Gary and I always have. There was some controversy on the show, as there always is, about whether or not I really wanted his company. That was never an issue for me; the only issue was that he had kids. After I got over that, though, I was really happy that he was coming. Gary was a bonus. With him hosting and moving the show along, the rest of us could just deal with making the troops laugh.

Florentine, DePaolo, Gary, and myself—a good start, but we still needed one more comic. The great Greg Fitzsimmons went through my mind, but Greg has a child. Bob Levy too was a guy the soldiers would love, but Bobby has a nine-year-old, so he was out of the question.

I wasn't sure what I was going to do until it just kind of happened. For the fourth time in the past six years, I did a benefit that Greg Fitzsimmons puts together in New York City. About eleven years ago, Gerry Red Wilson, a comedian he and I knew, died of spinal meningitis at thirty-six years old. He was a great, gregarious guy from Queens who died right when everything was going right for him. He had a fiancée who he'd proposed to on *The Tonight Show* and he was making a real name for himself. He had his own short-lived sitcom, but it was obvious that he was going on to do other sitcom work. Anyone who saw him knew that Gerry Red Wilson was going to be a very successful comic. Right after his girlfriend agreed to marry him, she and Gerry flew to Hawaii so he could appear in an episode of the new *Fantasy Island* series. He went, he did his thing, but while there he got very sick with what turned out to be spinal meningitis. His condition got dramatically worse very quickly and he slipped into a coma even before his fiancée could get him to the hospital. He died soon after.

Every year for the past ten years, his fiancée and Greg Fitzsimmons have held a benefit to support the Gerry Red Wilson Foundation, which helps raise awareness about spinal meningitis and funds research for a cure. I'm happy to say that his fiancée is now married and very happy and over the years the benefit has grown tremendously. It started out at Carolines but as of three years ago, it has become big enough to sell out the 1,100-seat Town Hall theater.

I did the benefit in 2008, while still looking for my last comic, and that's where I found him. Another guy who always does the show is arguably, along with Nick DePaolo, one of the best comedians of the last twenty years. He's also one of the nicest guys and has been a friend of mine for a long time. I'm in awe of this guy's talent, as many are when it comes to club comedy. His name is Dave Attell. Mainstream audiences know him as the host of the great

Comedy Central show *Insomniac,* and now he's hosting the new *Gong Show* on the channel too. But nothing can come close to capturing the unique experience of seeing Dave Attell in his element at a New York comedy club on, say, a Thursday night with a full room. Dave getting up to do a twenty-minute set is unequaled. In that environment there is no other comedian I'd rather see and that includes Richard Pryor and George Carlin. I know, that's a pretty emphatic statement to make, but it's true and I think a lot of comics would agree. You've got to believe me on this, and if you get the chance, go find out for yourself. If you were going to erect a Mount Rushmore dedicated to the greatest comedians of the last twenty years, DePaolo and Attell would be your Washington and Lincoln.

Anyway, when I saw Attell at the Gerry Red Wilson benefit he said to me, "Hey man, I hear you're putting together a troupe to go do stand-up for the troops."

"Definitely," I said.

"Man, I've been a bunch of times," Dave said. "And I'd like to do it with you. Do you mind if I'm a part of it?"

"Are you fucking kidding me?"

"No, are you sure?"

"Yeah, I'm sure!"

The next day, I called Conan Smith, very excited, to tell him that Attell wanted to do it. In my mind, this was it: Gary hosting, Jimmy Florentine, Nick DePaolo, Dave Attell, and myself. There wasn't a more heavenly lineup on earth for guys' guys and chicks who were soldiers. It was definitely my dream team.

I had put this thing together, so the USO asked that I name the tour. On a conference call with Conan and Tracy Thede, I said as a goof, "How about Operation Mirth?" It sounded kind of ironic, since "mirth" is an old-fashioned word that means gaiety and fun, which is not quite what any of our team is known for. I said it as a joke, Tracy giggled on the phone, and before I knew it there were fliers and shirts and hats going around that said "Artie Lange's Operation Mirth."

"There's just one thing you have to understand," Tracy said. "You can mention the tour on the air and you can mention who is going. But you are going to Afghanistan, you are going to the shit. You are not going to Iraq. You're not going to Baghdad and having a nice little trip. You're going out to obscure bases with only about eighty guys on them. Places with special ops, bases that never see shows."

If I hadn't already picked up on the vibe that we weren't exactly Robin Williams or Billy Crystal, that comment did it. "Well, that's great. We want to help," I said.

"These soldiers are going to love you so much just for showing up," Tracy said. "Before you go on stage, they'll give you a hug. But it's going to be a little dangerous, Artie. If you're okay with it, we'll send you to Afghanistan, but on the air, please just say that you're going to Iraq. We don't want people knowing that you're going there, and we don't want them to know the exact time, either."

We were scheduled to go from June 28 to July 4, 2008, which worked out perfectly. It was the first week of our two-week vacation from *Howard,* so neither Gary nor I would have to miss a day of work.

As the date drew closer, I got more and more nervous, and it was only a matter of time before I fell off the wagon again with heroin—bad. One night, weeks before, while I was shooting pool in this bar billiards league, what some of you might call "the wrong crowd" showed up. They're definitely the wrong crowd for me, because that night I fell off the wagon headfirst into a heroin binge that would last several months. But I'd made a promise to the USO, so I had to force myself to stop doing heroin and get myself together. Subutex, once again, did the job. When it was time to roll on June 28, I was allowed to take some Subutex with me and I was feeling well enough to get on the plane. It was tough, believe me,

but maybe some higher power helped me out. Of the many times I've needed an extra helping hand, this was one of them: That USO tour had become the single most important event in my career.

Our first leg was Newark to Frankfurt, Germany, a flight that Jimmy Florentine and I took together. We were supposed to meet up with the other guys in Frankfurt, but they were delayed. We spent our time with Jeff Anthony, an amazing Vietnam vet who was our USO guide and manager throughout the trip. From Frankfurt we took a flight to Istanbul, Turkey. Luckily, these first few legs were all commercial flights that we did in business class. There was a chance that DePaolo, Attell, and Gary might not meet us. If that was the case, Jeff informed us that we'd have to keep moving forward and that Jim and I might be responsible for doing all of the shows by ourselves until they caught up, but fortunately the others made it to Istanbul on time.

Next we flew to Kazakhstan, in Central Asia, where we slept on our first Army base. The arrangements were not nearly as bad as I'd thought they'd be. We stayed in a pretty clean, big Army barracks. We showered, slept, and got ready for our first engagement: one show for the entire base.

The first show was at 7 P.M., and it was packed—standing room only, a great turnout. There were about 800 people in a room that was meant to hold 600. We got the butterflies out during that show and found out what was cool to say and what wasn't. Because it was a tour I'd set up, I was the headliner, so I had to close. Let me tell you, following Jim Florentine, DePaolo, and Attell is no easy feat anywhere, and sitting there watching them perform that first time, I realized that it was going to be rough. That turned out to be a great thing, because it kept me focused on delivering the best set I could. Between that pressure and the Subutex, I felt great and had no heroin cravings. I had bigger fish to fry.

Gary took the stage, told a few jokes, and made the necessary announcements. Then Florentine did about fifteen to twenty minutes. Nick did the same, Attell did about the same, and then me. I was contracted to do thirty, thirty-five minutes.

Jimmy, God bless him, tore down all the taboos that first night. Everybody respected the ban on religious humor and didn't do anything anti-Bush, but starting with Jimmy at that very first show, we all did every other thing the USO had asked us not to do. And we could not have killed any harder. I looked at Jeff Anthony, thinking that this would be our first and last show.

"As long as nobody complains, you've got nothing to worry about," he said. "And judging by how hard they're laughing, I don't think anybody is about to complain."

Jimmy did sex stuff and amazing stuff about relationships, and they loved all of it. In our defense, we weren't completely blatant about it; we made an effort to get around the rules—with humor, of course. Our approach was best summed up by this joke Dave Attell told during his very first set:

"When we signed up for this tour, they said, 'You can't do any jokes about masturbation,'" he said. "So let me tell you a story about the time I was fucking a sock with shampoo in it."

I killed too, but there were a couple of lulls because I decided to tackle another taboo subject that nobody else had—racial comedy. Basically, it was stupid material that I love doing because it causes uptight white people to panic. That night I brought out gems like this one: "If Santa Claus was black there would be some problems. I don't think you could convince rednecks that once a year a black guy was going to break into their house late at night and leave them shit."

The next morning, we took our first true military flight. We walked into one of those huge planes that hold 500 soldiers, the type where the bottom of the plane drops down like a big ramp. I walked up into it thinking about that scene in *Close Encounters of the Third Kind* when the aliens come down a similar kind of thing. We took our seats, five out-of-shape comedians sitting up in front with 500 men and women in the Marines, Army, and Air Force behind us, ready to roll. These soldiers were not only in great shape, but they were young, kids in their twenties with sixty pounds of equipment on their backs. They were unbelievably heroic, ready to serve our country, and were so appreciative that we were there that I was incredibly moved.

There was a smoking hot chick, also about twenty, from Texas, who served as our sort-of flight attendant, except that unlike your average hot, young flight attendant, she was smart, tough, and military through and through. We knew her only by her nickname, Worm. She was *really* hot, and on the three-hour flight to Afghanistan, Jeff Anthony, our USO manager, could see that we all really liked her. I'm sure she could see it too, because our tongues were cartoonishly hanging out of our mouths. I couldn't help myself—I kept asking her to get up and get me more water, because that meant she'd have to bend over in front of us. She was clearly in better shape than all of us combined and could definitely kick our asses, but getting her to bend over for water was worth it. I was willing to risk the beating. I don't mind admitting that I jerked off to her that night with Dave Attell sleeping just eight feet away from me in our room. I never told Dave, and you might think I'm crazy for putting it in the book, but I'm not. I know Dave, and there's no way in hell he's going to ever read this.

Anyway, we landed in Kandahar, and let me tell you, that place was unique. We'd been warned by the soldiers at the base we'd just left, but honestly, no one can prepare you for the extra-special environmental eccentricities that await you when you touch down in Kandahar. The place literally tastes and smells like shit. You see, that's because there's a shit pond—literally, a reservoir of shit—in the middle of Kandahar. Every day around 6 P.M., when the wind blows just right, which, luckily for us, was when we were scheduled to start the second of our four *outdoor* shows, the air transforms into invisible shit. I'll say it again—nothing can prepare you for it. Right in the middle of Nick DePaolo's set, I breathed in and it tasted like I was biting into a steaming loaf of shit. This wasn't pleasant of course, but it did give us a heap of great material. All of us were experiencing it for the first time, which was funny for the soldiers, who'd had no choice but to get used to it. All kidding aside, it was so bad that I almost threw up. I wasn't sure I'd be able to make it onto the stage. I started thinking about what jokes I could make that involved throwing up, because as I saw it, there was like a seventy percent chance that I was going to vomit. Somehow I got through it. One of the best laughs I got came when I put a lit cigarette into my nose and coughed out the smoke. That was the only way I could handle the shit wind.

After every show on the tour, we did a meet and greet in a separate location where everyone who'd seen the show and everyone on the base could come and shake our hands and have us sign these Operation Mirth posters or whatever else they wanted signed. Those were my favorite moments—getting to talk to the troops, one-on-one. On the way to the meet and greet one night, twenty yards into the drive, an earsplitting siren went off, followed by an announcement: "Mortar fire coming in! Take cover immediately! Mortar fire coming in! Take cover immediately!" Without flinching, the driver pulled the big Hummer we were riding in over to the side of the road and told us not to move. A bunch of Marines, white and black, men and women, got us out of the truck and formed human shields around us. They walked us forward toward this aboveground bunker where we were going to wait this thing out because the base was under attack.

"Hey, man," I said to Chris, one of the black kids, "should we be worrying our asses off right now?"

"Artie," he said, "the way I look at it, I look at it like this. Don't stress it. If one of these motherfucking mortars hits you, you're gonna be *vaporized*. You won't feel a goddamned thing, man, because you're gonna be dust. In your case, you're gonna be a *lotta* dust, but you're gonna be dust all the same. You know what? If that happens, I'm gonna have to sweep that shit up, so I hope it doesn't, because you gonna be a lotta dust if you get vaporized, man! I wish you weighed a few less pounds, man, just in case you get hit. You would be one hell of a cleanup job, Artie. A hell of a lot of dust."

"Okay, I get it," I said, not really laughing because I was experiencing true fear. "Enough with the dust joke."

"Okay, man. Just look at it this way, Artie: If one of them *doesn't* hit you, then everything is cool. If you don't get hit, in a few minutes it's back to normal, everything's fine."

"Yeah, but what if one of them comes close? What if there's some shrapnel?"

This kid looked at me dead serious. "Artie, if that happens, me and my partner here will make sure you won't be touched. We'll take the hit." I'll never forget this. Here was a guy saying he'd throw himself in front of mortar fire to save *my* life, just because I'm an American citizen. It doesn't get more real than that. I'm a piece-of-shit, out-of-shape comedian; this guy's life means way more than mine does over there, but this Chris was willing to take that hit for me. And he was a black kid. The next time I hear somebody saying racist shit, I'm going to punch them in the fucking face. Actually, that's not true. I'll want to punch them in the face, but I'll probably pussy out and not do it and agree with the fucking racist shit they're saying so I don't get my ass kicked. But secretly I'll be disagreeing with them. I love black people, believe me, even more so now because one of them almost saved my life. But I fully intend to continue being the pussy that I am. Sorry, Chris.

Anyway, these guys got us to the bunker, and the attack continued for the next forty minutes. This structure was very claustrophobic, like an aboveground coffin made of concrete, about seven feet tall and ten feet wide and open at both ends. We were able to stand in it, but just barely. Manute Bol would have been fucked. We all sat in the interior of this thing, and we got great pictures of all of us in there, looking pretty scared. Once we got the all clear, they let us go. And that's when I understood what day-to-day life was like for these troops: We continued with the regularly scheduled program. We did the meet and greet and signed pictures for a while and carried on as if nothing had happened.

The next day, through some leaks in my agent's office or publicist's office or some people working for the Army or USO, Rush and Molloy in the *Daily News* ran pictures of Gary and me and an item about the mortar attack. We didn't find out about it until Nick DePaolo called home on a satellite phone that Jimmy Florentine had gotten from his brother before he left. Nick's wife was crying, thinking that it had been even worse than the paper let on. I'd just talked to my mother and sister a few days before, so when I got a chance to use the phone I called my great, beautiful friend Michelle in Florida, another one of the guardian angels in my life. When I found out that I wouldn't be able to make another call on the satellite phone because it would only last for short periods of time, I asked her to call my mother and sister to tell them I was fine.

The next day, we were going to a very remote place that I'm not allowed to name to do another show. We were told this was where the troops were really going to dig us. To get there, we had to take Black Hawk helicopters and we had to wear flak jackets and bulletproof vests. They had to sew three together to fit me, which was a great ego-boost and the big joke of the trip. Jeff Anthony showed us how to put them on, and off we went. If you ever have the chance to wear a flak jacket, don't. They are fucking uncomfortable. We did our show and were about to get on another helicopter to go to an even more remote base. I couldn't imagine what that was going to be like because where we were, there were only about eighty guys who'd just returned from doing hand-to-hand combat with the Taliban—I shit you not. Those guys thanked us up and down for making the trip, and when I told them where we were going next, these guys, who'd just faced off with the Taliban, couldn't believe it. Where we were was dangerous enough for them.

To get to the next location, we were required to have two Apache helicopters as an escort in addition to the armed Black Hawk helicopters. In the end we couldn't go because the Apaches had mechanical problems. Considering that there are two huge guns on each Black Hawk, the fact that we wouldn't be allowed to attempt the trip without the backup of two Apaches, hard-core armored Apaches, said it all. That fourth show had to be canceled.

Instead, we booked a meet and greet within driving distance of

Kandahar and returned there by helicopter. Two good old boys flew the Black Hawks and another two good old boys manned the guns in back. They were positioned on the outer sides of the copter, scanning the Afghani desert looking for Taliban who come out of water holes or just appear out of the desert from these little tents and caves. These guys had enormous M-60's, and they'd shoot at anything suspicious. When we got over the desert, one of the kids turned to me.

"Hey, Artie, you want to shoot this fucker?"

"Yeah! I'd love to."

"Come over here, man."

All the soldiers who took us around did a lot of subtle fat jokes with me, and this guy was no different. "First I've gotta climb over you. The war may be over by the time I do it, but I'm gonna have to climb over you."

Once he got over me, he said, "Okay, man, I'm gonna give you the gun and I want you to aim for that mountain."

I aimed for the mountain, which I assumed wasn't going to be a very difficult thing to hit, but it was. I swear to God, I came nowhere fucking near it—a mountain. I didn't care; shooting that thing was great. I fucking lost it. I had so much fucking fun shooting this huge M-60 out of a Black Hawk helicopter in the middle of the Afghani desert, I couldn't believe it. I was like some drunken cowboy just blasting away at a section of the desert with an amazing history. It was almost inappropriate. Our pilots pointed out ruins as we flew over, long bits of a wall that looked like a pile of rubble. That pile used to be one of Alexander the Great's castles. And there I was, shooting and missing the huge mountain just beyond it. After two minutes the kid had to cut me off.

"All right, Artie, calm down!" he said. "Calm down! We're gonna run out of ammo."

"Hey, man, that was fun!"

"I could see that."

"Hey, you said that the Taliban runs out of nowhere all the time—what if I accidentally killed a Taliban guy just now?"

The kid turned and looked out into the sun and the sand and then turned back to me and said: "Well, Artie, if you did, that's one less fucker I gotta kill!"

He started maniacally laughing, and as I enjoyed my own fantasy camp moment from *Platoon*, *Apocalypse Now*, and every other great war movie I've ever seen, I started maniacally laughing with him as if we'd gone through basic training together.

We landed back at the base, got reacquainted with the cool breeze of the shit pond, and the next day we were driven to a base about an hour outside of Kandahar, where we did a meet and greet, had dinner with the guys, talked, and took pictures. They hugged us and thanked us for coming. You could tell how much it was appreciated, which made the experience rewarding on a very personal level. I gave a lot of the guys I met there my phone number and offered to give them a tour of the Sirius studio when they got back. I've seen a few of them back here already. Right now I'm trying to get another kid Yankees tickets for next year, and despite the trip being over I will do anything I can to keep in contact. I have that much respect for these kids.

After that last visit, we returned to Kandahar, showered, and were all set to get our first of a few planes home. We were supposed to be back by July Fourth to have dinner with our families and enjoy the holiday, which, considering what we'd just done, would definitely be meaningful. Well, it didn't quite work out that way. We were cargo on military flights where we weren't exactly a priority, so we kept getting delayed. Show business people get their ass kissed in the States, but over there a piece of toilet paper being delivered to the soldiers had more pull than we did when it came to getting on one of those flights.

We waited for a full day after we'd been told that the next plane was ours. We played cards, we killed time, but twenty hours in a terminal in an Army airport in Bagram, Afghanistan, offers little entertainment or distraction after an hour, let alone twenty. In the end, we got out, but we missed the last flight out of Kazakhstan. When that happened, we officially weren't going to make it home for the Fourth, and I wasn't happy about that at all. My mother had planned a whole big party down at my new Shore house.

I was looking forward to my mother's sausage and fried peppers and bread and pasta, and I'll admit it, I lost it in the Kazakhstan airport. I threw shit around, I yelled, and I just got out of control. Everyone around me, who didn't exactly speak great English, looked at me like I was insane. Dave Attell, Gary, Florentine, and Jeff Anthony had to calm me down, and thank God I was surrounded by friends because they were the only reason I didn't get arrested. I know one thing for sure: If I had been arrested, I'd still be in a Kazakh jail right now. My friends kept the authorities from taking me away, and somehow they got me to relax a bit.

We weren't going anywhere, so the Army sent transport to take us back to the base until the next day. I'd had it, and as I'm known to do, which you obviously know if you've gotten this far, I looked around for some self-destructive relief. Gambling was out of the question since I wasn't interested in Kazakh horse and cart racing, and every woman in the vicinity who looked like a whore seemed like she'd last seen youth back when there was a czar in office. That left chemical relief, and drastic measures were necessary.

I told my friends I needed a stiff drink to chill out, so I went to this dinky little bar in the airport and ordered a double Jack Daniel's. As I chugged it and ordered another, I saw a shady-looking guy sitting there, eyeballing me. I knew right away what the deal with him was. I started talking to the bartender very loudly about where I could buy Valium or some other drug, and sure enough this guy came right over. I bought fifteen Valium off the guy and took twelve of them right there in one swallow of whiskey. That did it, all right. Suddenly this bare-bones airport lounge was completely interesting to me.

By the time we got back to the Army base, I was so fucked up that I was slurring my words and yelling at people for no reason at all. I tried to start fights with Gary and the other guys, all of whom are dear friends of mine. I was inventing stuff that they'd done that I was pissed about. I was just this Valiumed-up, fucked-up asshole who wanted to be rebellious, just like the douche bag I am.

"Look, man," Jeff Anthony said as we went through the gates. "We are on a military base. You are *way* too fucked up to be here right now, my friend. You're gonna get arrested if you don't watch yourself."

Jeff and the guys put me into what I'll call a "gentle headlock" and got me to bed, and thank God I passed out. I slept for twenty hours and when I woke up we had only about two hours to kill until our plane ride home. Crisis barely averted, but averted nonetheless.

We caught our plane to Istanbul where we had to bribe some guy $35 to get our exit visas. $35? What kind of pathetic bribe is that? It was such a scam—our visas were fine. The guys in the airport said that they were not fine, but for $35 they *could be* fine. Whatever. We slipped them the money and got the "right" visas. Then we flew out, had a two-hour layover in Frankfurt, and then flew to New York City, direct, for nine hours. I was in business class with Jimmy Florentine again and we watched *Shine a Light,* the Scorsese documentary about the 2007 Stones concert at the Beacon Theater in New York City. We watched it about three straight times, actually, and had fun bullshitting. Before that trip, I thought I knew everything there was to know about Florentine, but I was wrong. We got to know each other a little bit better and I'm glad for it.

It was such a successful trip. Now that we're home, I feel like I have a bond with those guys that will never be broken. When we landed, Gary and I still had six days of vacation to get ourselves together. But the best part was that Jeff Anthony told us right there in the airport that he'd spoken to Tracy Thede, who reported that they'd already gotten such amazing feedback and that the USO was unbelievably happy with the turnout. She called the tour a "smashing success" and said that we could return anytime we wanted. Everyone said that we'd go back together or on our own. I'm so proud of that—I really, really am.

A couple of weeks later I got a letter from Edward A. Powell, the president and chief executive officer of the USO.

Dear Artie,

Thank you for participating in your recent tour to Kazakhstan and Afghanistan and for taking the time to honor the men and women serving there. It meant so much to them and it reminded them that the USO supports them and their families wherever they serve. We look forward to future USO tours with you and wish you the very best.

> *With kind regards,*
> *Edward A. Powell*

That was a beautiful letter to get. It's displayed nicely on my refrigerator so I'll see it all the time.

Of all the fun things I've done in my career I'm most proud of my USO tour. My grandfather was a real war hero, and obviously I'm no hero—except when I'm trying to save drunken white-trash girls in taxicabs, but that's another story. I'm just glad that I possess a skill that enabled me to fulfill my dream. Despite a life of bad decisions that almost made it impossible, I ended up being asked to head up another tour almost the moment I touched down back home. It's nothing I'd ever take for granted, but when I stop to think about it, which I'm doing now, that kind of fucked-up shit is just what happens to me. That kind of fucked-up shit, both the good and the bad, is the story of my life.

I am glad to be ending this book on a positive note, which is rare but not impossible for me. But before I do, I need to say one more thing on the subject of our troops. When they start coming back, we cannot let this episode in our history mirror what happened after the Vietnam War. We cannot make the same mistake twice. Bob Costas did a great interview with Bruce Dern, an actor who was in the film *Coming Home,* which is about how Vietnam vets were treated in America after the war. At the end of the movie,

Bruce Dern's character feels such a sense of guilt about what he did in the war and whatever else he saw that fucked him up over there that he takes off his Marine uniform and runs into the ocean. He commits suicide. In this interview with Costas about the film, Bruce Dern said, "You know what? Whatever you feel about the sixties and Vietnam and Nixon, drugs, whatever else you think about that era, there's one thing everybody has to agree with. There should have been somebody there, supplied by the government or connected to the government in some way, to help guys like the character I played. They should have been there to put their arms around him and say, 'You don't have to kill yourself. What happened over there is not your fault.' The character represents just one of the thousands who did that, but they weren't in a movie."

I've been thinking about that film ever since I came back. We might not be prepared to deal with the kind of baggage these young kids will bring back from Iraq. When these American guys and girls from all backgrounds and races and of all ages come back to live among us again, no matter what the outcome of the crazy bullshit over there, our government has to provide some kind of outlet, some kind of expert who will throw their arms around these brave men and women and ask them how they feel about everything they've been through. These kids are going to need an outlet if they hope to lead normal lives. I hope that every single one of them comes home feeling like a hero, because that is what they are. And they must be treated that way.

If the government is too fucked up to do it, I am saying it now: We have to do it on our own. Every single one of us, as citizens who live here and lead lives untouched by the hell that rages on over there, must do our part. We should go right up to these vets from Iraq and Afghanistan and say, "Thank you, we love you, how are you feeling?" I'm hoping maybe they'll say something like this:

"Listen, it's okay. It wasn't easy over there, but we did what we had to do. We served, we risked our lives, and we did the best we could."

And when they do reveal their hardships, I hope it's nothing quite like this: "I was feeling fine about things, to tell you the truth, until Artie got political again in that motherfucking book of his. I picked that shit up to hear about his fucked-up life, and that asshole kept reminding me of the shit I'm trying to forget. Doesn't that douche bag know we don't need to hear that from a guy like him? Jesus Christ. How about telling a couple of dick jokes, Tubby?"

To our troops, I'd like to say this now: You're right, and I'm sorry. The third time is the charm, and it won't happen again. At least not in this book. Because as of now, this book is fucking over. You'll hear no more politics or anything else out of my fat jerk-off Jersey mouth, I promise you. Until next time that is. *Salud.*

The Last Word

As I finished writing this book, another drug-related problem came up, once again, in my life. It's too complicated a story to tell briefly, but put it this way: If I get a second book deal, it's going to be one hell of a good place to start. People always say to me, "Thank God you're in a business that is very forgiving when it comes to drug addicts." They say, "Look at Robert Downey, Jr.—that guy had a horrible problem with drug addiction. He was getting so fucked up he was passing out in strangers' houses, going to sleep in their kids' beds. He kept fucking up chance after chance. Now he's one of the biggest movie stars in the world!" Well, that might be true, but these people tend to forget one very important piece of that puzzle: Not everyone is Robert Downey, Jr. Yes, the guy had a tremendous problem with drugs, but he's also got tremendous acting talent.

Show business is a business—in fact, it's more business than it is show. And it's a business that's not very forgiving of those who don't bring in money. Drug addicts with talent who are good earners are good business, so they're forgiven. You can't let your drug problem get bigger than your talent or marketability because something very different happens to you then. Unfortunately, that is the norm, not the exception. For every Robert Downey, Jr., there are a hundred Jeff Conaways out there.

Before I sign off, I'd just like to say, if you enjoyed this book at all, if maybe you found something in these pages that gave you a chuckle or caused an eye to tear or taught you a lesson about what not to do, tell a friend about it. Don't give them your copy, please, that's a bad idea. I hope you found at least one story in here that you might want to reread. So no, don't give it away; tell your friends, all of them, that they should buy this book. It's fine to lie to them about how good it is—the important thing is to tell them to buy it. Because lately I'm starting to think that on the Show Business Drug Addict Forgiveness Meter, I'm inching closer to Jeff Conaway than Robert Downey, Jr. each and every day. . . . Well, I gotta go. Take it easy, and I hope to see you all back here next book.

—ARTIE LANGE

Acknowledgments

I'd like to thank the following people because without them this book would not have been possible: my book agent Richard Abate, my mother, my sister Stacey, Howard, Robin, Fred, and Gary, Benjy Bronk, Doug Goodstein, J.D., Teddy, Dan Zitt, Jared Levine, Michael Garnett, Stephen Levinson, Dana Cironi, my publisher Julie Grau, the co-writer of this and, I hope, my second book, Anthony Bozza, Michelle Stevens, all of my grandparents, including the recently passed Grandma Caprio, and of course my father, for providing me with so many of the fun memories in this book and in my life. I miss you very, very much, Pop.

Photo Credits

All photos courtesy of the author, with the following exceptions:

Photos courtesy of Howard Stern appear on pages ii, xi–xviii, 63, 79.

Photos courtesy of Dana Cironi appear on pages 153 and 266.

Photo courtesy of Mike Gange appears on page 131.

Stills from *MADtv* © 2004 *MADtv* © 1995, 1996 Quincy Jones/David Salzman Entertainment, appear on pages 135, 144, 169, and 181.

Stills from *Dirty Work* © 1998 Metro-Goldwyn-Mayer Pictures Inc., All Rights Reserved, appear on pages 211 and 234.

Photo courtesy of "Casino Rob" Paquette appears on page 247.

Photos courtesy of Gary Dell'Abate appear on pages 271, 282, and 290.

Insert

Page 8   © 2004 *MADtv* © 1995, 1996 Quincy Jones/David Salzman Entertainment (all photos)

Page 9   © 2004 *MADtv* © 1995, 1996 Quincy Jones/David Salzman Entertainment (top), *Dirty Work* © 1998 Metro-Goldwyn-Mayer Pictures Inc. All Rights Reserved. (bottom)

Page 10   Dana Cironi

Page 11   Dana Cironi (top)

Page 12   Doug Z. Goodstein (bottom)

Page 13   Dana Cironi (all photos)

Page 14   Howard Stern (top), Jared Fox (bottom)

Page 15   Gary Dell'Abate

Page 16   Gary Dell'Abate